Critical Philosophy of Race and

CW01095898

This volume by philosophers, sociologists, and historians on issues of race and racism examines central educational questions, contributing to ongoing discussions amongst educational theorists, philosophers, and practitioners.

Critical Race Theory and the Critical Philosophy of Race are now well established within North American academia – yet they are only recently beginning to make inroads in UK academia. The wide-ranging discussions in this collection explore conceptual, ethical, political, and epistemological aspects of race and racism in the context of discussions of pedagogy, curriculum, and education policy, across a range of educational settings. The questions and issues addressed include:

- why and how issues of race play out differently in different national and social contexts;
- the impact of the legacies of empire and colonialism on philosophy and education;
- the disciplinary boundaries and practices of academic philosophy;
- the philosophical canon;
- racial identities and their role in educational processes;
- diversity and difference in educational practices and curricula;
- whiteness and institutional racism; and
- the pedagogical issues raised by teaching young children about race and racism.

This book was originally published as a special issue of *Ethics and Education*.

Judith Suissa is Professor of Philosophy of Education at UCL Institute of Education, London, UK. Her research interests are in political and moral philosophy, with a focus on anarchist theory, questions of social justice, radical and libertarian educational traditions, utopian theory, the role of the state, and the parent-child relationship. Her publications include *Anarchism and Education: A Philosophical Perspective* (2006) and *The Claims of Parenting: Reasons, Responsibility and Society* (with Stefan Ramaekers, 2012).

Darren Chetty is a Teaching Fellow at University College London, UK. He has published academic work on philosophy, education, racism, children's literature, and hip-hop culture. He is a contributor to *The Good Immigrant* (edited by Nikesh Shukla, 2016) and he co-authored *What Is Masculinity? Why Does It Matter? And Other Big Questions* (with Jeffrey Boakye, 2019). Darren tweets @rapclassroom

Critical Philosophy of Race and Education

Edited by
Judith Suissa and Darren Chetty

Routledge
Taylor & Francis Group

LONDON AND NEW YORK

First published 2020
by Routledge
2 Park Square, Milton Park, Abingdon, Oxon, OX14 4RN

and by Routledge
52 Vanderbilt Avenue, New York, NY 10017

Routledge is an imprint of the Taylor & Francis Group, an informa business

First issued in paperback 2021

British Library Cataloguing in Publication Data
A catalogue record for this book is available from the British Library

ISBN 13: 978-0-367-34431-3 (hbk)
ISBN 13: 978-1-03-209047-4 (pbk)

Typeset in Myriad Pro
by Newgen Publishing UK

Publisher's Note
The publisher accepts responsibility for any inconsistencies that may have arisen during
the conversion of this book from journal articles to book chapters, namely the inclusion of
journal terminology.

Disclaimer
Every effort has been made to contact copyright holders for their permission to reprint
material in this book. The publishers would be grateful to hear from any copyright holder
who is not here acknowledged and will undertake to rectify any errors or omissions in
future editions of this book.

Contents

Citation Information

The chapters in this book were originally published in *Ethics and Education*, volume 13, issue 1 (March 2018). When citing this material, please use the original page numbering for each article, as follows:

Introduction
Editorial
Judith Suissa and Darren Chetty
Ethics and Education, volume 13, issue 1 (March 2018) pp. 1–3

Chapter 1
Is there such a thing as 'white ignorance' in British education?
Zara Bain
Ethics and Education, volume 13, issue 1 (March 2018) pp. 4–21

Chapter 2
Knowledge and racial violence: the shine and shadow of 'powerful knowledge'
Sophie Rudolph, Arathi Sriprakash and Jessica Gerrard
Ethics and Education, volume 13, issue 1 (March 2018) pp. 22–38

Chapter 3
Racism as 'Reasonableness': Philosophy for Children and the Gated Community of Inquiry
Darren Chetty
Ethics and Education, volume 13, issue 1 (March 2018) pp. 39–54

Chapter 4
Reconstructing a 'Dilemma' of racial identity education
Winston C. Thompson
Ethics and Education, volume 13, issue 1 (March 2018) pp. 55–72

Chapter 5

Teacher-led codeswitching: Adorno, race, contradiction, and the nature of autonomy
Jack Bicker
Ethics and Education, volume 13, issue 1 (March 2018) pp. 73–85

Chapter 6

Affect, race, and white discomfort in schooling: decolonial strategies for 'pedagogies of discomfort'
Michalinos Zembylas
Ethics and Education, volume 13, issue 1 (March 2018) pp. 86–104

Chapter 7

Race, pre-college philosophy, and the pursuit of a critical race pedagogy for higher education
Melissa Fitzpatrick and Amy Reed-Sandoval
Ethics and Education, volume 13, issue 1 (March 2018) pp. 105–122

Chapter 8

On intellectual diversity and differences that may not make a difference
Kristie Dotson
Ethics and Education, volume 13, issue 1 (March 2018) pp. 123–140

Chapter 9

Whiteliness and institutional racism: hiding behind (un)conscious bias
Shirley Anne Tate and Damien Page
Ethics and Education, volume 13, issue 1 (March 2018) pp. 141–155

For any permission-related enquiries please visit:
www.tandfonline.com/page/help/permissions

Notes on Contributors

Zara Bain is a PhD candidate in the Department of Philosophy at the University of Bristol, UK. Her current research focuses on the intersection of political philosophy and social epistemology, and seeks to provide a rigorous philosophical analysis of the concept of an 'epistemology of ignorance'.

Jack Bicker is a Senior Teaching Fellow at the Institute of Education at University College London, UK. His work encompasses critical theory, aspects of political philosophy, philosophy of mind, psychoanalysis, and developmental psychology.

Darren Chetty is a Teaching Fellow at University College London, UK. He has published academic work on philosophy, education, racism, children's literature, and hip-hop culture. Darren tweets @rapclassroom

Kristie Dotson is an Associate Professor in the Department of Philosophy at Michigan State University, USA. She researches epistemology, feminist philosophy (particularly Black feminism and feminist epistemology), and critical philosophy of race.

Melissa Fitzpatrick is a Graduate Teaching Fellow and PhD candidate in Philosophy at Boston College, USA. Her research interests include 19th and 20th century Continental philosophy, ethics and its history, the history of philosophy, and the philosophy of pedagogy.

Jessica Gerrard is a Senior Lecturer in Education, Equity, and Politics at the Melbourne Graduate School of Education at the University of Melbourne, Australia. She researches social inequality.

Damien Page is a Professor and Dean of the Carnegie School of Education at Leeds Beckett University, UK. He has conducted research in a range of fields such as teacher misbehaviour, organisational masculinities, and performance management in schools.

Amy Reed-Sandoval is Assistant Professor in the Department of Philosophy and Faculty Affiliate of the Center for Inter-American and Border Studies at the University of Texas at El Paso, USA. Her primary research interests are in the political philosophy of immigration, Latin American philosophy, philosophies of social identity, and feminist bioethics.

Sophie Rudolph is an Academic at the Melbourne Graduate School of Education at the University of Melbourne, Australia. Her research includes sociological and historical examinations of education and investigates issues of curriculum, pedagogy, and politics in education, policy, and practice.

Arathi Sriprakash is a Reader in Sociology at the Faculty of Education at the University of Cambridge, UK, where she helps convene the *Race, Empire and Education* collective.

Judith Suissa is Professor of Philosophy of Education at UCL Institute of Education, London, UK. Her research interests are in political and moral philosophy, with a focus on anarchist theory, questions of social justice, radical and libertarian educational traditions, utopian theory, the role of the state, and the parent-child relationship.

Shirley Anne Tate is Professor in Sociology, the University of Alberta, Canada. In her writing, research, and teaching she draws on Black feminist, gender, critical 'race', queer, post-colonial, and Caribbean decolonial theory within her overall focus on Black Atlantic diaspora studies and emerging identifications.

Winston C. Thompson is Assistant Professor in the Department of Educational Studies at the Ohio State University, USA. His scholarship focuses upon normative ethical and social/political questions of justice, education, and the public good, with recent efforts analyzing dilemmas of educational policy.

Michalinos Zembylas is a Professor of Educational Theory and Curriculum Studies at the Open University of Cyprus. He is also Visiting Professor and Research Fellow at the Institute for Reconciliation and Social Justice at the University of the Free State, South Africa, and Research Associate at the Centre for Critical Studies in Higher Education Transformation at Nelson Mandela Metropolitan University, South Africa.

Introduction

Judith Suissa and Darren Chetty

At a time when we are witnessing the rise of overtly racist political parties and movements in the US and Western Europe, with dangerously violent repercussions for people of colour and other minorities, engaging in a philosophical discussion of race and racism may seem, at best, a luxury, and at worst a dangerous distraction.

Yet Marx's Eleventh Thesis on Feuerbach notwithstanding, the editors and contributors to this volume would agree that it is important to understand what needs changing and why, and that philosophy can play a valuable role in this task. As Babbitt and Campbell noted as long ago as 1999, in the Introduction to the edited collection, *Racism and Philosophy*,

> Racism is not just a topic for ethics and political philosophy. The existence of systemic racism – its consequences for the structures of the societies in which philosophy is done, as well as for how philosophy has been done and by whom – has deep implications for epistemology, metaphysics, philosophy of mind, and philosophical methodology. (Babbitt and Campbell 1999, 1)

Exploring some of these consequences and meanings, and the way in which rigorous philosophical work can contribute to our understanding of 'race' and 'racism', is the focus of the Critical Philosophy of Race, now a well established academic field, albeit more so in the United States than in Europe. Yet at the same time, while, as the British Education Research Association puts it, '"Race" and ethnicity continue to be major factors influencing children's and adults' experiences of education at all levels and in a variety of respects' (https://www.bera.ac.uk/group/race-ethnicity-and-education), and while philosophers of education work across all the sub-disciplines of philosophy, philosophical work on race remains very marginal within philosophy of education, especially in the UK.

This point is reflected in the findings of the recent Runnymede Report commissioned by the Philosophy of Education Society of Great Britain.[1] One recommendation arising from this report is that if we want to make the spaces in which we do and teach philosophy more inclusive and diverse, we need to make room for a variety of voices drawing on different philosophical and inter-disciplinary work; exploring the myriad ways in which issues of race raise questions for us as philosophers and educators.

In the UK there is a long tradition of activist scholarship concerning the existence and effect of racism in the education system. Scholars such as C.L.R. James, Claudia Jones, Ambalavar Sivanandan, Stuart Hall, Paul Gilroy, Barry Troyna, Heida Safia Mirza, Bernard Coard and Gus John have addressed and explored many of the themes found in this special issue –how underlying racialised relationships of domination in society have shaped and influenced educational policy and practice and the extent to which they continue to do. The black British intellectual tradition has often operated outside of 'the ivory tower' both out of commitment to community struggles and, at times, out of necessity. Indeed Paul Warmington notes 'it might be argued that black British intellectual life and academia have intersected only fitfully' (Warmington 2014, 5). This volume is an attempt to build on and extend these intellectual conversations within the community of philosophy of education and philosophy more broadly, which, as Michael Peters put it in his recent Editorial for a special issue of *Educational Philosophy and Theory*, 'of all disciplines, [] has seemed most resistant to taking race seriously' (Peters 2015).

Likewise, while sounding a powerful warning of the very real dangers of contemporary racist currents in our educational institutions and in society more broadly, the contributors to this issue also recognise and celebrate the significant contributions and pedagogical interventions achieved by social movements such as Black Lives Matter, 'Why is My Curriculum White?', and 'Rhodes Must Fall' – whose voices form part of the critical discussion so necessary if we are to challenge the increasing resurgence of racist and xenophobic narratives about our past, our present, and our future.

In drawing together contributors from different cultural and disciplinary contexts, working within different intellectual traditions, we hope to show how philosophical conversations on race and racism, in dialogue with sociological research and historical enquiry, can inform and contribute to the endeavour to fight the structural racism that permeates the societies in which so many of us live, through an understanding of how it manifests itself in our pedagogical practices, curriculum, educational policy and institutions. The contributions range across the whole spectrum of educational practice. Winston Thompson, Kristie Dotson and Shirley Anne Tate and Damien Page all situate their discussions within the context of further or higher education, whether focused on issues of curriculum, institutional policy or pedagogy, and drawing on philosophical work on diversity, decolonisation, memory and knowledge. Sophie Rudolph, Jessica Gerrard and Arathi Sriprakash focus on the conceptualisation of knowledge and power that underlies so many debates about what and how to teach; Melissa Fitzpatrick and Amy Reed-Sandoval, Darren Chetty, Jack Bicker and Michalinos Zembylas all discuss particular aspects of classroom pedagogy, drawing on broader work to do with issues of identity, inclusion, dialogue, empowerment and affect.

The seminal work of Charles Mills informs many of these discussions. Zara Bain's opening article offers, for readers perhaps less familiar with this work, a systematic account of some of Mills' central ideas, and, for the first time, an explicit analysis of their relevance and implications for the British context. As Mills' own work has demonstrated, and as reflected in the discussions by Sriprakash et al., Dotson, Bain and Chetty, understanding the history of our educational, philosophical and social ideas and practices is a crucial element in developing a critical perspective on current debates. Indeed, reflecting on the electoral victory of Donald Trump and the Brexit campaign, Stuart Jeffries, in a recent interview about the relevance of the work of the Frankfurt School theorists for our contemporary age, notes the ease with which populist leaders speak and lie to voters, pointing out that 'this is a way of controlling people, especially people who don't have a sense of history' (Illing 2017).

Or, as James Baldwin put it,

> For history, as nearly no one seems to know, is not merely something to be read. And it does not refer merely, or even principally, to the past. On the contrary, the great force of history comes from the fact that we carry it within us, are unconsciously controlled by it in many ways, and history is literally present in all that we do. It could scarcely be otherwise, since it is to history that we owe our frames of reference, our identities and our aspirations. And it is with great pain and terror that one begins to realize this. In great pain and terror, one begins to assess the history which has placed one where one is, and formed one's point of view. In great pain and terror, because, thereafter, one enters into battle with that historical creation, oneself, and attempts to recreate oneself according to a principle more humane and more liberating; one begins the attempt to achieve a level of personal maturity and freedom which robs history of its tyrannical power, and also changes history. (Baldwin 1966, 173)

This is surely an important task for education; and, we would suggest, an important task for philosophers and theorists of education.

Note

1. http://www.philosophy-of-education.org/files/about/Runnymede%20PESGB%20Final%20Report.pdf

References

Babbitt, S. E. and S. Campbell, eds. 1999. *Racism and Philosophy*. Ithaca, NY: Cornell University Press.

Baldwin, J. 1966. "Unnameable Objects, Unspeakable Crimes." In *The White problem in America*, edited by Ebony, 170–180. Chicago: Johnson.

Illing, S. 2017. "If You Want to Understand the Age of Trump, Read the Frankfurt School." *Vox* 26 (12): 16 https://www.vox.com/conversations/2016/12/27/14038406/donald-trump-frankfurt-school-brexit-critical-theory.

Peters, M. 2015. Editorial, "Why is My Curriculum White?" *Educational Philosophy and Theory* 47 (7): 641–646.

Warmington, P. 2014. *Black British Intellectuals and Education: Multiculturalism's Hidden History*. Abingdon: Routledge.

🆔 http://orcid.org/0000-0002-4156-9477

1   Is there such a thing as 'white ignorance' in British education?

Zara Bain Ⓘ

ABSTRACT

I argue that political philosopher Charles W. Mills' twin concepts of 'the epistemology of ignorance' and 'white ignorance' are useful tools for thinking through racial injustice in the British education system. While anti-racist work in British education has a long history, racism persists in British primary, secondary and tertiary education. For Mills, the production and reproduction of racism relies crucially on cognitive and epistemological processes that produce ignorance, and which promote various ways of ignoring the histories and legacies of European colonialism and imperialism, as well as the testimonies and scholarship of those who experience racism in their everyday lives. I survey these concepts within Mills' work then marshal evidence in support of my claim that 'the epistemology of ignorance' and 'white ignorance' provide a useful framework for thinking through problems of racial injustice in British education.

Introduction

The evidence that racism exists within British education is overwhelming. While the way that racism manifests may have changed over the past three generations, becoming more 'subtle' and 'insidious' (Vincent et al. 2013), students and teachers of African, Arab, Asian and Caribbean descent – black, Asian and minority ethnic (BAME) students and teachers[1] – experience racism right across primary, secondary, and tertiary education.

In the summer of 2017, *Schools Week* reported a dramatic rise of over 50% in reports of racial hate crimes and subsequent arrests in schools between the years 2014–2015 and 2016–2017, based on freedom of information requests to the UK's 43 police forces (Camden 2017). The same year, the Scottish Parliament's Equalities and Human Rights Committee (2017) published a report on 'prejudice-based bullying' of children and young people in schools which claimed that children from black, Asian and minority ethnic communities are far more likely to experience racist bullying than their peers. In 2016, *Show Racism the Red Card Wales* revealed that teachers in Wales reported a rise in racist name-calling against both students and staff, as well as a lack of confidence, training and support among teachers on how to deal with racist incidents, despite the fact that over 90% of those surveyed strongly believed that anti-racist education should be incorporated into the curriculum (Lewis 2016). A common theme in the news coverage on these statistics was the claim these increases were part of an 'aftermath' or 'wake' of Brexit, whose campaigns and media coverage, founded on anti-immigration platforms, fuelled the normalisation of anti-immigrant views, speech and actions (Kroet 2016).

As well as racist name-calling, physical attacks or other forms of harassment, students who are racialised as non-white are likely to experience other forms of structural or 'institutional' racism. For example, recent UK government figures show that black Caribbean students were three times more likely than white British students to be permanently excluded from education, and twice as likely to face a fixed period of exclusion (UK Cabinet Office 2017, 23). In November 2017, Ofsted announced that it was encouraging its school inspectors to question Muslim girls in primary schools wearing the hijab as a measure against the 'sexualisation' of young girls, sparking an outcry from over 100 teachers and faith leaders who signed an open letter protesting that such action would be institutionally racist (Halliday 2017). Consider too, two key policy initiatives by the UK Government introduced since 2010: first, the introduction of statutory duties under the Counter-Terrorism and Security Act 2015 – the so-called 'Prevent' duty – where teachers and university staff are required under law to monitor student populations for signs of radicalisation into terrorism with the outcome that BAME students, especially Muslim students, are subjected to heightened surveillance (UCU 2015); and second, the collection of schools census data in which parents of school-age children are being asked to provide documentary evidence of their child's nationality and immigration status as part of the UK government's agenda of creating a 'hostile environment' for immigrants (Schools ABC 2017).

Also in 2017, the Runnymede Trust and the National Association of Teachers report (Haque and Elliot 2017) on the impact of racism on teachers in schools offered a similarly complex picture, with teachers from black, Asian and minority ethnic backgrounds identifying 'persistent discrimination, "microaggressions" and unfair and unequal treatment in their everyday teaching lives,' including 'being denied promotion without institutional clarity, cultural or racial stereotyping in terms of teaching roles… and a lack of support or firm action (e.g. zero tolerance) in relation to racist incidents against staff in school' (6). Demographically, the teaching workforce remains a predominantly white workforce (15), with significant disparities between the number of BAME students in primary schools (30.4%) and secondary schools (26.6%), the number of primary (6.5%) and secondary (9.6%) BAME classroom teachers, those in primary (5%) or secondary (6%) school senior leadership roles and primary (3.2%) or secondary (3.7%) BAME headteachers (14).

Universities do not fare much better. Annual demographic monitoring by the Equality Challenge Unit (ECU) reveals that for the period of 2015–2016, BAME academics are similarly chronically under-represented in teaching posts in universities, representing only 9.1% of UK academic staff, and only 8% of those holding professorships in UK universities. This is despite BAME students making up 23% of those undertaking undergraduate degrees and 16.9% of those in postgraduate study. In the case of women from BAME backgrounds, they make up only 4.1% of academic staff and 1.7% of all professorships in UK universities. BAME academics are more likely than their white counterparts to be on casual or temporary contracts, and are much less likely to be represented in academic senior management roles (ECU 2017). Similarly, and despite evidence that BAME pupils overall outperform their white peers in schools (UK Cabinet Office 2017), the ECU reports that white students are more likely than BAME students to achieve a 2:1 or a first in their undergraduate degrees, with 76.3% of white male students qualifying with a 2:1 or above compared to only half of black male students. BAME individuals are overrepresented within university admissions but under-represented in university teaching posts as well as being less likely than their white counterparts to either achieve top degree classifications or to continue to postgraduate study and on to become academics (ECU 2017).

The overall picture is clear: right across the educational pipeline, from primary to secondary to the university sector, black students and teachers experience systematic disadvantages compared to their white counterparts on top of the threat or presence of racist name-calling or assault.

Racism not only exists but endures in British education, despite decades of work of awareness-raising and policy-making aimed at promoting a 'tolerant' and 'multicultural' educational landscape. Why might this be? This paper seeks to argue that one way of making sense of the persistent existence of racism in British education – and indeed within Britain generally – is through the lens of the concept of 'white ignorance', introduced by Jamaican political philosopher, Charles W. Mills. 'White ignorance' identifies a phenomenon whereby contemporary and historical realities of racism are subject to the widespread, systematic and pernicious production of ignorance, as opposed to knowledge.

The paper will proceed as follows: in the first section, I offer an overview of the concept of 'white ignorance' and 'the epistemology of ignorance' in the context of Mills' work, as a sort of preliminary conceptual map for those who might encounter it while thinking through questions relating to 'race' and education. In the next section, I consider a range of evidence which I argue shows that systematic, pervasive and pernicious production of ignorance on matters relating to racism and its aetiology exists in British schools and universities, i.e. that 'white ignorance' exists in the British education system.

What is white ignorance?

In this section, I set up Charles W. Mills' account of 'the epistemology of igno-rance' and its connected concept 'white ignorance,' situating these concepts in the context of Mills' broader project of conceptualising the racialised political system of global white supremacy through social contract theory, ideology and social epistemology.

Mills works within the tradition of analytic political philosophy, and his work is framed within, and aimed at, the dominant concepts and theoretical frameworks of this tradition. Mills (2014) describes himself as using what Audre Lorde ([1984] 2007) calls 'the master's tools' to provide a political philosophical analysis of race and racism which he argues is endemic to Western liberal democracies. Contrary to the view prevalent within liberalism, racism is not an anomaly within an oth-erwise just political system, but the norm (1997, 2003, 2007a, 2007b, 2017). Mills' descriptively-oriented, naturalised account traces how the late fifteenth-century onwards marked the start of several hundred years of European colonisation and imperialism in which the violent theft and expropriation of lands, bodies, labour and resources of black and brown people created wealth and prosperity for coun-tries such as Britain, France, Belgium, Germany, Spain, Sweden, the Netherlands, and Italy, as well the British settler-colonies and ex-'Dominions' of the United States, Canada, South Africa, Australia and New Zealand. As these empires intersected the world, trading, fighting, annexing and ceding territories to one another, this gave rise to a global system in which the assumed superiority of phenotypically 'white' Europeans relied on the construction of a non-white 'Other' whose human-ity was sufficiently undermined to be eradicated, subjugated, and exploited for white profit, even in the midst of the construction of a 'white' European identity as benevolently paternalistic and morally superior. Thus, Mills theorises the political system of what European scientists and philosophers came to reify in terms of 'race', where 'bodies and bloodlines' (Taylor 2013) became markers for membership and standing within moral, intellectual and political communities.

This global political system is what Mills calls 'white supremacy': 'the system of domination by which white people have historically ruled over, and in certain important ways, continue to rule over nonwhite people' (1997, 1–2). This is 'the most important political system of recent global history', (1–2) despite, on Mills' reading, having been overlooked by mainstream and traditional political philos-ophy, 'taken for granted' (2). According to Mills, 'white supremacy' denotes:

> [A] political mode of domination, with … special norms for allocating benefits and bur-dens, rights and duties; [with] its own ideology and an internal, at least semi-autono-mous logic that influences law, culture and consciousness. (2003, 98)

White supremacy thus denotes a global political system in which power, resources, opportunities, and liabilities are distributed within this structure on the basis of 'race'. Mills (1998) follows radical black and colonial intellectuals, such as W. E. B. Du Bois and C. L. R. James in understanding

race in international terms, as a set of relations to be understood not merely locally …
but as the global outcome of historic processes of European imperialism, settlement
and colonialism. (126)

Race is thus understood as a 'social construction', a social not a biological category (Mills 1997, 1998, 2007a, 2015, 2017), and one whose history is inextricably
tied to the operations of the European global imperial project. White supremacy
is thus a political system that *racialises* persons, socially constructing them *into*
race, specifically hierarchies of racialisation framed around white superiority and
non-white inferiority. Mills (1997, 1998, 2003, 2007a, 2015) notes that naming
this political system 'white supremacy' was common pre-World War II, after which
the Allied fight against Hitler's application of colonial and imperial inventions in
Europe demanded the repudiation of German racism from the vantage point of a
white-washed, supposedly anti-racist position of moral superiority.

Mills argues that white supremacy names a racialised political system of domination that once existed and continues to exist (Mills 1997, 1998, 2003, 2015, 2017).
Many would claim that the end of the period of formal or legal *de jure* racial discrimination and the start of nominal equality for all persons regardless of their race
before the law, marked the end of white supremacy. Mills disagrees. He contends
that white supremacy – much like other forms of domination and oppression,
including those involving class and gender – is not solely constituted by one's formal or juridico-legal status. White supremacy is a multi-dimensional phenomenon
which operates in at least six areas: the economic, cultural, somatic (i.e. relating to
one's body or one's embodiment), cognitive-evaluative (i.e. pertaining to thinking
and valuing), and metaphysical (i.e. relating to one's status as a kind or type of being
in the world) (Mills 2003). Even with legal injunctions against racial discrimination
in the mid-twentieth century, Mills argues that de facto white supremacy continues into the latter twentieth-century and twenty-first century via these other five
dimensions. White supremacy thus admits of different periodisations – primarily
between the *de jure* and de facto phases – as well as different spatialisations, with
each political community within global white supremacy manifesting it in different
ways. So, the racialised political system – as well as the social processes of racialisation – in existence in the United States will differ in important ways from those
that exist in South Africa, Australia, Britain, France or the Netherlands (Wolfe 2015).
While Mills' project is predominantly focused on theorising global white supremacy,
as well as its operations in the United States and the Caribbean, his thesis is one
which not only permits, but insists, that any polity with a history of colonialism and
imperialism will be a racialised polity best characterised not merely in terms of its
liberalism, socialism or capitalism, but in terms of white supremacy.

'Whiteness' is a concept which is intimately connected to white supremacy.
Mills (2015) defines 'whiteness' in line with the work of scholars of critical race
and critical whiteness studies, to refer to people socially categorised as white
within a racialised social system (217). In his earlier work, Mills (1997) defines it
as 'a political commitment to white supremacy' (126–127), and argues that its

framing allows us to think of those persons who are racialised as white who could nevertheless refuse to 'consent' to whiteness by 'speak[ing] out and struggle[ing] against' white supremacy (107) rather than 'by accepting all the privileges' that come with being racialised as white under it. Whiteness, then, points not primarily to the *people* socially categorised as white, but to the processes of categorisation through which white power and white motivated self-interest circulate so as to reinforce themselves. Whiteness is a 'set of power relations' (127). The complexity of these processes is reflected in the complexity of the concept of 'whiteness', which others define variously as terror and supremacy, absence, norms, cultural capital, or contingent hierarchies (Garner 2007). Roughly speaking, the shift to talk of 'whiteness' provides a more accessible way of picking out the multidimensionality of white supremacy beyond the merely political to facilitate analysis of its social, economic and cultural aspects.

Throughout his work, Mills emphasises the central role of the cognitive, evaluative or epistemological dimensions of the racialised political system. It is here that he coins two interconnected concepts: 'the epistemology of ignorance' and 'white ignorance'. The epistemology of ignorance represents Mills' identification of a systemic, structural epistemological phenomenon within the racialised political system of white supremacy whose primary function is the production of ignorance, falsehoods, and distorted framings of facts in service of the production and reproduction of white supremacy. In this 'inverted epistemology' (1997, 18) truth is sacrificed in service of the continuation of white supremacy. 'White ignorance' names the same phenomenon, roughly speaking, but from 2007 onwards, Mills tends to use this label rather than its earlier alternative.[2]

White ignorance as a racialised social epistemological contract

In *The Racial Contract* (1997), Mills deploys a conceptual device central to post-Enlightenment political theory – the social contract – as a way of offering us 'X-ray vision' (5) into the internal workings of the global racialised political system. Typically, social contract theory allows political philosophers to model the origins of the polity as well as justifying its political authority over citizens on the grounds of consent by rational agents. In contrast with the hypothetical contracts of Hobbes, Locke, Kant and Rawls, Mills follows first Rousseau and then Pateman (1988) in analysing the structure of the polity in terms of a contract between some at the expense of others: in other words, a 'domination contract' (Mills 2007b). This 'anti-contractarian contractarian' project thus traces the origins of European and post-European polities in the existence of real-world contracts in which white Europeans entered into agreements with one another to construct polities, economies, and cultures in which darker peoples are denied full status as equal moral, political or intellectual persons (Mills 1997, 2000, 2015, 2017).

Alongside the moral and political contracts involved in traditional contract theory – the contracting of agents together to agree to abide by norms of moral conduct, as well as agreements to abide by political norms, such as obedience to the sovereign or the adjudication of the courts or other arbiters of justice under circumstances of conflict – Mills (1997) identifies an epistemological contract where particular 'norms and procedures' exist for determining what counts as 'moral and factual knowledge of the world' (17). Even within the traditional formulations of the social contract, Mills argues that the epistemological dimension of the social contract requires that in order to be 'granted full cognitive standing in the polity, the official epistemic community', one must 'agree' to this picture of human cognitive interaction with the world as depicting what is 'correct' or 'objective' (17–18). To be granted full cognitive standing within an epistemic community is to be recognised as an agent capable of possessing both moral and factual knowledge of the world, according to the standards of that epistemic community.

Within the racialised political system of the Racial Contract, however, the epistemological picture is 'more demanding' insofar as the epistemological requirements for membership of the polity will be determined by the standards – and interests – of the dominant racial group, i.e. white people. Consequently, within the Racial Contract Mills holds that

> one has an agreement to *mis*interpret the world. One has to learn to see the world wrongly, but with the assurance that this set of mistaken perceptions will be validated by white epistemic authority. (1997, 18)

What is taken to objectively represent the world as it is, is really a picture of the world generated by a particular viewpoint within it. Signatories to the Racial Contract will be invited to agree, among other things, that there will be claims that 'race' denotes a meaningful biological category; that if racial discrimination occurs then it is the fault of those whose 'race' makes their claims to entitlement to non-discriminatory treatment unjustified in virtue of lesser normative or metaphysical standing; that 'racism' denotes not a macro-level socio-structural phenomenon but an interpersonal dynamic influenced primarily by psychological or attitudinal facts about particular individuals; and that even if there were historical macro-level socio-structural forms of race-based discrimination in which people were sold, subjugated, displaced, killed, or otherwise brutalised and such activities were not only sanctioned by promoted by law, then the absence of such discriminatory laws in the present day means that racial hierarchies no longer exist; and that, given 'race's horrifying history', and that 'racism' simply *means* 'identifying persons on the basis of their race', the best course of action is a 'racial colour-blindness' where we do not 'see colour' at all. Such claims are, of course, either false or highly controversial and, at the very least, all loaded in such a way as to contribute to white benefit and non-white disadvantage.

Mills argues that under white supremacy, motivated group interest on the part of whites generates a 'cognitive model that precludes self-transparency and genuine understanding of social realities', resulting in 'an invented delusional world, a racial fantasyland' (1997, 18). Mills suggests that as a general rule, *white misunderstanding, misrepresentation, evasion, and self-deception on matters related to race* are among the most pervasive mental phenomena of the past few hundred years, a cognitive and moral economy psychically required for conquest, colonization and enslavement… in no way *accidental* but *prescribed* by the terms of the Racial Contract, which requires a certain schedule of structured blindnesses and opacities in order to establish and maintain the white polity. (19)

Officially sanctioned reality requires, among other things, the patterned insistence on particular narratives, facts, histories, and discourses and a similarly patterned rejection, obfuscation, denial or erasure of alternatives. Thus, under the racial-ised epistemology of white supremacy, as captured by the Racial Contract, the overriding epistemological impetus is one of the production and reproduction of ignorance, especially with respect to the realities of racism and the histories in which they originate.

White ignorance as ideology

Mills (2013) makes clear, in a response to Fricker (2013), who reads his account of white ignorance in terms of a cognitive tendency only on the part of white peo-ple, that white ignorance permeates the entire social system. This account offers an explanatory recasting of white ignorance into what might – following Shelby (2003) – more recognisably be called 'white racist ideology'. It deploys frameworks familiar from Marxist analyses to describe a situation in which *dominant group ide-ology* dominates *insofar as* it determines which narratives about the polity circulate widely and are accepted – and reinforced – as the official and correct story of social reality. Insofar as all members of the polity are socialised into white racial ideology, even members of oppressed social groups may be prone to white ignorance. The epigraph to Mills' book, *Radical Theory, Caribbean Reality* (2010) – an anthology containing multiple essays on Marxism and white supremacy in the Caribbean context – quotes Bob Marley's 'Redemption Song' with its famous line about the 'mental slavery' of colonised peoples. The oppression of people of colour is mental, psychological, intellectual, emotional, and epistemological, as much as it is eco-nomic, political, or juridical. Even while, as per standpoint theory, people of colour have a greater *interest* in being able to possess true beliefs and to eradicate false beliefs about contemporary and historical information about racism and white supremacy (Mills 1998; see also Harding 2004), the systematic promulgation of untruths and 'unknowings' that constitutes white ignorance provides precisely the conditions to make this hard to achieve (Mills 2010, 240-241); and attempts to do this will be met with resistance, marginalisation, suspicion and surveillance.

Why 'ignorance'?

It should be clear by now that the kind of ignorance Mills is talking about is some-thing more than a mere passive absence of knowledge, such as might occur in a situation about some piece of information one cannot yet know, such as what the future might hold. Mills directs our attention to an ignorance that is *active* and *dynamic* (2007a, 1), one that actively produces an absence of true beliefs and the presence of false beliefs – wrongly taken as knowledge – as well those 'conceptual frameworks' (2013, 38) which constitute a 'pervasively deforming outlook' (2015, 217).

This type of ignorance is one which *resists* and *fights back* (2007a, 1). Under traditional conceptualisations, ignorance result from a deficit of information – the absence of evidence, or convincing argument – and so can be eradicated by the presentation of new information. But active ignorance, especially when combined with motivated group interest, as in the case of white supremacy, is resistant to being defeated by the presentation of new information and is insensitive to countervailing evidence. Attempts to assert or promote anti-racist, decolonial knowledge at odds with the prevailing worldview commonly accepted under white ignorance will therefore result in the triggering of a range of discursive strategies whose function is to undermine, diminish, derail, or otherwise block such attempts. White ignorance can thus be understood as a *wilful ignorance*, the sort of ignorance where one should know better, and in which one's ignorance does not absolve one of responsibility for its harmful consequences (see Moody-Adams 1994; Mills 1997; 2003; 2007a, 2010, Applebaum 2010; Heffernan 2012).

One important reason for situating Mills' analysis of ignorance within his account of white supremacy – whether in terms of the social contract or ideology – is that it presses home the point that Mills is most concerned with the operations of ignorance at the macro, systemic or structural level (Alcoff 2007). Mills (2007a) offers a specifically epistemological analysis of ignorance, drawing on Goldman's (1999) model of a veritistic social epistemology which analyses social practices of knowing in terms of their ability to produce truth over falsehood. Goldman's framework offers the materials for a systems-oriented epistemological analysis, which Mills adapts as a means of

> looking at the 'spread of misinformation,' the 'distribution of error' (including the possibility of 'massive error') within the 'larger social cluster,' the 'group entity,' of whites, and the 'social practices' (some 'wholly pernicious') that encourage it. (2007a, 16)

Mills traces the development of the naturalistic approach within epistemology innovated by W. V. O. Quine which means that '[t]he Marxist challenge thrown down a century before [can] finally be taken up' (2007a, 14). Here, Mills' Marxist-informed political empiricism replaces Goldman's model of the social world with one which recognises the pervasiveness of interacting systems of group-based domination and oppression. Mills' naturalised, black radical social epistemology of ignorance cannot be divorced from the political conditions which ground social epistemological practices. Even while ignorance might be also be operative at the individual and group levels (Alcoff 2007), it is as a systematic phenomenon that it is most significant, impactful, and pernicious. At its root, the concern with ignorance is a concern for how socio-political epistemological processes and practices, such as denial, self-deception, obfuscation, mystification, idealisation, erasures, operate so as to uphold domination and oppression – in other words, ways or practices of *ignoring*.

White ignorance in British education

White ignorance, then, picks out a particular cognitive or epistemological phenomenon in a world structured in fundamental ways by the construction of racial categories and hierarchies within and through the European colonial imperial project. In the context of Mills' specific arguments, white ignorance is theorised either in the abstract, as a feature of racialised political systems *in general*; in the particular, such as in 2007s 'White Ignorance' with its focus on how white supremacy results in the racialisation of epistemological processes such as perceiving, remembering, or giving or receiving testimony in the United States; or in global terms, as in 2015s 'Global White Ignorance', where Mills argues that, much as white supremacy is global in scope, so too is white ignorance. Given that for Mills, the concept of 'white ignorance' is a means of fleshing out the cognitive or epistemological dimension of white supremacy, this latter claim would seem to follow.

White ignorance in Britain

One might thus argue for the existence of white ignorance in Britain fairly straightforwardly: Where white supremacy exists, white ignorance is likely to exist. Local political systems where global systems of racialised colonial-imperial domination once played, and continue to play, a significant role are themselves likely to be racialised political systems. Since one of the ways that a racialised political system (i.e. white supremacy) operates is via the cognitive or epistemological dimension (i.e. white ignorance), then for any polity where white supremacy exists, it is likely that white ignorance exists too. Britain is one such local polity; therefore, white ignorance is likely to exist in Britain.

Of course, this kind of logical derivation might seem to miss the point: aren't we more likely to discover whether white ignorance exists in British education empirically, rather than deriving conclusions from fairly abstract premises? Can we claim that Britain is a polity in which global systems of racialised colonial-imperial domination once played, and continue to play, a significant role? Is there evidence for the existence of white ignorance in Britain, especially in British education?

Arguably, Britain itself played an enormous role in the construction and development of that very same global racialised colonial-imperial system. The British Empire spanned the globe, and a great number of modern states are its ex-colonies: Hawaii, the United States, Canada, Nigeria, Ghana, South Africa, Zimbabwe, Australia, Jamaica and many other small island states in the Caribbean, as well as India, Pakistan, Bangladesh, Israel and Palestine.

Mills (2015) offers a framework for identifying instances of the 'racial erasure' that is central to white ignorance: erasing white racism as the ideological driver of modernity; denying white supremacy as a global system or, indeed, as a system whatsoever; whitewashing white atrocity; and eliminating non-white contribution. Ample evidence can be found of all of these categories of phenomena in the British context, although I offer only a cursory overview here.

The erasure of white racism was an essential part of the ideological basis of British Enlightenment and post-Enlightenment philosophy, such as we might find in the work of those founding fathers of social contract theory, toleration, or free speech. English philosopher John Locke was, for example, one of the shareholders in the Royal African Company, which 'transported more Africans into slavery than any other British company in the whole history of the Atlantic slave trade' (Olusoga 2016, 22); John Stuart Mill wrote in *On Liberty* that the famous 'Harm Principle', the basis of freedom of thought, expression, action and association for classical liberalism, ought not to extend to 'backward states' of 'race[s]' in their 'nonage' (Mill 1974, 69, 1998, 202, fn. 8). So too the denial, or at least erasure of white supremacy as a systemic or structural phenomenon. As historian Kathleen Paul (1997) illustrates, the now much-discussed British immigration and citizenship policies initiated in the early twentieth-century and developed throughout the Forties, Fifties and Sixties were expressly designed to reinforce or manage racialised hierarchies, negotiating the twin demands of maintaining at least soft political power in the white settler colonies and dominions of Canada, Australia, New Zealand and South Africa, while restricting the entry of British colonial subjects from Africa, India and the Caribbean who were deemed to be '"primitive of mind," "backward"… and "not our own people,"' even after a universalised formal citizenship was introduced across the United Kingdom and Colonies (22–23). British twentieth-century racism was perpetrated very much at the hands of state policies and systems, and not merely through interpersonal ill-will or prejudice. Similarly, examples abound of the whitewashing of white atrocity on the part of the British. As recently as 2011, as the result of a series of legal cases brought by members of the Kikuyu and Mau Mau tribes seeking justice for systematic brutalisation and torture at the hands of the British in the mid-twentieth century (Elkins 2014), the British government was forced to admit to the existence of at least two hundred feet of files on British colonial atrocities in Kenya at MI6's secretive Hanslope Park facility. This was despite both consistent denial of these British atrocities by ex-Prime Minister Gordon Brown, and the official Public Records office at Kew confirming the grounds of Brown's denial. As historian Ian Cobain (2016) recounts, this was just the tip of the iceberg: in preparation for the demise of the Empire and the onset of colonial independence, the British Foreign Office and its colonial agencies engaged in a decades-long project of burning, drowning, and confiscating any documentation which discussed – or even merely referred to documents which discussed – a wide range of systematic and brutal British activities during British rule. As for the elimination of non-white contribution to British life, the central thesis of historian

David Olusoga's *Black and British: A Forgotten History* (2016) is that despite evidence for a continued black presence in Britain since at least Roman times, black people have been 'expunged' from mainstream narratives of British history, a 'denial and disavowal' resulting in a 'distorted or diminished vision of our national past' which is 'not just a consequence of racism, but a feature of [it]' (10).

White ignorance in the British education system

There is also evidence of white ignorance at work in the British education system. The same systemic erasure, denial, obfuscation, forgetting, and idealisation which characterise national narratives exist within educational curricula and other sites of educational practice.

One notable recent example is highlighted by the 'Why is my Curriculum White?' (#whitecurriculum) movement which began at University College London (UCL) in 2014 and which has since spread across British universities and schools. In November of the same year, the 'Why is my curriculum white?' collective of academics and student scholar-activists released a video which sought to challenge the pervasive whiteness of their university experience. The #whitecurriculum movement argued that university curricula reproduce a racialised, Eurocentric worldview in which white people and their achievements are held as superior to those of people of non-European descent who are racialised as non-white. The result is that university curricula act as a vehicle for the transmission of whiteness – 'an ideology that empowers people racialised as white' ('Why is my Curriculum White?' Collective 2015). Such curricula set and adjudicate one's adherence to the intellectual conditions for the transmission and endurance of white supremacy and racism in British education and in Britain in general.

The movement's claims from the video and the various debates and events which took placed across the country might be summarised as follows:

- The white curriculum excludes or marginalises black scholars. White, male ('pale, male and stale') scholarship constitutes the majority of compulsory material in courses in History, Medicine, Mathematics, Philosophy, Politics, Economics and other academic disciplines. There is no reflection of the significant contributions made to these fields by non-European or non-white thinkers, and where they are included for study in these courses, they are either (a) offered as supplementary material to modulate discussions between white thinkers; (b) tend to be educated in British educational institutions, and can in many cases tend to reproduce a white worldview in their analysis and concerns; or (c) are used as a foil for white scholarship as a means of 'testing' ideas and, ultimately, showing how non-Eurocentric perspectives fail or are otherwise not to be taken really seriously.

- The white curriculum whitewashes and erases the role of British and European colonialism and imperialism. Either colonialism and imperialism is entirely absent from disciplinary narratives or, if present, its presentation tends to be framed as a project of benevolent improvement of inferior peoples – 'savages' – who required the steady hand of British and European paternalism, study and resource extraction before they could be bequeathed 'independence' as 'civilised peoples' from British rule. Similarly, the richness and sophistication of civilizations that the British destroyed is rarely taught. The white curriculum also functions so as to erase the role of universities in imperialism, despite being justifiably described as the 'research and development' wing of Empire (Willinsky 1998).
- The white curriculum is both a cause and consequence of the absence of black scholars in teaching roles in university classrooms. As noted above, black people are significantly underrepresented in academic posts, even while being overrepresented in causal academic contracts. White, as opposed to black, epistemic authority thus remains normalised in universities where not only black scholarship but black scholars themselves are absent and, where present, are forced to navigate the 'Antarctic' whiteness of academic disciplinary communities, practices, norms and canons.

The 'Why is my Curriculum White?' collective (2015) offers eight possible answers to the question of why the curriculum is white: (1) whiteness as the 'dominant framing position' is 'unmarked' and 'invisible', such that what it teaches 'hid[es] behind… universality, rationality and common-sense'; (2) a white curriculum was 'fundamental' to the 'ideological project' of capitalism which framed European economic models as 'morally and intellectually superior', defining 'progress, rationality and development' in ways antithetical to non-European and indigenous economic systems; (3) the white curriculum is intersectional, inasmuch as it is 'intrinsically linked to, and therefore reproduces, power and thought which is racialised as white, physiologically/physically fit, wealth-rich and heteropatriarchally/cisgenderly male'; (4) the white curriculum 'thinks for us so we don't have to', reproducing that logic of colonialism which held that the 'colonised do not own anything – not even their own experiences'. Instead, white commentators – anthropologists, historians, sociologists, cultural theorists, philosophers, and so on – are the only ones 'able fully to explain Black suffering' and the rightful inheritors of the right to produce true and objective knowledge; (5) the white curriculum is a product of the physically-rendered whiteness inherent in the built academic environment: 'every space of learning in Britain is constructed with the resources and the labour of the peoples of the Global South and in a manner that puts [them] as subordinate'; (6) the white curriculum instrumentalises the scholarship of black scholars to create a 'cognitive shelter' where we are 'guid[ed] in how to view marginalised perspectives – exactly as they are presented: as marginal'; (7) the white curriculum erases 'forms of knowledge production which emerge from community and grassroots academics', while 'reinforc[ing] the fallacy' of thinking as the preserve of Europeans and that 'while "the natives" may be able to run, fight and dance, what they could never do is think'; and finally (8), the white curriculum is white because 'the only way we can succeed is by reproducing whiteness – centering the "right" (i.e. white) voices and ideas to the exclusion of others'.

This central claim – that the white curriculum not only reproduces but mandates an ideological whiteness – clearly reflects many of the central claims within Mills' analysis of white ignorance. Indeed, Mills (2007a) specifically cites school textbooks as a crucial site for the management of colonial and imperial ignorance, albeit in the context of the United States (30). Moreover, if we return once more to the framework for identifying white ignorance provided by Mills (2015), we can interpret the claims of the #whitecurriculum movement in similar terms: in terms of the erasure of white racism as a central modern ideology, the denial or even outright erasure of white supremacy as a global (or local) system, the whitewashing of white atrocity, and the denial of non-white contribution.

Nevertheless, one might note that the language of 'white ignorance' is notably absent from the claims made by the #whitecurriculum movement. Why might this be? A number of plausible reasons exist, and perhaps surprisingly, point to some of what is useful about Mills' analysis. For one thing, an emphasis on 'white ignorance' may be considered by some to be a rhetorically inefficacious device for engaging with especially white audiences for whom mention of ignorance is associated with moral exculpation. Under this interpretation of white ignorance, white audiences may claim that they did not, and could not, have known better and, as such, that their 'white ignorance' gets them off the hook, morally speaking, for taking responsibility for the white curriculum and the project of dismantling it. Moreover, talk of 'white ignorance' may obfuscate the fact that colonialism, imperialism, white supremacy and racism are forms of what is arguably white *knowledge*.

These are undoubtedly good reasons for the rhetorical or even conceptual recalcitrance to deploy Mills' concept. However, as will hopefully be clear from the foregoing discussion, Mills' analysis has the resources to mitigate these concerns. White ignorance is not, no matter what white people might claim, morally exculpatory. White ignorance does, however, explain how and why it is that whiteness fosters and facilitates white denial of moral or political responsibility for racial injustice, both in general and in educational contexts. Mills also makes clear that central to the phenomenon of white ignorance is the presentation of falsehoods as knowledge, guaranteed by white epistemic authority. And while not his most well-known formulation of the concept, Mills explicitly suggests that 'white ignorance' can and in some senses should be understood in terms of ideology, a framework which permits certain manoeuvres to be made with the concept – an emphasis on socialisation of belief in contrast with the (albeit tacitly) voluntaristic model of the social contract, properly demarcating the scope of white ignorance as pervasive enough to permeate the entire polity. Thus, white ignorance as a framework highlights those processes of *active, resistant* and *systematic* ignoring which will be deployed to resist efforts such as those of the #whitecurriculum collective to name them to begin with.

The #whitecurriculum movement points to important pedagogical implications of adopting this conceptual framework as part of the ongoing project to understand and dismantle white supremacy. For example, anti-racist strategies which frame racism primarily as the consequence of 'implicit bias' can obfuscate the structural nature and aetiology of racism and its connection to socio-political systems (see Tate and Page in this volume), and prove ineffective absent the conscientious and deliberate 'unwhitening' of curricula, staff demographics, institutions and pedagogical practices.

Even with the backing of overwhelming evidence, claims to the existence of racism in British education are met with resistance. Merely descriptively speaking, we can say that there exists a pervasive and systematic set of practices in which the existence of racism, and the racialised political systems which produce and constitute it, are denied, diminished, misrepresented, erased. Therefore, white ignorance exists in the British education system.

Conclusion

The movement to reveal and interrogate the predominance of a #whitecurriculum in UK universities and schools can be read in terms of a movement dedicated to the identification and eradication of white ignorance. While it is not the only domain in which white ignorance operates, education plays a central role in the production and reproduction of white ignorance. Education constitutes a space in which students are led into a particular worldview – in which, to put it another way, students are offered the terms of an epistemological contract and there are consequences for refusing to be a signatory to it. Education is where people are taught what an objective and correct picture of the world looks like, as well as the methods appropriate to finding new knowledge, and applying existing knowledge to practical and intellectual problems. The #whitecurriculum movement presses home the point that to be educated in a racialised polity is to be educated into, and in confrontation with, white ignorance. The #whitecurriculum movement refuses such an education, insisting on its decolonised alternative. Anything less is a capitulation to white supremacy.

Educating for social justice requires educating in ways that are socially just insofar as we do all that is within our power to ensure that our pedagogy actively works against reproducing the epistemological systems that foster ignorance as a route to racial injustice. But, as Mills' analysis and the above discussion illustrates, this is no easy project. Naming white ignorance and its machinations is a necessary first step in the struggle for racial justice.

Note

1. From here onwards I use the term 'black' to denote persons of African, Arab, Asian or Caribbean descent.
2. Mills (2007a, 2007b) notes that white or racialised ignorance is not only form of an epistemology of ignorance and that gendered and classed epistemologies of ignorance also exist, as well as intersecting ignorance-systems such as will be experienced by black women subject to both racialised sexism and gendered racism. This elision of the two terms 'white ignorance' and 'epistemology of ignorance' is thus merely for ease of reference here.

Acknowledgements

Many thanks to the editors of this special issue for their invaluable feedback and committment to supporting disabled scholars, and to my PhD supervisors for their ongoing support.

Disclosure statement

No potential conflict of interest was reported by the author.

Funding

This work was supported by an Arts & Humanities Research Council South, West and Wales Doctoral Training Partnership Studentship, grant number 1502742.

ORCID

Zara Bain ⓘ http://orcid.org/0000-0003-3665-2839

References

Alcoff, L. M. 2007. "Epistemologies of Ignorance: Three Types." In *Race and Epistemologies of Ignorance*, edited by S. Sullivan and N. Tuana, 39–58. New York: SUNY.
Applebaum, B. 2010. *Being White, Being Good: Complicity, White Moral Responsibility and Social Justice Pedagogy*. Plymouth: Lexington Books.
Camden, B. 2017. "Racial Hate Crimes in Schools Surge in Wake of Brexit." *Schoolsweek*, June 18. https://schoolsweek.co.uk/racial-hate-crimes-in-schools-surge-in-wake-of-brexit/.
Cobain, I. 2016. *The History Thieves: Secrets, Lies and the Shaping of a Modern Nation*. London: Portobello Books.
ECU (Equality Challenge Unit). 2017. *Equality in Higher Education Statistical Report 2017*.
Elkins, C. 2014. *Britain's Gulag: The Brutal End of Empire in Kenya*. London: Bodley Head.
Fricker, M. 2013. "How is Hermeneutical Injustice Related to 'White Ignorance'? Reply to José Medina's "Hermeneutical Injustice and Polyphonic Contextualism: Social Silences and Shared Hermenuetical Responsibilities." *Social Epistemology Review and Reply Collective* 2 (8): 49–53.
Garner, S. 2007. *Whiteness: An Introduction*. Abingdon: Routledge.
Goldman, A. 1999. *Knowledge in a Social World*. Oxford: Oxford University Press.

Halliday, J. 2017. "Ofsted Accused of Racism over Hijab Questioning in Primary Schools." *The Guardian*, November 28. https://www.theguardian.com/education/2017/nov/28/ofsted-accused-racism-hijab-questioning-primary-schools.

Haque, Z., and S. Elliott. 2017. *Visible and Invisible Barriers: The Impact of Racism on BME Teachers.* The Runnymede Trust.

Harding, S. 2004. *The Feminist Standpoint Theory Reader.* Abingdon: Routledge.

Heffernan, M. 2011. *Wilful Blindness: Why We Ignore the Obvious at Our Peril.* London: Simon & Schuster.

Kroet, C. 2016. "UN Committee: Brexit Rhetoric Fuelled Hate Crime." *Politico*, August 26. https://www.politico.eu/article/un-committee-brexit-rhetoric-fueled-hate-crime-xenophobic-polish/.

Lewis, G. 2016. "Incidents of Racism in Schools up Post-Brexit." *Sec Ed*, September 26. http://www.sec-ed.co.uk/news/incidents-of-racism-in-schools-up-post-brexit.

Lorde, A. (1984) 2007. *Sister Outsider.* Berkeley, CA: Crossing Press.

Mill, J. S. 1974. *On Liberty.* London: Penguin.

Mills, C. W. 1997. *The Racial Contract.* New York: Cornell University Press.

Mills, C. W. 1998. *Blackness Visible.* New York: Cornell University Press.

Mills, C. W. 2000. "Race and the Social Contract Tradition." *Social Identities* 6 (4): 441–462.

Mills, C. W. 2003. *From Class to Race.* Lanham, MA: Rowman & Littlefield International.

Mills, C. W. 2007a. "White Ignorance." In *Race and Epistemologies of Ignorance*, edited by S. Sullivan and N. Tuana, 11–38. New York: SUNY.

Mills, C. W. 2007b. "The Domination Contract." In *Contract and Domination*, edited by C. Pateman and C. Mills, 79–105. Cambridge: Polity.

Mills, C. W. 2010. *Radical Theory, Caribbean Reality.* Kingston: University of the West Indies Press.

Mills, C. W. 2013. "White Ignorance and Hermeneutical Injustice." *Social Epistemology Review and Reply Collective* 3 (1): 38–43.

Mills, C. W. 2014. "Rousseau, the Master's Tools, and Anti-Contractarian Contractarianism." In *Creolizing Rousseau*, edited by J. A. Gordon and N. Roberts, 171–192. London: Rowman & Littlefield International.

Mills, C. W. 2015. "Global White Ignorance." In *Routledge International Handbook of Ignorance Studies*, edited by M. Gross and L. McGoey, 217–227. Abingdon: Routledge.

Mills, C. W. 2017. *Black Rights/White Wrongs: The Critique of Racial Liberalism.* NY: Oxford University Press.

Moody-Adams, M. 1994. "Culture, Responsibility and Affected Ignorance." *Ethics.* 104 (2): 291–309.

Olusoga, D. 2016. *Black and British: A Forgotten History.* London: Macmillan.

Pateman, C. 1988. *The Sexual Contract.* Stanford: Stanford University Press.

Paul, K. 1997. *Whitewashing Britain: Race and Citizenship in the Postwar Era.* New York: Cornell University Press.

Schools ABC. 2017. Accessed December 29, 2017. https://www.schoolsabc.net/

Scottish Parliament Equalities and Human Rights Committee. 2017. "It's Not Cool to Be Cruel: Prejudice-Based Bullying and Harassment of Children and Young People in Schools." http://www.parliament.scot/S5_Equal_Opps/Inquiries/EHRiC_5th_Report_2017_SP_Paper_185.pdf.

Shelby, Tommie. 2003. "Ideology, Racism and Critical Social Theory." *The Philosophical Forum* 34 (2): 153–188.

Taylor, P. 2013. *Race: A Philosophical Introduction.* Cambridge: Polity.

UCU (University College Union). 2015. *The Prevent Duty: A Guide for Branches and Members.*

UK Cabinet Office. 2017. "Race Disparity Audit: Summary Findings from the Ethnicity Facts and Figures Website." October. http://ethnicity-facts-figures.service.gov.uk.

Vincent, C., S. Ball, N. Rollock, and D. Gillborn. 2013. "Three Generations of Racism: Black Middle-Class Children and Schooling." *British Journal of Sociology of Education.* 34 (5–6): 929–946.

'Why is my Curriculum White?' Collective, UCL. 2015. "8 Reasons the Curriculum is White." *Novara Media*, March 23. See also 2014 'Why is my Curriculum White?' YouTube. Accessed December 29, 2017. https://www.youtube.com/watch?v=Dscx4h2 I-Pk

Willinsky, J. 1998. *Learning to Divide the World: Education at Empire's End*. Minneapolis: University of Minnesota Press.

Wolfe, P. 2015. *Traces of History: Elementary Structures of Race*. London: Verso.

2 Knowledge and racial violence

The shine and shadow of 'powerful knowledge'

Sophie Rudolph (iD), Arathi Sriprakash (iD) and Jessica Gerrard (iD)

ABSTRACT

This paper offers a critique of 'powerful knowledge' – a concept in Education Studies that has been presented as a just basis for school curricula. Powerful knowledge is disciplinary knowledge produced and refined through a process of 'specialisation' that usually occurs in universities. Drawing on postcolonial, decolonial and Indigenous studies, we show how powerful knowledge seems to focus on the progressive impulse of modernity (its 'shine') while overlooking the ruination of colonial racism (its 'shadow'). We call on scholars and practitioners working with the powerful knowledge framework to address more fully the hegemonic relations of disciplinary specialisation and its historical connections to colonial-modernity. This, we argue, would enable curriculum knowledge that is 'powerful' in its interrogation of racial violence, rather than in its epistemic reproduction of it.

Introduction: knowledge, power and race

Across institutions of politics, media, research and education, we are witnessing the surging political significance of debates about knowledge, truth, data and their relationship to racial violence. For example, recent months have seen attacks on journalists reporting on ethno-nationalism (BBC News 2017), government denials and misrepresentations of white supremacy (Shear and Haberman 2017), and the increasing use of data from public institutions and private citizens to surveil, threaten and demonise migrant communities (Yuval Davis, Wemyss, and Cassidy 2017). In the domain of education, debates about knowledge and racial violence have focused particularly on the epistemic legacies of colonialism and its formations of contemporary racism. Recent student movements to decolonise universities such as 'Rhodes Must Fall' and 'Why is my curriculum white?' have called on institutions to redress the exclusions of non-White histories, ideas and experiences in the formation of academic knowledge, spurring transnational debate on these issues (see Peters 2015; Joseph Mbembe 2016). The effective silencing of race and colonialism in school curricula is also being rigorously contested (Brown and Au 2014; Weiner 2014; Alexander and Weekes-Bernard 2017). And, as reflected by the present Special Issue, there has been a sustained interrogation of the ways in which disciplinary knowledge – the concepts and theories of sociology, philosophy, and so on – have been formed through colonial exploitation and racialised erasure (see for example, Connell 2007; Santos 2014; Bhambra 2016; Go 2016; Van Norden 2017).

Parallel to these interventions is an influential body of scholarship within Education Studies that, despite placing central importance on 'recovering' knowledge, has, we argue, ultimately failed to engage with the colonial formations of knowledge and its relationship to racial violence. We refer here to the concept of 'powerful knowledge' put forward by sociologist of education Michael Young and colleagues (see Young 2008, 2010, 2013; Young and Muller 2013; Young, Lambert, and Roberts 2014). The idea of 'powerful knowledge' has gained significant traction with school education policy actors, academics, and practitioners in different subject areas around the world (for example, Counsell 2011; Firth 2011; Rata 2012; Standish and Sehgal Cuthbert 2017). This includes the particular uptake of powerful knowledge in 'postcolonial' contexts, such as South Africa (see Hoadley 2015; Fataar 2016). Young has critiqued the field of education for its preoccupation with 'knowers' (the experiences of students and standpoint epistemologies), and has made an appeal to the field to 'bring knowledge back in' via a commitment to social realism (Young 2008). The 'powerful knowledge' position argues that some knowledge offers an objectively better basis for understanding the world than others and so a socially just education system is one which provides students with equal access to such 'powerful knowledge' through the curriculum. In particular, powerful knowledge is understood as 'specialised' knowledge, in that it is produced and legitimised by disciplinary communities, usually within universities.

There is indeed an imperative to remain committed to knowledge in collective educational projects, not least to guard against a 'post-truth' politics. In this paper we consider how awareness of the impact of colonial expansion and capitalist imperialism offers a different view of 'powerful knowledge', especially in attending to how its specialisation (i.e. its legitimation within disciplinary communities) is steeped in a hierarchical global economy of knowledge production (see Connell 2017). Expressed most clearly in the historical divisions of labour between the collection of data from the global South for the development of theory in resource-rich universities in the global north, this is an economy which proceeds from and perpetuates largely uninterrogated colonial epistemic logics of extraction, appropriation, containment, and control. This, we suggest, is not a matter of perspective or standpoint (positions that can be too easily dismissed as relativism from proponents of powerful knowledge), but rather, a matter of history. Thus whilst others have critiqued powerful knowledge for its focus on the cognitive rather than ethical purposes of schooling and its 'thin' articulation of social justice in postcolonial contexts (Zipin, Fataar, and Brennan 2015), or drawn attention to the tensions involved in extending powerful knowledge to disadvantaged students (Beck 2013), or reiterated the value of experiential knowledge and the importance of pluralist epistemologies (Catling and Martin 2011), we take a different approach.

Our interests lie in understanding the implications of colonial pasts/presents on disciplinary knowledge formation and use. This involves seeing how colonial violence – in the form of domination, erasure, dispossession, coercion, appropriation and assimilation – is bound by racial violences that are both physical and epistemic. Epistemic violence, in this context, is the ordering, classification, and naming that occurs through the practices of colonialism. The powerful construction of hierarchies of race through the lens of 'Western civilisation' has been a core technology of colonisation (Said 1978; Dirks 2001; Fanon 2008; Wolfe 2016; see also Willinsky [1998] on the epistemic project of imperialism as 'wilful knowledge'). Both the production and use of knowledge (disciplinary and non-disciplinary) have been implicated by these colonial and racial violences. For example, disciplines that are no longer considered viable, such as phrenology, demonstrate the explicit ways in which the racial violence of colonisation creates material and epistemic power relations that can endure and be re-formed today (see Rudolph 2018).

And so, in this paper we examine how disciplinary knowledge has both a 'shine' and a 'shadow' side that is historically knowable in accounts of disciplines more broadly (cf. Bhambra 2014b), but largely unaddressed in the powerful knowledge framework. The concepts of 'shine' and 'shadow' are mobilised here, following decolonial and Indigenous scholars, to demonstrate how knowledge claims associated with the disciplines (and thus, the concept of powerful knowledge) cannot be extricated from the power relations of colonial-modernity which hold the 'shine' of possibility whilst denying the 'shadow side' of colonial violence. Walter Mignolo (2000, 22), for example, invokes colonialism and modernity as two sides of the same coin in which coloniality is 'quite simply, the reverse and unavoidable side of "modernity" – its darker side, like the part of the moon we do not see when we observe it from the earth'. Working with this idea, Ahenakew and colleagues (2014, 219) suggest that the 'shine' of modernity, its 'dialectical and universal reasoning, reflected in modern institutions and forms of organisation such as nation-states and democracy', cannot be disconnected from its 'shadow': 'expansionist control of lands, racism and epistemic violence'. As Andreotti (2011, 386) offers, following Nelson Maldonado-Torres, 'if the darker side of modernity is forgotten, what results is a kind of universalism located in a "spaceless" realm'.

Our examination of the concept of 'powerful knowledge' finds that it evokes a faith in the shine of disciplinary knowledge without adequately attending to its shadow. In doing this, the power relations of colonialism are elided within the advocacy of 'powerful knowledge' creating the potential for its co-option into a cycle of epistemic violence and spaceless (and timeless) universalism that can enable collective modes of denial (see Cohen 2001). This unfortunately can permit and support as Mills (2007, 35) puts it, a 'white epistemology of ignorance'. While we are not suggesting the dismissal of disciplinary knowledge, and we in fact concur that disciplinary knowledge is often useful and powerful, we are also interested in its accountability to the very real legacies of the colonial past in the present. We therefore contend, as we explicate below, that *bringing history back in* to knowledge projects is required for working towards curriculum and educational justice. In attending to the history that has produced the disciplines that are central to the concept of 'powerful knowledge', the colonial relations of power become visible and the 'shadow' side of knowledge cannot be forgotten or overlooked. This, we argue, is knowledge that can be powerful in its interrogation of racial and colonial violence, rather than in its epistemic reproduction of it.

Powerful knowledge and the hegemonic relations of specialisation

Powerful knowledge is defined as being distinct from 'common sense' knowledge, and as systematic and specialised in terms of following the accepted but always refinable conventions of specialist (disciplinary) communities (see Young and Muller 2013). It is frequently contrasted with experiential, perspectival knowledge that is said to be foregrounded within curricula that purport to be grounded in a social constructivist epistemology (see Young 2008). The power of powerful knowledge, it is claimed, is its capacity to move students beyond their own experiences and into specialised knowledge communities which are said to offer better explanatory, moral and aesthetic understandings of our social and natural world. As Young writes, 'Powerful knowledge is cognitively superior to that needed for daily life. It transcends and liberates children from their daily experience' (2013, 118). The focus on specialisation is a key feature of powerful knowledge, and allows proponents to distinguish it from the 'knowledge of the powerful'. Young and colleagues suggest, for instance, that specialisation is a means to consider 'the features of the particular knowledge itself that is included in the curriculum and what it can do for those who have access to it' (2014, 74). In contrast, an emphasis on 'knowledge of the powerful' brings a heightened, and in Young et al.'s view, unhelpful focus on the 'who' of knowledge: the people and interests that select, frame and determine what counts as useful knowledge (ibid.). For Young, this focus leads to a conclusion that curriculum is 'always primarily a political instrument and not an educational instrument to support learning' (ibid., 73).

The binary position constructed by Young and colleagues between powerful knowledge on the one hand, and knowledge of the powerful on the other, limits analysis of curricula in ways that problematically bracket out the social relations in disciplinary communities that *do* impact the constitution, organisation, categorisation, and prioritisation of knowledge. Disciplinary knowledge is said to be produced through continual revision, through the 'strengthening' of conceptual and methodological coherence (Young and Muller 2013). However, there has been insufficient attention to how disciplinary communities – in which this process of specialisation takes place – are constituted by people, norms, histories, and politics.

Whilst proponents of 'powerful knowledge' acknowledge the 'internal rules' of hierarchy and solidarity in disciplinary communities, it appears that the powerful knowledge framework accepts these rules as a normalised 'pathos' (Muller 2014) rather than acknowledging their potential for epistemic violence.

We call on scholars and practitioners working with the powerful knowledge framework to address more fully the hegemonic relations – the cultural and social means of social dominance (Gramsci 1971) – within the process of specialisation. Unequal social relations are perpetuated in knowledge projects through their 'capacity to actively contain, educate, and reshape oppositional forces, to maintain them in their subordinate places' (Hall 2016, 169). Without a radical interrogation of hegemonic relations within processes of specialisation (for example, within universities), powerful knowledge is maintained *as* the knowledge of the powerful. This is precisely the concern of activists and scholars who are drawing attention to the racialised erasures and exclusions of histories and knowledge in the academy. That our university curricula are predominantly white is not an outcome of independent criteria for 'better' knowledge (to which the powerful knowledge framework seeks to defer), but a consequence of colonialism and racial domination in the epistemic communities of the academy. The establishment of the Western philosophical canon, for instance, is in and of itself a production of colonial exclusion (see Park 2013). The same could also be said in relation to the (past and present) academic marginalisation of, for example, the histories and literatures of women and of the poor and working classes, or non-heteronormative social analyses.

Yet, in its appeal for objectively 'better' knowledge, the powerful knowledge framework largely overlooks the ways in which the refinement of disciplinary knowledge is itself connected to social interests. As Lyn Yates (2018) points out in relation to the discipline of history, there is no way of adequately teasing apart social interests on the one hand and objectivity on the other, when it comes to the formation of knowledge. Yates writes,

> In the case of history as disciplined inquiry, the sharp distinction between so-called relativism and social interests on the one hand and reliable knowledge on the other does not work. History *is* disciplined and tested in the ways associated with those arguments about knowledge, but bringing new perspectives or understandings into being is also part of its core agenda. It is not *simply* about particular social interests: accounts have to be researched and supported in historically rigorous ways and can be challenged on similar grounds. (2018, 48, original emphasis)

Yates illustrates how the formation and ongoing development of disciplinary knowledge in history is thus always a contextual process. Unfortunately, many proponents of powerful knowledge treat such context as 'background' and not as central to the knowledge itself. By separating out 'powerful knowledge' and 'knowledge of the powerful' scholars such as Young appear to treat knowledge production and use (including the pedagogical 'acquisition' of knowledge) as somehow distinct. In contrast, we suggest this context is central to knowledge itself, and cannot be divided from its practices.

Thus, knowing this context is important for educators and those being educated. Disciplinary knowledge structures are based on an imagined European 'modernity' which is unhooked from the colonial contexts of its formation, and thus, from its potential for racial violence. As Bhambra (2014a, 419) argues, European development is often assumed to be an independent phenomenon, in which 'the rest of the world was external to these world-historical processes and that colonial connections and processes were insignificant to their development'. The social sciences, for example, have long crafted the majority world as a figure of the 'other': an object of study for Western knowledge and thus central to its development, but at the same time resolutely excluded (and denied) from it (see also Said 1978; Mignolo 2002). As Australian Indigenous scholar, Aileen Moreton-Robinson contends, an impulse and assertion of possession runs through this epistemic project of modernity, as seen starkly in the legitimization of settler-colonialism:

> It takes a great deal of work to maintain Canada, the United States, Hawai'i, New Zealand, and Australia as white possessions. The regulatory mechanisms of these nation-states are extremely busy reaffirming and reproducing this possessiveness through a process of perpetual Indigenous dispossession, ranging from the refusal of Indigenous sovereignty to overregulated piecemeal concessions. (Moreton-Robinson 2015, xi)

Work such as Moreton-Robinson's powerfully demonstrates the ontological effects of the epistemic project of modernity which 'are embedded everywhere in the landscape' (ibid., xiii) and which simultaneously disavow the existence of Indigenous sovereignties (ibid.). This is the deeply challenging 'shadow' side of modernity in which disciplinary knowledge and its process of specialisation is enmeshed. And yet, the powerful knowledge framework says little of, and much less accounts for, colonial-modernity in the formation of specialised knowledge.

What seems, then, to make 'powerful knowledge' powerful is not only its usefulness to society or refinement in form but two other key unacknowledged factors: (1) the silencing of its inherent possibility for racial violence and (2) the ways in which this silencing naturalises its hegemony. In other words, by not attending to the epistemic violence of disciplinary knowledge, the 'power' of 'powerful knowledge' rearticulates the shine/shadow problematic of colonial modernity. Below, we show how historical reflexivity is vital to both understand the shadow-shine relationship of knowledge and to address this silence. As we outline, we are not arguing for 'less' knowledge, or for all knowledge-claims to be 'relative', but for the powerful knowledge framework to see its shadow side in order to reconstruct curricular knowledge that is powerful in dismantling – not reproducing – the epistemic formations of colonial-racial hierarchies, dispossessions, and violence.

Bringing history back in: seeing the shadow side of knowledge

Historical reflexivity is more than contending with 'the past', as if history *only* represents events that have occurred in the past (see Rudolph 2016). It is about understanding history as also occurring in the present and future; and the present and future as being historical. As Ann Laura Stoler puts it,

> The present can never escape its relationship to the past, both in the ways we represent and understand the past in the present, and in the ways in which historical relations, traditions, understandings, habits and cultures reverberate and are sustained, in sometimes unexpected ways. (Stoler 2016, 33)

And as Bhambra suggests,

> the ways in which we understand the past are crucial to our understandings of ourselves and the world in which we live today and that if our understandings of the past are inadequate it follows that our grasp of the present will also be inadequate. (2007, 2)

Mignolo, Stoler, Moreton-Robinson and Bhambra in different ways suggest the need to attend to the historical relations that endure into the present when considering the ways in which knowledge is authorised and legitimised (see also Gerrard, Rudolph, and Sriprakash 2017).

By 'bringing history back in' to the debates about curriculum and knowledge, we may understand the constitution and capacities of knowledge more thoroughly. In this section we present three interweaving conceptual orientations that emerge from this historical reflexivity and which illuminate the capacity for knowledge to shine *and* produce a shadow. We suggest that these conceptual frames represent the different forms of violence that knowledge is capable of. First, that knowledge builds as well as ruins, which demonstrates the ways in which knowledge can perform erasure and dispossession in the process of generating use and value. Second, that knowledge opens up possibilities as well as holds things in place, which shows how knowledge can be coercive and dominating while at the same time offering possibilities for expansion of understanding. And third, that knowledge frees but also domesticates, which illustrates the capacity for knowledge to assimilate and appropriate people and ideas alongside its alleged intention to liberate. These three orientations, we suggest, offer an account of knowledge that more readily addresses its always-present possibility to cast both shine and shadow.

Knowledge builds as well as ruins

One of the greatest benefits of knowledge is that it builds. It builds understanding, it builds connections, it builds possibility. What Young and colleagues would understand as disciplinary knowledge – such as physics, mathematics, sociology, and biology – has played an integral part in literally building societies, cities, governments, medical developments, and modes of transport. However, in the act of building knowledge, a process of ruination inevitably also occurs. We suggest that the building of knowledge – and in particular the knowledge of the 'Western' academy and its disciplinary foundations – is also a project of ruination; one in which 'savages' and the 'civilised' appear, and in which other kinds of worlds, knowledges, existences, and cultures are actively refused and 'ruined'. Ruination in this sense is about the continuity of empire, and the enduring and transforming dimensions of the shadow side of colonial modernity. We take Stoler's use of 'ruins' here, as an active noun and verb referring 'to the enduring quality of imperial remains and what they render in impaired states' (ibid., 194). This is, as Stoler contends, not about '"leftovers" or relics', but a turn to 'what people are "left with"': to what remains, to the aftershocks of empire, to the material and social afterlife of structures, sensibilities, and things' (2008, 194). Rather than positioning this as something 'back there' in history, constituted in social relations long ago, we suggest with Stoler, that ruins are part of the active present.

The effects of the power relations that produce ruination in the building of knowledge are complex, containing both pain and possibility. This is illustrated in the Australian context by Torres Strait Islander scholar, Martin Nakata, who argues that increased awareness of Torres Strait Islander culture, and 'inclusion' of this culture into educational spaces in settler colonial Australia

> has mostly resulted in ways for researchers and practitioners to explain the Islander's existence, the Islander's resistance, and the Islander's failure. Relevance or sensitivity to cultural differences alone however does not change traditional classroom practices from alienating the Islander in formal learning processes. (2007, 179)

Here, Nakata points to the ways that inclusion of knowledge of Indigenous peoples in Australian schooling systems has the capacity to build understanding and awareness but at the same time the schooling structures and classroom practices alienate Indigenous peoples, their very presence a reminder of the destruction caused by colonialism and the portrayal of Indigenous knowledges and subjectivities as inferior.

The hegemonic forces of colonial-modernity and its forms of knowledge acquisition and ruination elide these disciplinary formations. Through the act of colonial construction and destruction, the resulting knowledge becomes simultaneously both empowering and alienating. Central to this are the ways in which existing knowledge traditions and disciplines require the mediation, and evocation, of hegemonic power. As Fanon argues, 'To speak means to be in a position to use a certain syntax, to grasp the morphology of this or that language, but it means above all to assume a culture, to support the weight of a civilization' (2008, 8). So-called objective description, as Fanon points out, obfuscates the relations of power that create the platform, perceived necessity, and audience for such 'description'. Practices of building (and using) disciplinary knowledge can simultaneously participate in ruining, destroying and silencing other forms of knowledge that become unrecognisable and are thus dismissed as 'undisciplined' or lacking 'objectivity' and not capable of offering power. There is a need, therefore, to understand the 'epistemic dimension' of colonialism (Mignolo 2002, 64), and its enduring processes of ruination, erasure and dispossession as influential shadow sides of disciplinary formation.

Knowledge opens up possibilities as well as holds things in place

There is a complex dynamic in the ways in which knowledge shines in its capacity to open possibilities, whilst at the same time holding things in place. Access to education and knowledge is generally regarded as a universal human right precisely because it is seen as opening up possibilities. The struggles for universal access to schooling since the later half of the twentieth century illustrate the value accorded to disciplinary knowledge for participation in society (see for example, Campbell and Proctor 2014). However, the widening of school and university participation has brought new contestations to knowledge and the formation of disciplinary knowledge. The establishment of new academic disciplines through the second half of the twentieth century (such as Women's Studies, Indigenous Studies, Critical Race and Whiteness Studies, Queer Studies and Postcolonial Studies) represents the inadequacy of older disciplines to account for and develop knowledge that adequately speaks to the diversity of human experience. These disciplines sought to open up further possibilities for knowledge at the same time as directly contesting the ways in which disciplines can hold power relations in place in damaging ways. Human experience, then, is an essential element of the theories that drive the development of disciplines (see for example Ahmed 2017) and therefore we contend that the distinction made by Young between disciplinary knowledge and 'pupils' everyday experience' (Young 2013, 102) is neither uncomplicated nor so neatly polarised; and nor is the production, use and pedagogical acquisition of knowledge.

A number of new disciplinary formations have sought to critically engage with the harm of reification of particular epistemologies, ontologies and subjectivities within disciplinary knowledge. For example, Australian Indigenous researcher Maggie Walter works with Indigenous statistics to suggest that statistics can help understand possibilities for Indigenous peoples to transform their social realities but also cautions against assumptions of objectivity: 'Separating social phenomena from their moral, political and cultural social landscape is not possible: objectivity or value-neutral knowledge is a research disingenuity' (2010, 53; see also special issue by Garcia, López, and Vélez 2018). She examines how the politics of data reveals a tendency to hold a simplified racial image of Indigenous people in place, including selective usage and interpretation of data, simplistic presentation of data, morally undemanding interpretations of data and dichotomous entrenchment (i.e. Indigenous compared to non-Indigenous) (2010, 49–52).

Audra Simpson, an Indigenous scholar from North America, is similarly engaged in the discipline of anthropology – deeply aware of both its shine and its shadow. On the one hand she states that she found the anthropological analyses of the Iroquois 'exceedingly ritualistic and procedural, and so much so that they privileged particular communities and people in ways that stressed harmony and timelessness' (2007, 68). Thus knowledge that was generated about the Iroquois through disciplinary rigour and specialisation also produced a 'knowing of' the subject that involved cementing categorisations that were, and are, in fact fluid and negotiated (and often far more complex). However, on the other hand, through more recent reforms in the discipline of anthropology in which empire and colonialism are increasingly accounted for, Simpson finds some possibilities: 'critiques and philosophical trends outside of and within anthropology that have embedded the discipline within the history of colonialism, have highlighted ethics and form, and pluralised the places and peoples that are now considered viable for ethnographic analysis' (2007, 69; see also Simpson 2014).

Thus, with Ruha Benjamin, we ask 'who and what are fixed in place – classified, corralled, and/or coerced…' (2016, 150) through the refinement and reform of disciplinary knowledge? Benjamin, addressing science and technology studies, argues for understanding the 'carceral imaginaries' in which technoscientific knowledge seeks 'to contain individual bodies *and* collective visions of the future' (ibid., 151). Technology is, for example, one of the many conduits through which forms of racial domination are 'upgraded'. As Benjamin writes of the shadow, or as she calls it 'underside', of technoscientific development:

> Visions of development and progress are too often built upon forms of social and political subjugation that require upgrading in the form of novel techniques of classification and control. When scholars set out to study the values, assumptions, and desires that shape science and technology, we must also remain attentive to the racial anxieties and fears that shape the design of technoscience. (Benjamin 2016, 149)

While disciplines such as phrenology that explicitly invoked ideas of racial inferiority and superiority have been rejected, as Bhambra, Simpson and Walter's scholarship highlights, racial anxieties and fears have shaped many disciplines, including anthropology, biology, history, sociology and neuroscience (see also, Gould 1981; Willinsky 1998). Such anxieties cannot simply be renounced as existing 'back there' in the past or as unimportant 'context'; as having no impact on the ongoing processes of knowledge creation and refinement.

Indeed, the academic categorisation, counting, labelling and measurement of 'colonial subjects', illustrated through the work of both Walter and Simpson for example, was done in the name of disciplinary rigor. But it was also done within a wider colonial project of containment, subjugation, and – ultimately – possession, based on constructed racial hierarchies that privileged the European coloniser. In other words, the basis of knowledge specialisation does not adequately ensure against violence. Expert communities have converged on very dangerous ideas of inferiority and 'abnormality' through acceptable systematic applications of knowledge and research criteria (see Said 1989; McNiven and Russell 2005); rigorous treatments of 'evidence' (and now data) that do not critically approach the very definition of 'evidence'. To put it simply, there is nothing about specialised knowledge that ensures that it is not the 'knowledge of the powerful,' carrying past and present enactments of racial violence.

Knowledge frees as well as domesticates

Knowledge has liberating capacities. The freeing potential of knowledge is captured in the idea of 'speaking truth to power' in the tradition of critical pedagogy,
or in the reconstructive possibilities enabled by seeing and knowing injustice.
Knowledge can mobilise and connect, and thus knowledge can bring about
change. This is a key argument of proponents of powerful knowledge, who suggest that it is through powerful knowledge that *genuine* freedom is possible: '…it is
only through the boundaries of the disciplines that genuine freedom, unforeseen
expanded possibilities, can be generated' (Young and Muller 2013, 247). Yet, while
knowledge may have the capacity to free, it also has the potential to domesticate.
We draw here on the work of Ghassan Hage (2017) who examines the notion of
domestication in a similar way to how we are attempting to understand disciplinary knowledge: as both necessary and flawed, with the capacity to elicit power
as well as violence. Hage notes how domestication can be the act of making a
home, or homeliness, however it 'paradoxically, is also a mode of domination,
control, extraction, and exploitation' (2017, 91). He draws the concept of domestication into dialogue with settler colonialism to show the generalised features of
domestication: 'inhabiting the world by occupying it' (ibid., 94).

Hage's critique of generalised domestication trains our attention to the forces of
normalisation and acceptance within the educational project of powerful knowledge: we are to be 'at home' with occupation and the taming of the Other within
disciplines and their translations into school curricula. This 'homeliness' produces
the fantasy of domestication as mutually beneficial, and even *genuinely* freeing: 'a
relation of domination that aims to be lived as a relation of nondomination' (Hage
2017, 91).[1] Disciplinary knowledge has a domesticating impulse in that it seeks to
offer knowledge that is useful and powerful, thus increasing comfort and a sense
of homeliness in the world. However, the ways in which 'powerful knowledge' is
advocated to address inequality can slip towards generalised domestication: 'the
act of occupying a space by declaring one's own interest as its primary organizing
principle' (Hage 2017, 94–95). Hage warns that the fantasy of mutual benefit locks
us into a cycle of normalised knowledge-for-control: 'the fact that we are not able
to think of solutions, or worse, we are unable to ask questions, other than through
and within the categories of generalized domestication' (ibid., 126).

We suggest that this can have two key concerning, potentially violent, effects:
assimilation and appropriation. First, the governance of the Other through the
epistemic projects of colonialism (for example, as demonstrated by Walter [2010]
and Simpson [2007] above) is deeply assimilationist: unable to think beyond the
fantasy of mutual benefit in the process of domination. Indeed, the claim that
'nothing else seems to be on offer' for a just curriculum, apart from the powerful knowledge framework (Young and Muller 2013, 247), seems to reflect a similarly worrying assimilationist approach. Second, appropriation occurs through
the polarised assumption that 'powerful knowledge' is more 'objective', more

'specialised' and more 'powerful' than 'community knowledges'. This is a paradox-ical assumption that rests on the appropriation of community knowledge and community experience within disciplinary (and thus 'powerful') knowledge. For example, McNiven and Russell (2005) outline the ways in which colonial tropes about the Other have been central to the development and specialisation of disci-plines such as anthropology and archaeology. Images of the Other, along with their own specialised and honed knowledge systems, are domesticated (dominated, controlled, extracted and occupied) and woven into the process of disciplinary specialisation. To create such a strongly polarised distinction between 'powerful knowledge' (disciplines) and general knowledge produced through communities and experience is to expunge the power relations that are so central to the devel-opment of the capacity of 'powerful knowledge' to be powerful.

As Hage notes,

> polarization is a process driven by the domesticator that has an interest in the polarity. To speak of polarization as opposed to just difference is to speak of a difference where a force is aiming to evacuate each element of what makes it similar to the other. (2017, 98)

When difference is understood in this way through polarisation, communities can be divided and students have to choose between artificial poles rather than being able to understand the interrelated nature of knowledge and the power relations that can keep inequality in place. Arguably, the restricted frame of powerful knowl-edge – namely its blindness to the shadows of colonial-modernity and to the hegemony of its specialisation – reflects the domesticating desire: it sets out to "recover' an omnipotence we never had' (Hage 2017, 126).

Conclusion: knowing history and the powerful interests of knowledge

> To accept one's past – one's history – is not the same thing as drowning in it; it is learning how to use it. An invented past can never be used; it cracks and crumbles under the pressures of life like clay in a season of drought. (Baldwin 1995, 80–81)

In this paper we have sought to engage productively with the ways in which dis-ciplinary knowledge is sutured into the past and present practices of colonial violence. The context for our contribution is the significant political debates sur-rounding the nature of knowledge and truth, and in particular the many con-temporary struggles over the continuing colonial legacies within university and school curricula. Specifically, we address the debates within the field of education prompted by the conceptual development of 'powerful knowledge', which posi-tions itself as the means by which knowledge can come 'back into' educational con-siderations (Young 2008). In our discussion, we have suggested that the conceptual development of powerful knowledge unfortunately constructs a false binary that posits powerful knowledge as concerned with the 'what' of knowledge, and critical accounts of knowledge as too overly concerned with the 'who' of knowledge. This polarising position seems to enable powerful knowledge to bypass the political nature of knowledge and the interwoven practices and processes of knowledge production and use. The result is that disciplinary and specialised knowledge is reified as in and of itself somehow capable of transcending 'knowledge of the powerful' to become 'powerful knowledge' for all.

We suggest that ultimately powerful knowledge fails to see the violence that is inherent in its production, and the perpetuation of that violence that occurs through such silencing. As we have outlined above, there is no way that disciplinary knowledge can escape its enduring connections to colonialism, and – effectively – its links with 'knowledge of the powerful': knowledge that was and is generated through relationships (often violent ones) with the peoples and cultures marginalised through colonialism. In this way, 'powerful knowledge' is in danger of performing Baldwin's edict of cracking and crumbling under the pressures of life. We suggest that the obfuscation of the exclusions and violence of colonial-modernity, including the use and development of disciplinary knowledge, is a form of invention. It is a form of invention that retains the progressive impulse (or shine) of modernity, without recognising the destruction (or shadow) of modernity. Further to the notion that knowledge contains both power and violence, we have shown that at times disciplinary knowledge formation also relies on violence to produce power. We argue, therefore, that when the kinds of violences we have discussed in the sections above are not ethically and politically engaged, the power of knowledge can become co-opted into a cycle of epistemic violence, driven by histories of colonisation and dispossession.

Key to the problems we have identified with 'powerful knowledge' and its reliance on disciplinary knowledge being an objectively better basis for understanding the world, is that it fails to account for the relationships that occur through the production and use of knowledge, and the power and politics that infuse such relationships. In doing this it repeats violent histories of misrecognition. We suggest, therefore, that more just curricula would make visible the politics of knowledge production and the power relations that underpin such politics. It would seek to make students aware of connections between different forms of knowledge similar to that argued for by Bhambra in relation to sociology (2014b). In this way it would guard against both polarisation and relativism, each of which position difference in ways that tend to divide and engender competition, that are in turn bound within legacies of racialisation and violence.

The historical reflexivity that we have advocated, which is based on an understanding of the interwoven nature of the past, present and future allows us to see both the power *and* violence of knowledge, its shine *and* its shadow side. It also allows us to consider how we can *work with* (rather than ignore) the multiple relationships that occur in the production of knowledge: relationships between violence and power; between experience and theory; between community and institution; between past and present; and between privilege and marginalisation. This then, is not a call to reject the disciplines nor an argument that suggests that disciplinary knowledge is not powerful. Instead it is an appeal to ward against the invention of a disciplinary past that overlooks the colonial and racialising practices that have contributed to their power. Our focus here has been on the colonial logics of epistemic power in the formation and use of knowledge, but the analysis presented also extends to the multiple ways in which power circulates and sticks within knowledge: 'whiteness', 'heteronormativity', 'masculinity', and class-based 'elitism', to name just a few. By foregrounding multiplicities *and* relationality, we believe disciplinary knowledge can really be more meaningful and more powerful for *all*, rather than be an assimilative solution to inequality that does not truly contend with the politics and power of social relations and knowledge production.

We therefore suggest the need to turn towards, not away from, the historical relationship between disciplinary knowledge and colonial-modernity in order to address the stark inequalities of our world and to create stronger communities of knowledge. This position requires that any theory of knowledge interested in social justice and power must attend to the *interests* of knowledge as constitutive of knowledge itself. The interests of knowledge cannot be dealt with by creating a binary between the 'who' and the 'what' of knowledge, as Young attempts to do in the distinction between 'knowledge of the powerful' and 'powerful knowledge'. Interests are invariably embedded within knowledge processes (or 'specialisation') as we have delineated above; knowledge is *interested*.

Note

1. As Helen Ngo (2017) has recently discussed, processes and practices of racialisation also contribute to racialised bodies feeling not-at-home in body and lived environment, reminding us of the paradoxical effects of domestication that Hage points to.

Acknowledgements

The authors would like to thank the Guest Editors, as well as John Beck, Lyn Yates and Fazal Rizvi for their helpful comments on earlier drafts. The authors are responsible for the argument presented here, and any limitations or insufficiencies in the analysis.

Disclosure statement

No potential conflict of interest was reported by the authors.

ORCID

Sophie Rudolph ⓘ http://orcid.org/0000-0001-6542-8858
Arathi Sriprakash ⓘ http://orcid.org/0000-0003-3655-0605
Jessica Gerrard ⓘ http://orcid.org/0000-0001-9011-6055

References

Ahenakew, C., V. Andreotti, G. Cooper, and H. Hireme. 2014. "Beyond Epistemic Provincialism: De-Provincializing Indigenous Resistance." *Alter Native* 10 (3): 216–232.

Alexander, C., and D. Weekes-Bernard. 2017. "History Lessons: Inequality, Diversity and the National Curriculum." *Race Ethnicity and Education* 20 (4): 478–494.

Ahmed, S. 2017. *Living a Feminist Life*. Durham, NC: Duke University Press.

Andreotti, V. de O. 2011. "(Towards) Decoloniality and Diversality in Global Citizenship Education." *Globalisation, Societies and Education* 9 (3–4): 381–397.

Baldwin, J. 1995. *The Fire Next Time*. Modern Library ed. New York: Modern Library.

BBC News. 2017. "Gauri Lankesh: Indian Journalist Shot Dead in Bangalore." September 6. Accessed November 6, 2017. http://www.bbc.co.uk/news/world-asia-india-41169817

Beck, J. 2013. "Powerful Knowledge, Esoteric Knowledge, Curriculum Knowledge." *Cambridge Journal of Education* 43 (2): 177–193.

Benjamin, R. 2016. "Catching Our Breath: Critical Race STS and the Carceral Imagination." *Engaging Science, Technology, and Society* 2: 145–156.

Bhambra, G. 2007. *Rethinking Modernity: Postcolonialism and the Sociological Imagination*. Hampshire: Palgrave McMillan.

Bhambra, G. 2014a. "Postcolonial Entanglements." *Postcolonial Studies* 17 (4): 418–421.

Bhambra, G. 2014b. *Connected Sociologies*. London: Bloomsbury.

Bhambra, G. 2016. "Comparative Historical Sociology and the State: Problems of Method." *Cultural Sociology* 10 (3): 335–351.

Brown, A. L., and W. Au. 2014. "Race, Memory, and Master Narratives: A Critical Essay on U.S. Curriculum History." *Curriculum Inquiry* 44 (3): 358–389.

Campbell, C., and H. Proctor. 2014. *A History of Australian Schooling*. Crows Nest: Allen & Unwin.

Catling, S., and F. Martin. 2011. "Contesting Powerful Knowledge: The Primary Geography Curriculum as an Articulation between Academic and Children's (Ethno-) Geographies." *Curriculum Journal* 22 (3): 317–335.

Cohen, S. 2001. *States of Denial: Knowing about Atrocities and Suffering*. Malden, MA: Polity Press.

Connell, R. W. 2007. *Southern Theory: The Global Dynamics of Knowledge in Social Science*. Sydney: Allen & Unwin.

Connell, R. W. 2017. "In Praise of Sociology." *Canadian Review of Sociology* 54 (3): 280–296.

Counsell, C. 2011. "Disciplinary Knowledge for All, the Secondary History Curriculum and History Teachers' Achievement." *Curriculum Journal* 22 (2): 201–225.

Dirks, N. 2001. *Castes of Mind: Colonialism and the Making of Modern India*. Princeton: Princeton University Press.

Fanon, F. (2008) 1952. *Black Skin White Masks*. Translated by C. L. Markmann. London: Pluto Press.

Fataar, A. 2016. "Towards a Humanising Pedagogy through an Engagement with the Social-Subjective in Educational Theorising in South Africa." *Educational Research for Social Change* 5 (1): 10–21.

Firth, R. 2011. "Making Geography Visible as an Object of Study in the Secondary School Curriculum." *Curriculum Journal* 22 (3): 289–316.

Garcia, N. M., N. López, and V. N. Vélez. 2018. "QuantCrit: Rectifying Quantitative Methods through Critical Race Theory." *Race Ethnicity and Education* 21 (2): 149–157. doi:10.1080/13613324.2017.1377675.

Gerrard, J., S. Rudolph, and A. Sriprakash. 2017. "The Politics of Post-Qualitative Inquiry: History and Power." *Qualitative Inquiry* 23 (5): 384–394.

Go, J. 2016. *Postcolonial Thought and Social Theory*. Oxford: Oxford University Press.

Gould, S. J. 1981. *The Mismeasure of Man*. New York: W. W. Norton & Company.

Gramsci, A. 1971. *Selections from the Prison Notebooks*. New York, NY: International Publishers.

Hage, G. 2017. *Is Racism an Environmental Threat?*. Cambridge: Polity Press.

Hall, S. 2016. *Cultural Studies 1983: A Theoretical History*. Durham, NC: Duke University Press.

Hoadley, U. 2015. "Michael Young and the Curriculum Field in South Africa." *Journal of Curriculum Studies* 47 (6): 733–749.

Joseph Mbembe, A. 2016. "Decolonizing the University: New Directions." *Arts & Humanities in Higher Education* 15 (1): 29–45.

McNiven, I., and L. Russell. 2005. *Appropriated Pasts: Indigenous Peoples and the Colonial Culture of Archaeology*. London: Rowman & Littlefield.

Mignolo, W. D. 2002. "The Geopolitics of Knowledge and the Colonial Difference." *South Atlantic Quarterly* 101 (1): 57–96.

Moreton-Robinson, A. 2015. *The White Possessive: Property, Power, and Indigenous Sovereignty*. Minneapolis: University of Minnesota Press

Mills, Charles. 2007. "White Ignorance." In *Race and Epistemologies of Ignorance*, edited by Shannon Sullivan and Nancy Tuana, 11–38. Albany: SUNY Press.

Mignolo, W. 2000. *Local Histories/global Designs: Coloniality, Subaltern Knowledges, and Border Thinking*. Princeton, NJ: Princeton University Press.

Muller, J. 2014. "The Pathos of Specialised Knowledge." In *Educational Research in South Africa: Practices and Perspectives*, edited by C. Wolhuter, A. Fataar, S. Motala, and V. Wedekind, 1–10. Potchefstroom: Platinum Press.

Nakata, M. 2007. *Savaging the Disciplines, Disciplining the Savages*. Canberra: Aboriginal Studies Press.

Ngo, H. 2017. *The Habits of Racism: A Phenomenology of Racism and Racialized Embodiment*. Lanham: Lexington Books.

Park, P. K. 2013. *Africa, Asia, and the History of Philosophy: Racism in the Formation of the Philosophical Canon, 1780–1830*. Albany: Suny Press.

Peters, M. 2015. "Why is My Curriculum White?" *Educational Philosophy and Theory* 47 (7): 641–646.

Rata, E. 2012. "The Politics of Knowledge in Education." *British Educational Research Journal* 38 (1): 103–124.

Rudolph, S. 2016. "The Logic of History in 'Gap' Discourse and Related Research." *The Australian Educational Researcher* 43 (4): 437–451.

Rudolph, S. 2018. "The past in the Present: Identifying the Violence of Success and the Relief of Failure." In *The Relationality of Race in Education Research*, edited by G. Vass, J. Maxwell, S. Rudolph, and K. N. Gulson, 145–155. London: Routledge.

Said, E. 1978. *Orientalism*. London: Routledge & Kegan Paul.

Said, E. 1989. "Representing the Colonized: Anthropology's Interlocutors." *Critical Inquiry* 15 (2): 205–225.

Santos, B. 2014. *Epistemologies of the South: Justice against Epistemicide*. Boulder, CO: Paradigm.

Shear, M., and M. Haberman. 2017. "Trump Defends Initial Remarks on Charlottesville; Again Blames "Both Sides."" *New York times*, August 15. Accessed November 6, 2017. https://www.nytimes.com/2017/08/15/us/politics/trump-press-conference-charlottesville.html

Simpson, A. 2007. "On Ethnographic Refusal: Indigeneity, "Voice" and Colonial Citizenship." *Junctures: The Journal for Thematic Dialogue* (9). http://junctures.org/index.php/junctures/article/viewFile/66/60.

Simpson, A. 2014. *Mohawk Interruptus*. Durham: Duke University.

Standish, A., and A. Sehgal Cuthbert, eds. 2017. *What Should Schools Teach? Disciplines, Subjects and the Pursuit of Truth*. London: UCL IOE Press.

Stoler, A. L. 2008. "Imperial Debris: Reflections on Ruins and Ruination." *Cultural Anthropology* 23 (2): 191–219.

Stoler, A. L. 2016. *Duress: Imperial Durabilities in Our times*. Durham, NC: Duke University Press.

Van Norden, B. W. 2017. *Taking Back Philosophy: A Multicultural Manifesto*. New York: Columbia University Press.

Walter, M. 2010. "The Politics of the Data: How the Australian Statistical Indigene is Constructed." *International Journal of Critical Indigenous Studies* 3 (2): 45–56.

Weiner, M. F. 2014. "(E)Racing Slavery: Racial Neoliberalism, Social Forgetting, and Scientific Colonialism in Dutch Primary School History Textbooks." *Du Bois Review: Social Science Research on Race* 11 (2): 329–351.

Willinsky, J. 1998. *Learning to Divide the World: Education at Empire's End*. Minneapolis: University of Minnesota Press.

Wolfe, P. 2016. *Traces of History: Elementary Structures of Race*. London: Verso.

Yates, L. 2018. "History as Knowledge: Humanities Challenges for a Knowledge-Based Curriculum." In *Knowledge, Curriculum and Equity: Social Realist Perspectives*, edited by B. Barrett, U. Hoadley and J. Morgan, 45–60. London: Routledge.

Young, M. 2008. *Bringing Knowledge Back in: From Social Constructivism to Social Realism in the Sociology of Education*. London: Routledge.

Young, M. 2010. "The Future of Education in a Knowledge Society: The Radical Case for a Subject-Based Curriculum." *Journal of the Pacific Circle Consortium for Education* 22 (1): 21–32.

Young, M. 2013. "Overcoming the Crisis in Curriculum Theory: A Knowledge-Based Approach." *Journal of Curriculum Studies* 45 (2): 101–118.

Young, M., D. Lambert, and C. Roberts. 2014. *Knowledge and the Future of School: Curriculum and Social Justice*. London: Bloomsbury.

Young, M., and J. Muller. 2013. "On the Powers of Powerful Knowledge." *Review of Education* 1 (3): 229–250.

Yuval Davis, N., G. Wemyss, and K. Cassidy. 2017. Everyday Bordering, Belonging and the Reorientation of British Immigration Legislation. *Sociology*: 1–17. doi:10.1177/0038038 517702599.

Zipin, L., A. Fataar, and M. Brennan. 2015. "Can Social Realism Do Social Justice? Debating the Warrants for Curriculum Knowledge Selection." *Education as Change* 19 (2): 9–36.

3 Racism as 'Reasonableness'

Philosophy for Children and the Gated Community of Inquiry

Darren Chetty (iD)

ABSTRACT

In this paper, I argue that the notion of 'reasonableness' that is, for many, at the heart of the Philosophy for Children (P4C) approach particularly and education for democratic citizenship more broadly, is constituted within the epistemology of 'white ignorance' and operates in such a way that it is unlikely to transgress the boundaries of white ignorance so as to view it from without. Drawing on scholarship in critical legal studies and social epistemology, I highlight how notions of reasonableness often include consensus, 'racialised common sense' and the 'typical' view. In addition the promotion of particular dispositions on the grounds of 'reasonableness' both promotes stability and limits how one may think otherwise. Thus, P4C practices that fail to historicise, examine and challenge prevailing notions of reasonableness establish an epistemically 'gated' community of inquiry.

Introduction

In her article in this special issue, Zara Bain notes,

> Educating for social justice requires educating in ways that are socially just insofar as we do all that is within our power to ensure that our pedagogy actively works against reproducing the epistemological systems that foster ignorance as a route to racial injustice. (Bain 2018)

In this paper, I argue that the notion of 'reasonableness' that is, for many, at the heart of the Philosophy for Children (P4C) approach particularly and education for democratic citizenship more broadly, is constituted within the epistemology of 'white ignorance' (Mills 2007) and operates in such a way that it is unlikely to transgress the boundaries of white ignorance so as to view it from without. Thus, P4C practices that fail to historicise, examine and challenge prevailing notions of reasonableness establish an epistemically 'gated' community of inquiry.

Specifically, I will argue that whilst racism is often assumed to be the preserve of unreasonable individuals, an understanding of the world informed by Charles

Mills' *The Racial Contract* permits us to see that reasonableness might be conceived as both structured by 'white ignorance' produced by 'the racial contract' and as a tool for maintaining 'white ignorance' by rendering actions intended to disrupt and dismantle white supremacy as 'unreasonable', whilst posing as a conceptual and philosophical norm that sits 'outside of ideology'. In order to begin to do this I will first offer a brief overview of the notion of 'reasonableness' as discussed in P4C scholarship, before turning to critical legal studies and social epistemology. I will then explore the ways in which some of the assumptions reflected in these debates are echoed in the practice of the community of inquiry, as an example of a pedagogical approach, P4C, explicitly committed to using philosophy to further the values associated with life in democratic, pluralistic societies.

Reasonableness as an educational aim

I wish to situate this discussion within a broad consensus in educational philosophy, theory and policy, whereby the notion of 'reasonableness' is viewed as an important educational aim and value. This sometimes appears as part of a defence of the need for schools in liberal societies to cultivate civic virtues (see e.g. Callan 1997) as part of a defence of the importance of critical thinking, or as an element of democratic education. In this paper I will focus on the way in which 'reasonableness' has been developed and defended by scholars arguing for the value of teaching philosophy in schools within the 'Philosophy for Children' or P4C tradition as an example of an educational practice committed to the value of democracy and the role of philosophy in nurturing and sustaining democratic institutions and values. While this paper will, I hope, be of particular interest to practitioners and scholars of P4C, it should also be relevant to those with an interest in education for democracy.

In earlier work, I have focused on issues to do with the choice of resources within P4C practice, especially with young children (see Chetty 2014). I argued that the popularity of certain books amongst P4C practitioners as useful sources for enquiring philosophically about racism lent some weight to claiming that the idealised community of inquiry – a truly egalitarian space, where the path of inquiry is not blocked and where all assumptions are examined – might actually sometimes be operating as a 'Gated Community of Inquiry'. I drew on work on gated communities to explore how this spatial metaphor can be a fruitful way of thinking about how race and racism is dealt with in educational practices such as P4C, where, as Joanna Haynes and Karin Murris write, 'Race and racism often crop up as problematic "no- go" areas' (Haynes and Murris 2011, 296). As Atkinson and Flint point out, concerns about safety and security in gated communities enable 'social distance to be maintained' (Atkinson and Flint 2004, 875). In such a social climate the unfamiliar is viewed with suspicion and as a potential intruder whose presence is illegitimate. Thus the gated community can, they argue, be viewed as a 'cognitive shelter'.

As well as the materials selected as starting points for philosophical inquiry, I have also explored in other writing (see Chetty and Suissa 2016), how a sense of discomfort, particularly the discomfort of P4C practitioners racialised as white, may contribute to the philosophical consideration of racism being pushed to the margins or even beyond the intellectual boundaries of the community of inquiry.

In what follows, I build on some of this earlier work, as well as on the work of theorists working within the field of critical philosophy of race and social justice education (see e.g. Applebaum 2010; Boler and Zembylas 2003; DiAngelo 2011; Leonardo 2009) in order to explore the way that reasonableness *itself* is constituted and understood and how this can limit the possibilities for discussing and addressing race and racism within educational practices that see philosophical thinking as vital to education, and particularly to education for democracy.

It is increasingly difficult to speak of 'Philosophy for Children' as if it is a uniform set of principles and practices. In their Editorial for the 2011 special issue of the *Journal of Philosophy of Education* entitled 'Philosophy for Children in Transition', Nancy Vansieleghem and David Kennedy explore the various different developments within the broad field of philosophy for and with children 'after Lipman', noting that these multiple views yield significant implications 'as a discourse, a methodology, a philosophical enterprise, and a form of biopolitical production' (Vansieleghem and Kennedy 2012, 179, 180).

Whilst the philosophical novels written by Matthew Lipman are still widely used in many countries, in others they are rarely if ever, seen; rather picturebooks, retellings of myths, films, poetry and other works of art are used as starting points for philosophical inquiry. The extent to which teachers work with questions created by students varies – some P4C advocates regard this as central to their practice, others suggest supplying students with a philosophical question can be a more philosophically productive approach, at least in the early stages of building a 'community of inquiry'.[1] Lipman's original P4C programme was clearly indebted to John Dewey and the American pragmatists. Subsequent P4C scholars have drawn upon analytic and continental philosophers and on a growing range of theoretical perspectives. However, whilst some scholars of P4C give 'reasonableness' less attention in their work it remains significant in current P4C scholarship, and is discussed in three chapters of the recent *Routledge International Handbook of Philosophy for Children (2017)*.

As previously mentioned, Matthew Lipman, who began his work on the original P4C programme in the late 1960s, saw a very close relationship between reasonableness and critical thinking, citizenship education and democracy, arguing that 'Critical thinking improves reasonableness, and democracy requires reasonable citizens so critical thinking is a necessary means if our goal is a democratic society' (Lipman 1991, 244). In a slightly different, and even stronger, formulation, he states: 'I take it that in a democratic society there is a maximum premium on the cultivation of reasonableness. The goal of education should therefore be the development of reasonable individuals' (Lipman 1991, 64).

Both Tim Sprod and Michael Pritchard add moral education to the list of educational goals for which 'reasonableness' is central. In his highly influential work *Reasonable Children: Moral Education and Moral Learning,* Pritchard claims that reasonableness is educationally desirable, though it 'is rare even in adults' and is 'not an all-or-nothing concept' (Pritchard 1996, ix). As Sprod notes, despite the book's title, Pritchard avoids offering a definition of 'reasonableness', preferring instead to offer what he terms a 'a rough demarcation' (Sprod 2001, 13). This decision by Pritchard is far from atypical amongst scholarship related to P4C, leading Renia Gasparatou to conclude that 'The ideal of *reasonableness* seems to provide some common ground, yet the way P4C theorists characterize reasonableness can be rather vague …' (Gasparatou 2016, 105). A concept that is at once so important and so nebulous is deserving of closer attention.

Splitter and Sharp view reasonableness as an aspect of rationality but claim that it goes beyond it. 'As an educational ideal, reasonableness goes beyond rationality which is all too-too-often rigid, exclusively deductive, ahistorical and uncreative' (Splitter and Sharp 1995, 6). In contrast to rationality, 'reasonableness' is seen by Lipman as being comprised of critical *and* creative thinking, where the 'twin pillars of critical thinking are reasoning and judgment' (Lipman 1991, 65).

The suggestion that 'reasonableness' is, unlike rationality, not ahistorical is in keeping with some of Lipman's discussion, although this too seems vague at times. For example, Lipman writes that, '[r]easonableness certainly does not exclude cultural literacy, but neither does it specify such literacy in terms of a particular set of contents'. (Lipman 1991, 65) whilst noting somewhat ambiguously that '[w]e are rapidly moving toward a multicultural world'. Lipman does not discuss what he means by this, nor indeed the history that might have lead us to conceive of our world as monocultural. Elsewhere, Lipman acknowledges criticism of his desired aim for education to produce 'reasonable, judicious and creative individuals'; namely, that it 'emphasizes method at the expense of content' but sees such criticism as mistaken. Rather, he argues,

> It is not unusual to find people who are learned but reason poorly and lack judgment. But I cannot imagine anyone being reasonable without acquiring the amount of content a reasonable person ought to have. If knowing too little is injudicious, then surely that is something a judicious person will endeavour to avoid. (Lipman 1991, 92)

Lipman appears to envisage that a child who has an education aimed at cultivating reasonableness will 'endeavour to avoid' lacking the necessary knowledge. Given that this quote appears in a section where Lipman argues that schools should prioritise cultivating higher-order thinking, it is not clear exactly what knowledge Lipman thinks should be on the curriculum. This may go some way to explaining why whilst he includes knowledge as an element of reasonableness, subsequent P4C scholarship has not tended to explore the relationship between knowledge, the school curriculum and reasonableness. The element of this relationship that I focus on here is the sense in which pedagogical spaces conceived as communities of inquiry may reflect and reproduce the kind of 'knowledge' that can be better understood as a form of ignorance which, as Charles Mills argues, serves an ideological function. As Mills' analysis of white supremacy as a racialised political system of domination shows, the maintenance of this system involves an epistemological contract that establishes 'norms and procedures' for determining what counts as 'moral and factual knowledge of the world' (see Mills 1997, 17; Bain, this issue).

The distinction between reasonableness and rationality is perhaps also in need of further attention. Terri Field, in an article that is cautiously optimistic about the potential of P4C, raises questions as to whether P4C's advocacy of reasonableness will allow for voices that have been excluded by reason or whether Lipman's P4C project, informed as it is by American pragmatism, is subject to at least some of the same criticisms as those made by feminist philosophers about reason (Field 1995).

Indeed, whilst Lipman and others have argued that reasonableness is complex and mulitilayered, the vagueness of what precisely reasonableness entails increases the possibility of it being reduced to proceduralism. Thus, the SAPERE Handbook deals with the complexity of reasonableness by advising teachers working with students, '... to reflect on the very idea of reasonableness and on what counts as good reasoning' (SAPERE 2010, 23). The Handbook does not give teachers a clear indication of what is meant by reasonableness. At the same time it offers some suggestions/guidelines for ground rules for developing a community of inquiry. These include 'encouraging positive body language, such as eye contact and smiling' and considering the use of 'time out' or 'extra thinking time' if 'someone breaks the rules'. Given the educational aim of cultivating reasonableness through the community of inquiry, these rules and sanctions can presumably be viewed as both reasonable and likely to foster reasonableness.

The social nature of reasonableness

Whilst acknowledging the literature that discusses 'reasonableness' as multi-layered, my 25 years of involvement with P4C as a trainee, practitioner and trainer has lead me to believe that the two aspects of reasonableness most prevalent in P4C practice and scholarship in the UK and mostly likely beyond are as follows: (1) reasonableness is constituted and understood through dialogic inquiry in a community of inquiry that is (2) governed by imposed or negotiated ground rules which are intended to be reasonable and foster reasonableness.

The role of philosophical dialogue or 'the experience of trying to reason together, as a community' (Lipman 2003, 21) in cultivating reasonableness is a consistent theme in P4C literature, with Splitter and Sharp viewing reasonableness as 'primarily a social disposition'. (Splitter and Sharp 1995, 6). Most recently Caralho and Medonça put this in the strongest terms when they claim that, 'it is not possible to educate for reasonableness without educating persons to think (and feel, and act) for themselves through an ethical experience of dialogue with others' Costa-Carvalho and Mendonça 2017, 128).

Before discussing how discussions between children in a classroom might foster reasonableness, Pritchard briefly discusses how some committees might be good illustrations of reasonableness – where group deliberation might inform social policies – and considers how committees may ensure that they offer reasonable recommendations. Many of his suggestions relate to openness to reasons, willingness to compromise without compromising personal integrity, and dispositions conducive to dialogue. However he also acknowledges that '[r]epresentative membership can be expected to contribute to the reasonableness of a committee's recommendations' (Pritchard 1996, 11). This consideration for who is (and is not) present within a deliberative setting, and the extent to which this may affect the constitution of reasonableness, is a further area of P4C scholarship which, I contend, has received insufficient attention. For in the case of classroom deliberative dialogue we are faced with a challenge concerning representativeness. A legacy of segregated housing, whether through racial laws (in the US or South Africa for example) or house prices makes it rare to find a classroom where the students are representative of the nation in which they are located with regards to race and class. There is a greater likelihood that the students will be representative of the immediate locality (notwithstanding the existence of private schools and, in the UK, faith schools), but it is questionable as to whether that local population has itself been shaped through reasonable circumstances. Given that deliberative dialogue is seen by P4C scholars as having a central role in the development of reasonableness in children, the question of representativeness and the non-ideal conditions that impede it are important for considering the detrimental impact this may have on the views and testimony that students will encounter in the community of inquiry.

A racially representative classroom is not the norm in the UK (where I live and teach), in the USA (where P4C originated) or in South Africa (where I retain family connections and where a growing amount of P4C work is happening). Nor indeed is it the norm at P4C related conferences. Indeed at the most recent ICPIC[2] Conference, one of the key-note speakers noted – not entirely accurately – that there were no Black people present. If representativeness is important for reasonable deliberation, educators faced with unrepresentative classrooms and educational spaces presumably need to take active steps to bring in perspectives that are insufficiently represented, particularly when their under-representation may be related to historical oppression and marginalisation.

The teacher's role in the community of inquiry is described by Lipman's successor at the Institute for the Advancement of Philosophy for Children, Maughn Gregory, as to 'shore up the fairness and reasonableness of the discussion' (Shaughnessy 2005, 2). This is not a straightforward task. While the question of what notion of reasonableness teachers are most likely working with is an empirical question beyond the scope of this paper, it is worthy of some research attention, not least because, as Lipman, Sharp and Oscanyan put it, 'the teacher is the one who has to make the judgment as to whether a particular personal account should be capitalized upon or squelched' (1980, 92). My observation, from working with teachers, is that they will often take their cue from everyday language usage of 'reasonableness', which often reflects how the term is used in policy and the law. For this reason, in this next section I focus on discussion of reasonableness and race in critical legal studies.

Reasonableness and the law

In *Reasonableness, Racism and The Articulation of Bias*, a study of the use of reasonableness in criminal law, Nicola Y. Wright, uses the term 'reasonable man' to mean 'the anthropormorphism of the law's devotion to "reasonableness and rationality", as well as its claim of "neutrality" and "objectivity"' (Wright 1996, 2). In order to test whether a person has acted as a reasonable person would, it has for some time been common in UK courts to refer to 'The man on The Clapham Omnibus'. This derives from a time when Clapham was seen as part of the suburban commuter belt of London. The man in question is said to be reasonably intelligent and educated. Jody Armour finds similar use of personifications in US law: 'the ordinary prudent man', 'the average man', 'the man in the street', and the 'man who takes the magazines at home, and in the evenings pushes the lawn mower in his shirt sleeves' (Armour 1997, 22). The last of these three mostly clearly implies, like the Victorian commuter to London, a person who is gendered, classed and raced. In *Negrophobia and Reasonable Racism*, Armour highlights court cases where lawyers representing white defendants who have shot a black person argue that they did so out of reasonable fear of attack and in so doing 'exploit the racial fears of jurors in asserting the reasonableness of their fear of supposed assailants who are Black' (Armour 1997, 4). Armour concludes, 'Certainly the reasonableness standard, in its classic formulation (e.g. the 'average man'), privileges the perspective of the majority'. He posits the idea of the 'reasonable racist'. By this he means someone who holds racist beliefs but who holds that s/he can be excused for them because they can be shown to be typical, majority views and 'blame is reserved for the (statistically) deviant' (Kelman 1991 cited in Armour 1997, 19). Armour summarises his argument thus,

> The legal definition of reasonableness is uniquely insidious in that it takes the merely typical and contingent and presents it as truth and morality, objectively construed. For example, according to legal usage, the 'objective' standard of reasonableness encompasses those beliefs and attitudes that are shared by most people. (Armour 1997, 26)

Armour argues that the role of the courts is often taken to be to *observe* rather than *define* the attributes of the reasonable man. Whilst we have already seen that P4C scholarship advocates a more nuanced 'multilayered' sense of reasonableness than that of 'the reasonable man', it is still a useful exercise for educators to identify elements of the practice that might be implicitly working with this understanding of reasonableness. A common implicit argument in P4C scholarship is that in order to address continuing racism it is the cultivation of reasonableness that is required.

However, I suggest, reasonableness as commonly understood in the law may not only be shaped by a racist past but help secure a racist present.

Racialised common sense

This critical perspective on the association between the notion of reasonableness, the claim to neutrality, and the perspective of the majority suggests the educational significance, when it comes to cultivating genuinely democratic dialogical deliberation, of attending not just to the question of who is present in the community of inquiry, but to the underlying relationships of domination and their historical roots. For even if we were to find a classroom where the make-up of students is representative of the nation in which they live (leaving aside for now questions of why the historically contingent and often unreasonable boundaries of the nation should be our measure), we still find ourselves in a situation, the representative constitution of which may mask the relationships of domination that characterise the society in question. In this sense, such a classroom may be seen as a non-ideal situation, within which the avowed educational starting-point of reasonableness and neutrality serve as an ideal analogous to the role of ideal theory in Mills' criticism of liberal theory, where, as he notes, 'Obviously such a starting point crucially handicaps any realistic social epistemology, since in effect it turns things upside down. Sexism and racism, patriarchy and white supremacy, have not been the exception but the norm' (Mills 2007, 17).

It may be objected here that in the context of P4C, given its concern with relationships amongst reasoners, the suggestion that majority perspectives will be privileged in philosophical enquiries is overstated. It is important to note that whilst certain perspectives might be in the majority in a community of inquiry, the emphasis given to reason in P4C enables a minority perspective to be heard, considered and judged persuasive by a majority – *if* it is adjudged to be the most reasonable perspective. However, Meira Levinson sounds a note of caution about this, when she observes that in multiracial classrooms,

> differences of opinion and priorities in part reflect differences in life experience that lead members of different racial/ethnic groups to 'read' the world in different ways. The problem, however, is that this often results in majority group members judging minority perspectives as being totally irrational, as well as unreasonable. (Levinson 2012, 75, 76)

Furthermore, as the analysis of white ignorance reveals, the prevailing notion of reasonableness can involve not just a cognitive model or a set of procedural norms, but also an accepted set of behaviours. Thus a standard of reasonableness might serve to limit the extent to which a person from, say, a racially minoritised perspective can argue, challenge and disagree with what is taken to be 'reasonable' with regard to racism. In further exploring how such processes may play out in pedagogical situations, it is helpful to consider what Alexis Shotwell terms 'racialized common sense' (Shotwell 2011).

As Shotwell explains, in a passage clearly evoking Mills' notion of 'white ignorance',

> Common sense is formed at the fulcrum of what we care to know, and what we cannot know under current conditions, what we refuse to know, and what we would have to transform ourselves in order to know. When we have commonsense knowledge, we do seem to know something, frequently even in a strong sense of the term 'know' – but this knowledge is frequently a product of and productive of inequitable social worlds. As a norm, an epistemology of ignorance perpetuates the common sense it describes. (Shotwell 2011, 37)

An example of the way in which such 'racialized common sense' can serve to block discussions of racism on the part of people from racialised minorities can be glimpsed in Leonardo's observation that 'Anyone who has performed a radical racial analysis has faced … a scenario where the messenger is dismissed because the message produces psychological dissonance between a white subject's desire for racial justice and her inability to accept radical change' (Leonardo 2009, 82).

On the face of it philosophical inquiry should help us to examine 'racialised common sense' assumptions. However, in social contexts structured by the operation of white supremacy as a racialised system of domination involving the epistemic aspects described in Mills' analysis of white ignorance, our guiding notion of 'reasonableness' may itself be infected with racialised common sense. As Shotwell writes, 'The close link between reason, white, and what it is to be human – or the extent to which those three attributes end up being coterminous – should give us pause' (Shotwell 2011, 61).

In a similar analysis, David Theo Goldberg explores how representations in racial discourse 'draw their efficacy from traditions, conventions, institutions, and tacit modes of mutual comprehension' (1993, 46). Goldberg frames this underlying stratum as the pre-conceptual plane that underlies and shapes modernity's common sense (38, 43).

What this discussion suggests is that, in the context of attempts at dialogue and deliberation that invoke, explicitly or implicitly, normative notions of reasonableness, there is a danger that reasonableness can imply a prioritisation of stability; a notion that, in turn, may suggest not moving too far from where we are and not looking too closely at how we got here. A crucial step in correcting this potential bias is insisting on the importance, especially in an educational context, of historical perspectives. Yet, as I discuss in the next section, it is this perspective that is arguably missing from many approaches to philosophical dialogue as a means to cultivating reason and enhancing democracy.

The problem of ahistoric reasonableness

Marguerite and Michael Rivage-Seul discuss a P4C project implemented in Guatemala in 1987, 2 years after the election of civilian president Vincio Cerezo, after 30 years of military dictatorship. Whilst they see much that is positive in P4C, they view it as lacking some of the essential qualities for democratic education offered by educators working in the Freirian tradition:

> The founding belief seems to be that teaching children to think reasonably, responsibly and philosophically can eventually empower the Guatemalan majority to take advantage of democracy's promises. The implication is that democracy is not being realized because of deficiencies in reasoning on the part of Guatemalan adults. Hope for democracy's full implementation are thus pinned on elementary schoolchildren, who, despite the fact that most attend school for no more than a few years, are to bring reason to Guatemala's political processes in a generation or so. (Rivage-Seul and Rivage-Seul 1994, 45)

They go on to make the more disturbing criticism that,

> Indeed, if we consider *the structured silences in the P4C program we see how pretensions to uncommitted objectivity actually help* the Guatemalan government establish locally and internationally its claim that it is in fact democratic. Moreover, regardless of whether one agrees or disagrees with the claim, *accepting its practical validity and leaving it unquestioned represents a political option on the part of P4C in support of* the Cerezo government and against the dissenting constituency represented by Bermudez and by the Guatemalan Army of the Poor. Acceptance effectively comprises an option in support of the Guatemalan ruling classes. (Rivage-Seul and Rivage-Seul 1994, 57; my emphasis).

Marguerite and Michael Rivage-Seul argue that Lipman's P4C program does not engage with history. 'While laudably characterized by dialogue, such pedagogy ignores the historicity of what is known' (Rivage-Seul and Rivage-Seul 1994, 48).

It is perhaps not surprising that significant criticisms of Lipmans's P4C program have tended to come from Latin America, and have often placed P4C in the context of US 'interventions' – whether military, political or educational – in the region. While these criticisms highlight the hypocrisies and contradictions in the US self-image as a democracy, in the context of the present discussion I want to focus on the way in which they reveal the ways in which white ignorance may be operating to reflect and reinscribe relations of domination, whether at a global or a local level. In this sense, Rivage-Seuls' analysis has affinities with Mills' discussion of the 'management of memory', and with the related analysis of 'technologies of colonization' developed by De Lissovoy.

Reasonableness in education is explored by Noah De Lissovoy with regard to race as follows:

> In this way, the reasonable as an ideological formation in education does not simply distort a more authentic reason, but rather serves as a technology of colonization. It is not simply that elites operate according to a rationality that privileges their own class-racial interests, but rather that the violation of communities of color becomes the positive content of good sense in White politics and policy, according to the Manichean logic of colonial society outlined by Fanon (1963) … Activists for equity in education who seek to intervene in official policy-making circles need to realize that they confront not only political headwinds, but also a form of rationality that depends on the abjection of the poor, Black and Brown as the condition of its own dubious virtue. (De Lissovoy 2016, 353)

Furthermore, the criticisms of P4C as a practice that is guilty of 'ahistoricity', whether or not they can be fairly made of Mathew Lipman's work, are echoed in critical discussions of the discipline of philosophy itself. As Carlos Sanchez puts it, many professional philosophers believe that 'if a thinking situates itself, embodies itself, or historicizes itself, then it is not profound, and worse, not philosophy' (Sánchez 2011, 40, cited in Dotson, 2013, 14).

Much of Charles Mills's work is devoted to showing how philosophers have dehistoricized race. In *The Racial Contract* Charles Mills points out that the fact that the discussion of race and racism is so often absent from western philosophy might lead one to think that race and racism have been marginal to the history of the West. But in actuality, we need to understand how the 'exclusion or marginali- zation of race and its typically sanitized, whitewashed, and amnesiac account of European imperialism and settlement, is deeply flawed and misleading'. Reflecting on some of the explicit expressions of racist and colonial attitudes in Kant's work, he observes that 'white academic philosophy as an institution has had no interest in researching the implications of, and making known to the world this dimension of Kant's work', Mills (1997, 71). As a result, when one considers the historical com- plicity of academic philosophy in obscuring and excluding matters of racialisation from that which is considered to be 'proper' study, it becomes easier to understand the expressions of surprise, bewilderment, and alarm that have arisen from both media commentators and professional philosophers, in response to calls to decol- onise philosophy courses at universities in the UK and beyond.

This discussion also has important implications for questions of who is included in the academic philosophy community, and who is excluded from it. In her 2012 paper 'How is this Paper Philosophy?' Kristie Dotson 'answers a call made by Anita Allen to genuinely assess whether the field of philosophy has the capacity to sus- tain the work of diverse peoples' (Dotson 2013, 3). Drawing on Gayle Salamon's 'Justification and Queer Method, or Leaving Philosophy' Dotson argues that aca- demic philosophy privileges a 'culture of justification' where justification is 'making congruent' one's position with acceptable norms (Salamon 2009, 226). As Dotson explains,

> Typified in the question, 'how is this paper philosophy', is a presumption of a set of com- monly held, univocally relevant, historical precedents that one could and should use to evaluate answers to the question. By relying upon, a presumably, commonly held set of normative, historical precedents, the question of how a given paper is philosophy betrays a value based on performances and/or narratives of legitimation. Legitimation, here, refers to practices and processes aimed at judging whether some belief, practice, and/or process conforms to accepted standards and patterns, i.e. justifying norms. (Dotson 2013, 5)

I detect a similar attitude and set of assumptions in the words of an established P4C practitioner and writer who responded to one of my earliest attempts to philoso- phise about race in the community of inquiry with the observation that, though socially significant, race is not philosophically interesting – whereas 'differences is'.

I suggest that here we have an example in the community of inquiry of the same problem that Mills highlights, and that can be seen as a specific example of the operation of white ignorance.

It is perhaps not too great a leap to conclude that, according to this person, my thoughts were presumably then not philosophical. What if similar thoughts were expressed by a child in a classroom? The above discussion suggests that in a classroom where children are engaged in a philosophical inquiry structured by norms of 'reasonableness', the constitution of certain contributions as 'unreasonable' may serve to exclude perspectives offered by pupils from racialised minorities, and in so doing, to both mask and perpetuate racialised structures of domination.

Dotson makes the important point that 'one has to examine closely who has the burden of destabilising norms any given time and whether this a worthy activity for the targeted populations. Diverse practitioners may disproportionally shoulder it' (Dotson 2013, 15).

This burden may go some way to explaining the continuing absence of people of colour at P4C seminars and conferences. It may also explain why so few philosophers of colour have embraced P4C despite the liberatory potential claimed by many of its advocates. But even more than this it should raise questions about who is shouldering the burden for doing the philosophical labour in our classrooms.

Crucially, for our discussion of the operation of philosophical dialogue in P4C and other educational contexts, De Lissovoy argues that a kind of thinking that would break with reasonableness 'will show up in the first instance as unreasonable' (2016, 346). What might such 'kinds of thinking' look like, and how might we come to see them as pedagogically valuable? In the next section, I explore the possibility that, as part of the necessity of revealing and addressing the historical processes that come to constitute forms of white ignorance, and that therefore may inflect dominant notions of 'reasonableness', disruptions initially perceived as 'unreasonable' may have an educational value.

'Unreasonable' disruptions of Denial/white ignorance/reasonableness

The recent 'Rhodes Must Fall' campaign at Oxford University may be an example of unreasonable public pedagogy. In reality, the campaign's very name is a demand for an 'unreasonable' action – the removal of a statue. This is sufficiently unreasonable behaviour to be newsworthy. Newspaper articles covered the campaign. Think-pieces were produced in broadsheets and online platforms. Many of them focused primarily or exclusively on the 'unreasonableness' of the demand to take down the statue of Cecil Rhodes. Some articles however did not avoid engaging with the campaign's justifications for its demands. Articles detailing Cecil Rhodes' behaviour and writings appeared. So too did articles pointing out that the taking down of statues is not the sole preserve of ISIS, and also exploring how the demand to 'remove' a statue is not equivalent to a simple act of destruction and can express a more complex and nuanced political position. For example, there is a complex history of removing statues celebrating Nazism and Soviet Communism in post-war Europe. In Lithuania and Hungary[3] there are memorial parks where one can visit the statues to communism that were erected and, after the fall of communism in the country, removed but not destroyed. Implicit in the park is the idea that the statues are worthy of being taken seriously as historical artefacts even as they are not worthy of remaining in place as celebrations of deeply oppressive ideals. Might we say the same of Cecil Rhodes? And if not why not? These are important moral questions, which are best answered with sufficient historical knowledge. These are questions which many of us concerned about social justice and education asked ourselves and each other. These are questions brought into public consciousness by 'unreasonable pedagogy'. The campaign did not succeed in its stated aim to relocate the statue. However Oriel College's backtracking on its offer of a six-month consultation period due to concern that it would lose donors revealed how the preservation of wealth impacts decision-making now as it did in Rhodes' era[4] (Telegraph).

The campaigners could have limited their concerns about Oxford University's relationship to racism and colonialism to a 'reasonable' course of action. I speculate that had they done so, the issues would have reached far fewer people and generated less discussion. They might have attempted to educate people only by means of more traditional academic practices, such as running seminars, lectures, writing historically informed papers about Cecil Rhodes, the University's relationship with colonialism, and so on. A series of student-run debates might have been held perhaps even with a number of sympathetic academics in attendance. If the institution was put under great pressure it may have commented on these discussions. It might have pointed out how proud it was that the fine tradition of debate at Oxford was being continued. In other words, without even needing to engage with substantive issues, it could communicate a congratulatory message to students for their conduct – conduct that is in keeping with the norms of the institutions. And given that the institution has historically defined those norms, this message could be read as a self-congratulatory message for the continuation of reasonableness in the institution. However, if this were to have happened, it is unlikely that anyone outside of Oxford University would ever have become aware of the debates taking place. The willingness of donors to threaten to withhold funds and the seemingly crucial role that would play would not have been revealed to the wider public.

As a result we might reflect on how starting in a place that appears at first *unreasonable* might help us to perceive the historical and social processes that contribute to our conception of reasonableness. Therefore possibilities for coming to know the world – and for challenging white ignorance and its political consequences – might be limited by an emphasis on a procedural notion of reasonableness that forecloses opportunities for inquiry and for knowing.

Conclusion

Laurence Splitter and Ann Margaret Sharp note, '[t]he concept of a "reasonable person" lies at the heart of P4C and, arguably, of education itself and the ideal of democracy' (Splitter and Sharp 1995, 6).

They go on to argue that reasonableness is linked to, but goes beyond, rationality, which they view as 'all-to-often rigid, exclusively deductive, ahistorical and uncreative'. As Tim Sprod notes, they argue that reasonableness is 'not just process oriented (requiring sufficient knowledge or content as well)' (Sprod 2001, 13).

In the above discussion, I have attempted to attend to the process element of reasonableness whilst also making a case for giving knowledge a greater status than the brackets above might imply. I have explored the ways in which the prevailing notions of reasonableness operating within everyday language, within academic philosophy, and within philosophical inquiry in the classroom, reflect layers of complex historical and social meaning. Specifically, I have suggested that reasonableness, so construed, can be understood as constituted by and reinscribing the epistemological features of white ignorance.

If reasonableness is, unlike reason, not ahistoric, then the cultivation of reasonable citizens presumably includes a commitment to the teaching of history. This seems vital to Mills' discussion of 'The Racial Contract', and indeed to much work in the critical philosophy of race. It raises questions then for how P4C practitioners, programmes and theorists engage with history as a subject of study and understand its place in philosophy and the community of inquiry.

Advocates of P4C would then be well served by historicising the movement itself, perhaps, given his influence on Matthew Lipman, beginning with the philosophy of John Dewey.

> I think that the great John Dewey never saw white supremacy as a major priority in his wrestling with philosophical and democracy. I think that is sad … you can't really be wrestling with American democracy unless you also come to terms with its legacy rooted in slavery, Jim Crow, and so on. So in that regard I think, despite his greatness and his genius, it is a major silence … (West 2004, 226)

The cultural milieu in which deliberation takes place is often one of white supremacy and white ignorance. The school curriculum is an element of this. Dialogical deliberation is thus limited in its scope for examining this milieu given that it is governed by reasonableness. That is not to say it is impossible, but rather that it is highly unlikely.

Notes

1. 'A group of people used to thinking together with a view to increasing their understanding and appreciation of the world around them and each other' (SAPERE 2010, 15).
2. ICPIC is the International Council for Philosophical Inquiry with Children. Conferences are held biennially. In 2017 the conference was held in Madrid.

3. See http://grutoparkas.lt/en_US/ and http://www.mementopark.hu.
4. http://www.telegraph.co.uk/education/universityeducation/12129261/Finally-Oriel-College-should-have-stood-up-to-Rhodes-Must-Fall-long-ago.html.

Acknowledgement

I would like to thank Judith Suissa for her editorial guidance and comments on an earlier draft of this paper.

Disclosure statement

No potential conflict of interest was reported by the author.

ORCID

Darren Chetty iD http://orcid.org/0000-0002-8943-6876

References

Applebaum, B. 2010. *Being White, Being Good: White Complicity, White Moral Responsibility, and Social Justice Pedagogy*. New York: Lexington Books.
Armour, J. D. 1997. *Negrophobia and Reasonable Racism*. New York: New York University Press.
Atkinson, R., and J. Flint. 2004. "Fortress UK? Gated Communities, the Spatial Revolt of the Elites and Time–Space Trajectories of Segregation." *Housing Studies* 19 (6): 875–892.
Bain, Z. 2018. "Is There Such a Thing as White Ignorance in British Education." *Ethics and Education* 13 (1).
Boler, M., and M. Zembylas. 2003. "Discomforting Truths: The Emotional Terrain of Understanding Difference." In *Pedagogies of Difference: Rethinking Education for Social Change*, edited by P. Trifonas, 110–136. New York: Routledge.
Callan, E. 1997. *Creating Citizens: Political Education and Liberal Democracy*. Oxford: Clarendon Press.
Chetty, D. 2014. "The Elephant in the Room: Picturebooks, Philosophy for Children and Racism." *Childhood & Philosophy* 10 (19): 11–31.
Chetty, D., and J. Suissa. 2016. "No Go Areas: Racism and Discomfort in the Community of Inquiry." In *The Routledge International Handbook of Philosophy for Children*, edited by M. Gregory, J. Haynes, and K. Murris, 11–18. Abingdon: Routledge.
Costa-Carvalho, M., and D. Mendonça. 2017. "Thinking as a Community: Reasonableness and Emotions." In *The Routledge International Handbook of Philosophy for Children*, edited by M. Gregory, J. Haynes, and K. Murris, 127–134. Abingdon: Routledge.
De Lissovoy, N. 2016. "Race, Reason and Reasonableness: Toward an 'Unreasonable' Pedagogy." *Educational Studies* 52 (4): 346–362.
DiAngelo, R. 2011. "White Fragility." *The International Journal of Critical Pedagogy* 3 (3): 54–70.
Dotson, K. 2013. "How is This Paper Philosophy?" *Comparative Philosophy* 3 (1): 121–121.
Field, T. 1995. "Philosophy for Children and the Feminist Critique of Reason." *Critical and Creative Thinking* 3 (1): 9–12.
Gasparatou, R. 2016. "Philosophy for/with Children and the Development of Epistemically Virtuous Agents". In *The Routledge International Handbook of Philosophy for Children*, edited by M. Gregory, J. Haynes, and K. Murris, 103–110. Abingdon: Routledge.

Goldberg, D. T. 1993. *Racist Culture*, 91. Cambridge, MA: Blackwell Publishers.

Haynes, J., and K. Murris. 2011. "The Provocation of an Epistemological Shift in Teacher Education through Philosophy with Children." *Journal of Philosophy of Education* 45 (2): 285–303.

Kelman, M. 1991. "Reasonable Evidence of Reasonableness." *Critical Inquiry* 17 (4): 798–817.

Leonardo, Z. 2009. *Race, Whiteness, and Education*. New York and London: Routledge.

Levinson, M. 2012. *No Citizen Left Behind*. Vol. 13. Cambridge, MA: Harvard University Press.

Lipman, M. 1991. *Thinking in Education*. New York: Cambridge University Press.

Lipman, M. 2003. *Thinking in Education*. 2nd ed. New York: Cambridge University Press.

Lipman, M., A. M. Sharp, and F. S. Oscanyan. 1980. *Philosophy in the Classroom*. Philadelphia, PA: Temple University Press.

Mills, C. W. 1997. *The Racial Contract*. Ithaca: Cornell University Press.

Mills, C. W. 2007. "White Ignorance." In *Race and Epistemologies of Ignorance*, edited by S. Sullivan, and N. Tuana, 13–38. Albany: SUNY Press.

Pritchard, M. S. 1996. *Reasonable Children: Moral Education and Moral Learning*. Lawrence: University Press of Kansas.

Rivage-Seul, M., and M. Rivage-Seul. 1994. "Critical Thought and Moral Imagination: Peace Education in Freirean Perspective." In *Politics of Liberation: Paths from Freire*, edited by C. Lankshear and P. McLaren, 41–61. London: Routledge.

Salamon, G. 2009. "Justification and Queer Method, or Leaving Philosophy." *Hypatia* 24 (1): 225–230.

Sánchez, C. A. 2011. "Philosophy and the Post-immigrant Fear." *Philosophy in the Contemporary World* 18 (1): 31–42.

SAPERE. 2010. SAPERE Handbook to Accompany Level 1 Course. 3rd ed. SAPERE.

Shaughnessy, M. F. 2005. "An Interview with Maughn Gregory: About Philosophy, Critical Thinking and Higher-Order Thinking." *The Korean Journal of Thinking & Problem Solving* 15 (1): 115–125.

Shotwell, A. 2011. *Knowing Otherwise: Race, Gender, and Implicit Understanding*. University Park: Pennsylvania State University Press.

Splitter, L., and A. M. Sharp. 1995. *Teaching for Better Thinking: The Classroom Community of Enquiry*. Melbourne: Acer.

Sprod, T. 2001. *Philosophical Discussion in Moral Educations: The Community of Ethical Inquiry*. London: Routledge.

Vansieleghem, N., and D. Kennedy. 2012. *Philosophy for Children in Transition; Problems and Prospects*. Oxford: Wiley-Blackwell.

West, C. 2004. "Afterword: A Conversation between Cornel West and Bill E. Lawson." In *Pragmatism and the Problem of Race*, edited by B. Lawson and D. F. Koch. Bloomington: Indiana University Press.

Wright, N. Y. 1996. "Reasonableness, Racism and the Articulation of Bias." Unpublished thesis. University of Ottawa, Canada.

4 Reconstructing a 'Dilemma' of racial identity education

Winston C. Thompson

ABSTRACT

In this paper, Thompson engages the fact that educators perceive themselves to be faced with an apparent dilemma regarding racial identity education. On one hand, their political obligations may incline them to teach racial identity so as to avoid reifying the reality of a racialized system of power. On the other hand, honoring their epistemic obligations to accurately represent the realities of the world may incline them to teach racial identity in a less consequentialist manner, prioritising the goal that students do not suffer hermeneutical injustices as they grapple with racial identities/consequences. Thompson argues that these seemingly opposed obligations can be united, by attending to their underlying claims. In closing, Thompson provides an example of an educational event that coheres with these conclusions.

Introduction

Some educators claim to be conflicted in regards to their educational obligations related to race. In my own experiences teaching preservice practitioners at a predominantly white university in the northeastern United States, I have heard well-intentioned educators express various formulations of this ongoing sense of tension.[1] This conflict surfaces in numerous accounts of classroom life, but also seems to emerge in the experiences of the family, institutions of civil society, and the like.[2] This conflict of racial identity education is, by popular accounts of those afflicted, owed to a frustration regarding the degree to which they believe they have what are essentially contradictory educational obligations related to teaching children about race. These increasingly race-aware educators, many of them new to the ethical language of social justice aims, perceive themselves as obliged to (1) keep students from entering into a racial identity and (2) bring students into a racial identity. Simply put: they take themselves to be morally hamstrung as they cannot meet both obligations at once. Or can they?

In this article, I engage this perceived dilemma, analysing elements of its construction and suggesting a new perspective on its constituent claims in the service of providing educators (broadly construed) some helpful analytic tools for their present circumstances and future actions. In this I will engage versions of the constituent pieces of the dilemma that are often voiced by my ethically-minded preservice educators, analysing why these issues might so often recur in their perceptions, and offering one potential response to the perceived dilemma. As this work is but one example of a response to the claims that I have encountered, it should be read as a general framework for educators who wish to think about their own or others' relationship to these issues and is intended for any parties searching for conceptual tools in aid of navigating the same.

My work in this paper will proceed across the sequence of the five sections that follow this introduction. In section two, I will further describe the core dilemma of this paper's consideration. As this dilemma is articulated in various ways by various educators, I will provide context for these reports (suggesting something of their value) while streamlining their most salient portions into an essential description. My description aims to sharpen the reader's attention to the sense of moral/ethical obligations (and their constituent pieces) that constitute the core of the dilemma. In order to pursue the aims of this article, in this and all subsequent sections, I charitably interpret the views (e.g. perceived claims, obligations, etc.) of those who perceive themselves as burdened by the central dilemma, even if I do not find these especially compelling. Section three provides an inexhaustive list of complicating factors that one might generally consider in making decisions regarding explicitly and intentionally engaging race within educational contexts. This listing provides analytic fodder for the remainder of the article. Section four attends to a number of the dimensions of consideration mentioned in the previous section, arguing that they give further substance to the description of the dilemma offered in section two. They are the constituent pieces of the dilemma's content. Section five shows that the perception of the dilemma can be avoided when its constituent pieces are reorganised and reconsidered. In this, I aim to show the educator's moral/ethical obligations are not in rigid tension and may indeed be mutually pursued. I conclude in section six by presenting an example of a pedagogical practice that honors the claims of the described 'dilemma', further showcasing the possibility presented by section five.

In advance of the main content of the article, a few remarks are necessary. First, though portions of my analysis might apply to other types of group-based identities, I do not claim to offer an analysis that is generalisable in this way; my attention in this work is firmly focused upon race. In this regard, my attention is very much circumscribed. That said, it should be noted that I will use a fairly capacious view of race that contains little more than the claim that race, however it is conceptualised, is tied to systems of power (Omi and Winant 1986; Bell 1992; Smedley 1993; Garcia 1996; Mills 1997, 1998; Shelby 2005). Though I cannot offer additional detail within this article, this view aligns with most foundational premises of mainstream racial scholarship, while remaining functionally agnostic about many of the details that might suggest one or another nuanced and competing racial theory. The article proceeds in this manner so as to preserve the degree to which multiple (though not all) accounts of race might find traction within the presented arguments.

Additionally, while the article does draw upon understandings of race that are rooted in a North American context, I do not intend my comments to be limited to only that region. Though race operates in specific ways in North America, much of what I detail can be readily applied to the specific racialised circumstances of numerous locations throughout the world, especially so for Western contexts. For this reason, dismissing this work's problem and analyses as the business of a uniquely 'American' ethical dilemma would be a mistake.

Describing the dilemma

Context and potential significance

The discourse around both race and the preponderance of relative disadvantage that accompanies some racial identities (i.e. those attached to 'minority' racial groups) has been rather present within mainstream spaces (i.e. those occupied by members of the majority racial group in Western contexts) in recent years (Vance 2016). In the US, for example, this focus might be explained by the mainstream foregrounding of race in the wake of the election of that country's first black president in 2008, the ubiquity of digital recording devices and the accompanying rise in so-called 'citizen reporting' of instances of racial violence at the hands of police officers, or any number of factors (Ibid). Whatever the origins for this focus, it is amid that attention to the lived realities of race and racialised trends of experience that educators have had cause to squarely address the question of 'what to tell the children?'. In what follows, I ask why that question matters (or, perhaps said differently, 'what might it represent?') and identify one potential response, suggesting that this response is especially relevant to the subject of subsequent sections of this article.

Questions of 'what to tell the children about race' are often found in reference to the concentrations of disadvantage that negatively impact members of racial minority groups (i.e. under conditions of racialised systems of power). One familiar example of this invocation might be found in the parent who feels some tension between the desire to, on the one hand, provide their child the explanatory resources necessary to interpret the race-sensitive systems of power that surround them and the desire to, on the other hand, either keep their child (1) insulated from complicity/contribution to the injustices of those systems and/or (2) for the moment, free from the knowledge that they have a hierarchical identity status that is unlike that held by some others (whether that might be a source of guilt, shame, or both, likely depends on the racial identity options available to the child).[3] That such a parent might struggle (perhaps, deliberating with family members, friends, other parents, etc.) to make the 'right' choice about what their children ought to be told about race suggests something of the perceived moral ambiguity of the situation. Never mind, of course, that research has shown that even fairly young children have an awareness of race that exceeds the expectations of adults around them, educators continue to struggle with their potential obligations related to bringing children into understandings of race and racialised identities (Tatum 2007; Winkler 2009; Delpit 2012).

Before turning to the central dilemma of this article, which is a subset of the practical ethical dimensions of this more general concern, allow me to offer a brief statement about the context and potential importance of this larger question. I would like to suggest (though not fully defend within the pages of this article) that the degree of handwringing regarding the question of what to tell the children about race may well be indicative of the significance of the query. Though a sense of these moral tensions is often invoked in relation to how one ought to (or ought not) bring children to the social facts of race, the question of 'what to tell the children' may well represent a rather fundamental worry, a pervasive preoccupation that tends to be primarily communicated as concern for the education of children. Said differently, the ongoing engrossment with questions of racial education may be reason to consider whether the concern relates only to young children as students of race.

Consider, for example, acclaimed author Ta-Nehesi Coates' award-winning memoir, *Between the World and Me* (2015). On the surface, the text is a missive from the author to his son (a literal example of what to tell the child/ren), explaining the social realities of race through reflection on the author's lived experiences and observations of the world. More fully explored, and perhaps evidenced by the record-breaking sales the book has enjoyed from adults with and without explicit roles as educators, the text does not demonstrate only what one might tell children about race (Alter 2015). Instead, the text serves as a meditation on how we, adult members of this flawed world, might continually attempt to make some sense of its racialised systems and structures. Asking the question of what to tell the children about race is especially significant as it may well represent our own discomfort in our abiding efforts to navigate our relationship with race in this world. Arguably, this partially explains the appetitive fervor around Coates' book, as Coates, one of the most celebrated contemporary writers on the subject of race, offers a relatively clear (and, perhaps, cautiously hopeful – or maybe 'hopefully cautious') path forward regarding these issues.[4]

In some sense, then, the question of 'what to tell the children' might be understood as an anxiety regarding what to teach children, others, and, ultimately, *ourselves,* about race, its consequences, and our related normative obligations. Unsurprisingly, given its potential significance, this general question is not easily answered (owed in part to reasons offered in section three) and, in one particular application, seems to give rise to a perceived dilemma for well-meaning educators.

The dilemma

Against the backdrop of this general question of what to tell the children, race-aware preservice educators in my courses report perceiving a particularly sharp moral dilemma. These educators take race to be a feature of social life that visits unequal distributions of burdens and benefits upon persons. In light of this, they recognise a moral imperative to attend to (and are beset by a moral uncertainty regarding) the ways in which they enact what might be referred to as racial identity education.

By use of the term 'racial identity education', I wish to highlight the notion that an education about race necessarily influences a student's racial identity and, as such, is educational activity in the service of creating/endorsing that identity. Decisions about how to teach race contain content about racial identity. That is, one learns portions of one's racial identity – the contours, the logics, the potentially embodied social facts – as one more broadly learns about race. Even educator decisions to remain silent on particular subtopics of a race curriculum impact a student's sense of race and their relationship to their own racial identity (Helms and Cook 1999). For example, not engaging race in the curriculum may communicate that race is a topic unworthy of focused study, implying that racialised identities have little explanatory salience regarding historical, social, and personal circumstances. As such, an educator's conscious choices in racial education may have unintended (though oftentimes foreseeable) consequences for a student's racial identity (Blum 2012). Given that developmental psychology has a strong tradition of work on racial identity development/formation, one may draw upon that rich conceptual legacy to delimit this wider educational category.[5]

As race-aware educators engage the work of teaching children (or other students) about race, their obligations in a process of racial identity education may seem to pull in two incompatible directions. Firstly, they perceive a need to educate students about race such that the students can pursue a more desirable racial future. Secondly, they perceive a need to educate students about race such that the students can more fully engage with the realities of their circumstances.

Stemming from the first obligation, educators wish to educate in an instrumental or consequentialist fashion, as labour in the construction of a more 'socially just' future. Educators who hold only this obligation may well call for 'colour-blind' racial identity education (in the pedagogical *process* and/or the outcome-oriented *product* of the education). From this perspective, the good educator is one who pursues a socially desirable 'post-racial' future. Therefore, one views education as a potential tonic for the social problems of race, which can be combatted by a generation (or *n* generations) of persons who have not learned strong commitments to particular racial identities. In addition to this larger social goal, these educators might take issue with curricula that suggest some racial determinism for individual students of colour. The implied or explicit argument is that some race-sensitive curricula might influence students to think of themselves as perpetual victims in a larger system of race-based social disadvantage, such that the curriculum itself has a deleterious effect on students' sense of their social/political/economic potential.[6] John Huppenthal, former Superintendent of Public Instruction in Arizona, captures this view well in response to a description of racial minority student outcomes in a canceled racially-focused Mexican-American Studies curriculum:

> To tell young kids that the whole deck - that they can't get ahead, that they're victims […] it defies what we know. We know that you can engage in America. You can get ahead – that these kids can succeed. (NPR 2012)

On both the social and individual scale, this obligation directs educators to consider their efforts as contribution to the construction of a self-determined potential future.

The second obligation is based in educators' sense that they have a duty to prepare students for the reality of the world they currently inhabit, a world marked by racial power and disadvantage. As such, racial identity education organised in response to this obligation is primarily concerned with the veracity of the curriculum (rather than its potential social impact). Educators who hold only this obligation may well call for lessons that do not deemphasise the stark realities of race. As one educator reports in relation to her racial minority student outcomes:

> You need to understand being Black ... the struggles that Black people have gone through ... [As a Black person], you need to learn how to deal with adversity because you're going to be faced with it big time. (Hambacher and Thompson 2015)

This sense of obligation has an almost deontological character as the role of educator carries with it a corresponding duty to remain faithful to the subject matter, faithful to the truth of the world. The good educator, under this perspective, is one who prioritises her student's ethical/epistemic status as a knower in the world, even though this might be painful for the student. Miranda Fricker's compelling work on the concept of 'hermeneutical injustice' is helpful here as the educator is concerned with the ethical status of the student as a knower of her experiences in the world. As a person in a racialised world, the student ought to be educated in a manner that allows her to reasonably accurately interpret her experiences within this world, and to be recognised as doing so (Fricker 2007).[7] Summarised, then, this obligation directs educators to safeguard the accuracy of their representations of the present world.

Though a good many educators might perceive themselves to have one or the other (or, indeed, none) of these general obligations regarding racial identity education, we shall concern ourselves with the subset of educators who struggle with the ethical ambiguity of perceiving themselves to have a combination of both. In the service of formalising the obligations of this dilemma, it will be helpful to represent the major core of the perceived dilemma's tension. Some race-aware educators perceive themselves to have the following two ethical obligations:

> *The Political Obligation*: One ought to teach race (and racial identity) in a manner that prioritises desirable political consequences. Avoiding the reification of systems of racialised

power, one ought to educate students for creating and inhabiting a more socially just (i.e. race neutral) world.

The Epistemic Obligation: One ought to teach race (and racial identity) in a manner that prioritises one's epistemic and educational duties to accurately represent the world. One ought to avoid one's students' experiencing hermeneutical injustices as they grapple with racial identities (and their consequences) in this racialised world.

Given these formalised statements, do educators have a justifiable basis for the moral hesitation often whispered within the ranks of teacher education programmes?

As mentioned in the introduction, my own experiences teaching predominantly white cohorts of future educators has presented many instances in which these preservice educators express their perceptions of a tension between these two obligations. They report that, on the one hand, they feel obliged to teach their own students in ways that do not endorse racialised identities; this strategy is intended to dismantle racialised systems of power (or, at the very least, avoid active complicity in those systems). On the other hand, they report discomfort with that duty as they perceive themselves to have an obligation to accurately teach their students about the (social) facts of the world. For many of these preservice educators, it would seem that this second obligation may result in an education that further embeds students within racialised identities such that, by so doing, it contributes to reifying racialised systems of power. For these preservice educators, this is the core or their perception of a dilemma.

The fact that these preservice educators perceive some tension between these two commitments ought not be undervalued. For many of the preservice educators with whom I work (and others like them), race, power, and social justice are relatively novel concerns, such that their early engagements with moral reasoning on these subjects may well set the tone for their continued work on and through these issues. Taking seriously the fact that they find these obligations to be a source of moral frustration, I resist providing neatly-packaged answers, opting instead to encourage them to further consider the claims upon which their sense of moral turmoil rest.

In the service of addressing that specificity of this perceived dilemma, I now turn to an analysis of a few perceived factors that often complicate the entire subject of race for educators. To better analyse the ethical dilemma of racial identity education, it shall be useful to identify some of the perceived complicating factors that make education about race, generally, such a difficult topic for well-intentioned educators.

Complicating factors

In what follows, I offer an inexhaustive list of complicating factors that can influence decisions regarding explicitly and intentionally engaging race within educational contexts. As issues of race are over determined and have their sources in numerous (often overlapping) factors, I select these dimensions due to their applicability to our current work. This listing provides analytic fodder for the remainder of the article by discussing perceived barriers to ethical conduct in racial identity education. I submit that these factors are perceived to complicate this educational work in either/both process and product. That is to say, some ethical ambiguities of *what* to teach about race and *how* to teach it have a basis in perceptions of these factors. For our purposes, the following descriptions (which draw upon my experiences with nearly racially-homogeneous groups of pre-service educators) of these likely interrelated dimensions of consideration are best understood with these qualifications held firmly in mind.

Epistemological dimensions

The processes of education may be frustrated by uncertainties regarding whether one is socially well-positioned to appropriately know the subject of study, in this case: race (Sullivan and Tuana 2007). This uncertainty might be placed upon the educator, the student, or, in the autodidactic case, the unified both. Take note, I present the epistemological factor as one that may frustrate regardless of *how* it might do so (either in fact or merely only in perception of a potentially paralysing inability to understand that which is taught). The notion that our racial identities complicate what we might know (or impact the ignorances that might restrict all but our must careful actions), suggests that we might also be limited in what we might learn (or learn well). One might readily imagine educators wondering whether racial identities can limit one's epistemic horizons. University educators may well be familiar with students who seem nervous when speaking on the subject of race, yet simultaneously optimistic about the possibility that they might learn something in their moment of vulnerability. These students often qualify their views by stating something resembling the following: 'As a [member of a particular racial group], maybe I just can't see it accurately, but I understand things in the following way …'. While this sense of uncertainty could stimulate motivation for students to learn, a similarly uncertain educator might feel unequipped to teach race, given their own racial identity.[8]

Diagnostic dimensions

Diagnostic issues are a portion of much educational activity, as educators often need to identify various dimensions of their students' educational need (Sparks 2015). By invoking that fact here, I wish to suggest that the diagnostic problem, rendered as a complication that is related to the epistemological issues (see above) regarding assessing the potential and current status of a student of the subject of race, is an additional source of consternation for many learners and educators of race and racial identity. The worry might be expressed as a concern that attempting to determine a person's status as a student of race (and as a holder of a racialised identity that is partially the product of educational experiences) fails to provide any useful traction. Perhaps it injures the dignity of a student by suggesting that one or another relationship with race is deficient? Or maybe the diagnosis does little more than presume one's immediate or eventual participation in a system that may be morally suspect? Said differently, the act of diagnosing a student's facility with the subject of race (and racial identity) may be perceived to lack the necessary normative force to be of much use. For example, an educator of a small child might diagnose that child as not yet understanding race very well. Even so, in light of the worries of this diagnostic factor, one might concurrently claim that the child has no moral need to *better* understand such a (morally) 'bad' concept. In part, one's ability to helpfully diagnose the student's status suffers from a lack of clear educational aims on the subject of race (see below).

Teleological dimensions

Closely related to the previous two issues, the teleological factor frustrates educators and learners who are uncertain of what racial education ought to have as a worthwhile educational aim. Should an education about race result in a non-racialised future? A colourblind present? A racial sensitive present? A racialised future in perpetuity? Something else entirely? In relation to this factor, educators might contend with the question of whether the activity of educating another person (or, perhaps, even oneself) about race, serves to reify the 'fact' or social 'reality' of this morally dubious topic? Efforts in responding well to race might be flummoxed by difficulties in identifying the ethically appropriate ends of, and efforts within, the educational process. Should schools or other institutions explicitly teach students how to conceive of or inhabit their racial identities? Are these educational institutions negligent if they do not do so explicitly? Absent an explicit racial curriculum, how might those judgements be complicated by the potential (or certainty) of implicit lessons entailed within the structures of the institutions?

Ontological dimensions

For many, the ontological problem of educating about race and towards racial identity might be simplified into a question of what one truly takes race to be (James 2012). This is to ask, is there some biological, morphological, or physiological basis for race, or does it exist only as real social fact?[9] If so, would that make race any less 'real' in our experiences and as an educational subject? Does educating one about race reify its reality (echoing some of the factors that have been previously described above)? Can the results of such educational activity be anything more than only the assertion of one view (amongst a potential many)?

Perhaps a good number of these worries are laid bare by public responses to the case of Rachel Dolezal. Dolezal, who identifies as racially black though her biological family asserts that they and she are racially white as defined by generally held standards, became the focal point for public discussions of the ontological status of race (Brubaker 2016). That abiding discussion suggests pervasive uncertainties about whether an objective essence to racial categories exists. The case may give one pause in regards to the degree to which such identities might be real and therefore appropriate subjects for legitimate study (and potential endorsement). For our current purposes, this suggests something of a basis for a hesitation one might have regarding race as an educational subject.

Alethic dimensions

Related to (yet distinct from) the previous descriptions, the truth status of claims regarding race, racial identity, and racial consequences may present a barrier for educators and students of race.[10] Even when taking the ontological query as a settled issue, one might nonetheless experience distress over whether there is a single truth to be known (or theory of what that truth might indicate or identify about those claims) regarding racial topics. Perhaps there are many parallel truths about race such that one's racial education might well be wholly dissimilar from one's neighbour yet hold an equivalent truth status despite this difference in content? How might that circumstance confound an attempt at racial education (especially given the impact that such an education might have on racial identities)? Must an education in race and racial identity necessarily push towards a truth, even under conditions in which there is no *single* truth to be known? How might that worry frustrate the ethical obligations that exist in a racialised society comprised of diverse persons attempting to coherently approach shared problems (see below)?

Social dimensions

Finally, for many potential educators and students of race, the underlying hesitations may be more indeterminately social, such that questions about conducting a racial education express and/or represent social facts and/or relationships in the past, present, or expected future that appear costly or overly burdensome. This social category may well contain some elements of other categories listed above, though its essence may rest in the fact of their interplay with other actors within the shared setting of our social environment. Said differently, the work of racial identity education may simply be complicated by the fact that it cannot take place in some purely 'academic' context; it happens in a messy social world.

It should be noted that I do not mean to suggest that educators only explicitly or consciously navigate these six dimensions (or some subset). I wish only to assert that in situations of uncertainty regarding racial identity education, these are some of the background conceptual influences that might complicate one's engagement with that project. For our present purposes of responding to the perceived dilemma of the incompatibility of the Political Obligation and the

Epistemic Obligation in relation to racial identity education, an understanding of these dimensions may be analytically beneficial.

Dimensions of the dilemma?

To recall our central dilemma, racial identity educators perceive themselves to be faced with a tension between the Political Obligation and the Epistemic Obligation, such that they are unable to proceed in an ethically appropriate manner. In this section, I shall engage the complicating dimensions mentioned in the previous section, arguing that they give further substance to the description of the obligations with the dilemma offered in section two. Said differently, these factors provide foundational claims upon which the dilemma's content is based. Let us review each obligation, in turn.

The Political Obligation draws upon epistemological considerations in order to claim that (E1) 'We don't know the degree to which our knowledge is bounded by our racial identity'. Additionally, in light of the fact that, per the social considerations of the endeavor, (S1) 'We occupy a world deeply marked by racialized systems of power', it is not surprising that (A1) 'We disagree about the truth status of contentious racial claims'. The Political Obligation builds upon these claims while also drawing upon the diagnostic considerations to remind us that (D1) 'We have little cause for confidence in assessments of what students ought to ultimately learn about race and racial identity'. Instead, even in the light of all this, the teleological dimensions of our considerations suggests that (T1) 'We can pursue desirable social and political consequences, namely, a more just world, when we engage in racial identity education'.

The above, taken in sum, may lead an educator to adopt a consequentialist view of ethical action in racial identity education. Acknowledging difficulties in knowing, assessing, and agreeing upon issues of racial identity in this contested social context, the educator might instead prioritise the outcomes of the educational project resulting in the articulation of *The Political Obligation* that:

> One ought to teach race (and racial identity) in a manner that prioritises desirable political consequences. Avoiding the reification of systems of racialised power, one ought to educate students for creating and inhabiting a more socially just (i.e. race neutral) world.

As such, the educator may perceive that they ought to keep their students from committing to inhabiting a racial identity, as holding such an identity sacrifices the possibility of a more just future world.

Conversely, the Epistemological Obligation draws upon ontological considerations in order to claim that (O2) 'Despite ambiguities regarding the reality of race, one may still be confident about the realities of its effects'. Building upon this, epistemological considerations of the endeavour recognise that (E2) 'Even though race might impact what we know about ourselves and the world, that need not prohibit potential students from its study'. Regardless of the fact that, according to alethic considerations, (A2) 'Educators and students might have or be in pursuit of nonidentical truths about race and racial identity', they might still conduct that work together. One's work in this process is aided by the diagnostic factors which suggest that (D2) 'Observations of hermeneutical struggles might present educators with the evidence necessary to recognise their educational duties to students'.

The above, taken in sum, may lead an educator to adopt a deontological view of ethical action in racial identity education. Acknowledging possibilities for engaging in educational work towards reducing hermeneutical injustices, even under the potential limitations that render race a complicated educational subject, the educator might prioritise the process of their educational activity resulting in the articulation of *The Epistemic Obligation* that:

> One ought to teach race (and racial identity) in a manner that takes seriously one's epistemic and educational duties to accurately represent the world. One ought to avoid one's students' experiencing hermeneutical injustices they grapple with racial identities (and their consequences) in this racialized world.

As such, the educator may perceive an obligation to bring their students into a racial identity, as holding such an identity is necessary for making sense of their racialised experiences in the world.

In this, we have identified 9 claims (labeled E1, S1, A1, D1, T1, O2, E2, A2, and D2) as constituent portions of the obligations that form the perceived dilemma of racial identity education. Assembled as they are (i.e. as The Political Obligation and The Epistemic Obligation) these claims seem at tension with one another.

But must their underlying claims be?

Redefining the issues

Taking the work of the last section as a point of departure, this section aims to reconcile the seemingly conflicted claims that constitute the two obligations (i.e. The Political Obligation and The Epistemic Obligation) of the dilemma of racial identity education. In what follows, I will suggest that these claims can be rearranged such that the resulting obligations are more clearly compatible with one another.

The claims, as understood in the previous section, are:

- (E1) We don't know the degree to which our knowledge is bounded by our racial identity
- (S1) We occupy a world deeply marked by racialised systems of power
- (A1) We disagree about the truth status of contentious racial claims
- (D1) We have little cause for confidence in assessments of what students ought to ultimately learn about race and racial identity
- (T1) We can pursue desirable social and political consequences, namely, a more just world, when we engage in racial identity education
- (O2) Despite ambiguities regarding the reality of race, one may still be confident about the realities of its effects

- (E2) Even though race might impact what we know about ourselves and the world, that need not prohibit potential students from its study
- (A2) Educators and students might have or be in pursuit of nonidentical truths about race and racial identity
- (D2) Observations of hermeneutical struggles might present educators with the evidence necessary to recognise their educational duties to students

The Political Obligation is founded upon E1, S1, A1, D1, and T1; while The Epistemological Obligation has O2, E2, A2, and D2 as its basis.

But, if we group these claims differently, we find that new obligations emerge.

One can acknowledge that (E1) 'We don't know the degree to which our knowledge is bounded by our racial identity'. Nonetheless, (E2) 'Even though race might impact what we know about ourselves and the world, that need not prohibit potential students from its study'. These two uncertainties cohere with the notion that (A2) 'Educators and students might have or be in pursuit of nonidentical truths about race and racial identity'. These point towards the *Open-mindedness Obligation:*Given the ambiguities of racial identity and its impact on our knowledge, one ought not for this reason restrict the study of race nor commit to authoritative accounts of racial identity education's necessary outcomes.

Additionally, one can acknowledge that (S1) 'We occupy a world deeply marked by racialised systems of power', yet (O2) 'Despite ambiguities regarding the reality of race, one may still be confident about the realities of its effects'. Said differently, that power is felt even if the source of that power is not fully understood. In light of this confidence about the real effects of that power, we can directly respond to it through educational activity; (T1) 'We can pursue desirable social and political consequences, namely, a more just world, when we engage in racial identity education'. These claims point towards the *Advocacy Obligation:*

In consideration of the pervasiveness of racialised systems of power, racial identity education ought to consider the impacts it can have on that power's real effects in the world.

And finally, one can grant that the degree to which (A1) 'We disagree about the truth status of contentious racial claims' results in the fact that (D1) 'We have little cause for confidence in assessments of what students ought to ultimately learn about race and racial identity'. However, that uncertainty about the ultimate learning outcomes of racial identity education does little to blunt the fact that (D2) 'Observations of hermeneutical struggles might present educators with the evidence necessary to recognise their educational duties to students'. Said differently, one need not reply upon clearly defined ideals to motivate educational action under non-ideal circumstances.[11] These claims point towards the *Engagement Obligation:*

In circumstances of abiding disagreement regarding issues of truth and knowledge of race and racial identity, one ought to engage in racial identity educational activity those persons seeking to understand their own experiences in a racialszed world.

Taken together these three obligations (i.e. The Open-Mindedness Obligation, The Advocacy Obligation, and The Engagement Obligation) represent a major accomplishment in response to the perception of the dilemma to which we are attending. They hold the underlying claims of the former obligations (i.e. The Political Obligation and The Epistemic Obligation) without the sense of incompatibility that marked the experiences of educators attempting ethical conduct in regards to racial identity education.

This reconstruction frees these educators from making a choice about whether or not to bring students into a racial identity. Instead, they have reason to view the issue of racial identity education as more complex than they might have first assumed. In the service of discussing this complexity, I will provide an example of a pedagogical exercise that conforms to the new obligations provided above.

A concluding example

During the spring semester of 2017, The University of New Hampshire was host to a cascade of racially charged events, which included incidences of brownface, racial slurs, vandalism, and more (NHPR 2017; WMUR 2017). In the wake of these disturbing happenings, faculty and staff convened a 'teach-in' during the fall of 2017. By popular accounts, the educational event was intended to create a space in which students might address and process elements of the racial context of the campus while becoming better educated about their racial roles therein (and beyond). I submit that this special educational event conforms to the three obligations offered in the previous section. In what follows, I will describe why this is the case and how it might serve as a model for educators in various contexts. I will conclude with reflections on the general value of this point, especially as it may be of value to the predominately white cohorts of preservice educators who have expressed the sense of moral dilemma at the core of this article.

The educational event at the University of New Hampshire rather directly took race and the racialised identities of its students as its subject of study. That these students largely appeared to be members of the majority racial group, gave context to the educational potential of the event, especially as it relates to their sense of the experiences of others and their own roles in racialised systems of power in their communities. The event coheres with the redefined obligations of racial identity education in the following ways:

In line with the Open-Mindedness Obligation, the event had no formal attendance restrictions for members of the community and consciously avoided the pursuit of a single authoritative result for its attendees. While the central issue of power in the racialised context of the campus was explored, the event was structured so as to allow all interested students to do the hard work of constructing their own views on the matters of fact. By providing those facts for students (i.e. reports of minority students' experiences, the histories of cultural practices and traditions, etc.), the event offered all voices an opportunity to attempt to make sense of the various pieces of knowledge (and positions from which they were known) present in the room.

Cohering with the Advocacy Obligation, the event did not seek to only have students learn about race and their racial identity. The educational event was also about better understanding one's classmates and improving one's understanding of oneself. In the exchange, some students at this predominately white campus voiced the realisation that, though they did not think of themselves in racialised terms, their actions impacted members of other racialised groups in ways that were now demonstrable to them – as were being articulated by classmates in the event. Without suggesting that all disagreements about race were resolved, one can be confident that the event led to a greater sense among the white attendees of the salience of one's racial identity status in regards to non-white attendees' patterns of experience. This result is especially meaningful, given the nearly racially homogenous demographics of the campus, which may limit opportunities for casual engagement with and reminders of the experiences of others.

Finally, the Engagement Obligation was met by the decision to host the educational event itself. The campus's community had been in a state of tension and turmoil, with many students at a loss for how to make sense of what they were experiencing. A group of faculty and staff members was able to recognise that the campus community was attempting to understand its racialised circumstances, such that these group members were moved to create an educational space in which to do so. The campus was calling for an opportunity to question, study, and learn in this way.

Educators might take the example of the educational event described above as one model of a promising educational encounter with race and racial identity. Rather than telling students what they racially must or must not be/come, this educational approach recognises their yearning to better make sense of the world (and their roles with it) and provides them with an opportunity to ethically (in its processes) navigate that difficult set of question themselves, while moving towards (as product) answers that contribute to their ethical relationships with others. Though the specific features of such racial identity work may shift according to its variables (institutional context, age, specific social histories of race, etc.), the underlying commitment to the fact that students must do much of the strenuous labor of making sense of race and their racialised selves is key.[12]

Perhaps recognition of that laborious educational task returns us to an earlier statement of the significance of the questions which stem from the anxieties of race as an educational subject impacting our identities.[13] Thinking once again about the central concerns of the perceived dilemma at the core of this article, I wonder if the predominately white preservice educators in my courses so often express moral perplexity about 'what to tell the children' regarding race due to the fact that they are, to some degree, actively navigating questions of what to tell themselves about race in this world of racialised systems of power.

As race is increasingly undeniable as a subject of attention within the societies that have made it so, growing numbers of persons are confronted with the task of making sense of themselves in its shadow (Stone 2016). Though there may be few simple answers to the educational questions they pursue, our sense of what educators owe to students may illuminate something of what we all owe to ourselves. Conceivably our central educational obligation in response to these racialized systems and structures is to take up this unending work, continually probing, studying, and educating ourselves about race and our racial identity. As the educators endeavour to bring students into this constant curriculum, perhaps we owe it to ourselves to commit to the same course of study.

Notes

1. According to recent demographic data published in the New York Times (Ashkenas, Park, and Pearce 2017), the student population of the University of New Hampshire has a higher percentage of white persons than its peer institutions (some of which are located within states that have higher percentages of white persons in their state populations than the state of New Hampshire). Among flagship state universities, one would be hard-pressed to identify a university in the United States with a higher proportion of white students.
2. The pre-service educators with whom I work state that they (and other well-intentioned educators within their networks) wrestle with the central dilemma of this article. They generally claim to be hobbled in their attempts to 'do the right thing'. As such, I draw from their statements in this article's pastiche constructions of the views held by some educators. I do not take these views to necessarily reflect their most carefully considered and constructed premises and conclusions but, instead, aim to represent the loose set of claims that recur in their moments of moral uncertainty as educators aware of race.
3. The general underlying factors of this example will be expanded upon in subsequent portions of this text.
4. Coates' work might be read as imploring his son (and us all) to recognise the value in straining and fighting for better days, but to accept that they are highly unlikely. This lesson is also signaled by the title of Coates' previous book, *The Beautiful Struggle* (2008).
5. This field is too expansive to capture here, but good work can be found in Helms (1990), and Tatum (1997); among others.
6. On a related point, one might also invoke the memorable image of DuBois' ([1903] 1994) character, John. Well-educated, he ultimately suffers due to his increasingly clear vision of racialized systems of power and is alienated from his community and life prospects.
7. Though Fricker is concerned with the person as knower, the person as student (i.e. one who comes to know) likely also carries ethical obligations for those who educate her.
8. See pieces within this issue that engage Charles Mills' fine work on the concept of white ignorance.
9. Though one might question the ontological status of race, one need not also question the fact of its effects. Through analogy, Elizabeth Anderson captures this nicely in noting: '[T]hat demons don't exist doesn't imply that demonized people don't exist'

(Anderson 2010, 161). See also Mills, C. "'But What Are You Really?' The Metaphysics of Race', in Mills (1998).

10. Though not labeled as such, work on this subject might be found in (and in the exchanges between) epistemological and ontological work on race. See McPherson (2015) or Haslanger (2000).
11. I (2015) explore related conceptions of ideal and non-ideal approaches to education.
12. Arendt ([1954] 1977) reminds us of a similar duty when she notes that educators must not attempt to realise their own visions of utopia through the education of their students. Rather, students must be allowed to form their own perceptions of the world and a future worth creating.
13. See Section 2.

Disclosure statement

No potential conflict of interest was reported by the author.

References

Alter, A. 2015. "Ta-Nehisi Coates Wins National Book Award." *The New York Times*, November 19.
Anderson, E. 2010. *The Imperative of Integration*. Princeton, NJ: Princeton University Press.
Arendt, H. 1954 [1977]. "The Crisis in Education." In *Between Past and Future*, edited by HannahArendt. New York, NY: Penguin Books.
Ashkenas, J., Haeyoun Park, and Adam Pearce 2017. "Even With Affirmative Action, Blacks and Hispanics are More Underrepresented at Top Colleges Than 35 Years Ago." *The New York Times*, August 24.
Bell, D. 1992. *Faces at the Bottom of the Well: The Permanence of Racism*. New York, NY: Basic Books.
Blum, L. 2012. *High Schools, Race, and America's Future: What Students Can Teach Us about Morality, Diversity, and Community*. Cambridge, MA: Harvard Education Press.
Brubaker, R. 2016. *Trans: Gender and Race in an Age of Unsettled Identities*. Princeton, NJ: Princeton University Press.
Coates, T. 2008. *The Beautiful Struggle: A Father, Two Sons, and an Unlikely Road to Manhood*. New York, NY: One World.
Coates, T. 2015. *Between the World and Me*. New York, NY: Spiegel & Grau.
Delpit, L. 2012. *Multiplication is for White People: Raising Expectations for Other People's Children*, New York, NY: The New Press.
Dubois, W. E. B. 1903 [1994]. *The Souls of Black Folk*. New York, NY: Dover Publications.
Fricker, M. 2007. *Epistemic Injustice*. Oxford: Oxford University Press.
Garcia, J. L. A. 1996. "The Heart of Racism." *Journal of Social Philosophy* 27 (1): 5–46.
Hambacher, E., and Winston C. Thompson. 2015. "Breaking the Mold: Thinking Beyond Deficits." *Journal of Educational Controversy* 9 (1): 1–17.
Haslanger, Sally. 2000. "Gender and Race: (What) are They? (What) do we Want Them to Be?" *Nous* 34 (1): 31–55.
Helms, J. 1990. *Black and White Racial Identity: Theory, Research, and Practice*. Westport, CT: Praeger.
Helms, J. E., and Donelda Cook. 1999. *Using Race and Culture in Counseling and Psychotherapy: Theory and Process*. Needham Heights, MA: Allyn & Bacon.
James, M. 2012. "The Political Ontology of Race." *Polity* 44: 106–134.
McPherson, Lionel K. 2015. "Deflating 'Race'." *Journal of the American Philosophical Association* 1 (04): 674–693.

Mills, C. 1997. *The Racial Contract*. Ithaca, NY: Cornell University Press.

Mills ,C. 1998. *Blackness Visible: Essays on Philosophy and Race*. Ithaca, NY: Cornell University Press.

NHPR. 2017. *Incidents at UNH Force Difficult Dialogue about Race and Diversity*, Last modified May 18, 2017. http://nhpr.org/post/incidents-unh-force-difficult-dialogue-about-race-and-diversity.

NPR (National Public Radio). 2012. "Mexican American Studies: Bad Ban or Bad Class." *NPR*, Last modified January 18, 2012. https://www.npr.org/2012/01/18/145397005/mexican-american-studies-bad-ban-or-bad-class

Omi, M., and Howard Winant. 1986. *Racial Formation in the United States*. New York, NY: Routledge Press.

Shelby, T. 2005. *We who are Dark*. Cambridge, MA: The Belknap Press of Harvard University Press.

Smedley, A. 1993. *Race in North America: Origin and Evolution of a Worldview*. Boulder, CO: Westview Press.

Sparks, S. 2015. "Comparing Assessments." *Education Week* 35 (12): S3.

Stone, Z. 2016. "The Rise of White Guilt Book Clubs." *OZY.COM*, Last modified December 9, 2016. http://www.ozy.com/fast-forward/the-rise-of-the-white-guilt-book-club/72400.

Sullivan, S., and Nancy Tuana, eds. 2007. *Race and Epistemologies of Ignorance*. Albany, NY: State University of New York Press.

Tatum,B. 1997. *Why are all the Black Kids Sitting Together in the Cafeteria: And Other Conversations About Race*. New York, NY: Basic Books.

Tatum, B. 2007. *Can We Talk About Race? And Other Conversations in an Era of School Resegregation*. Boston, MA: Beacon Press.

Thompson, W. C. 2015. "Rawls, Race, and Education: A Challenge to the Ideal/Nonideal Divide." *Educational Theory* 65 (2): 151–167.

Vance, J. D. 2016. "Why Race Relations Got Worse." *National Review*, August 29.

Winkler, E. 2009. "Children are not Colorblind: How Young Children Learn Race." *PACE* 3 (3): 1–8.

WMUR. 2017. "Students, Faculty at UNH Discuss Recent Racial Incidents." *WMUR*, Last modified May 11, 2017. http://www.wmur.com/article/protests-held-at-unh-over-recent-racial-incident/9639777.

5 Teacher-led codeswitching
Adorno, race, contradiction, and the nature of autonomy

Jack Bicker

ABSTRACT

Drawing on respective ideas from within both liberal political philosophy and Frankfurt School critical theory, this paper seeks to examine claims about autonomy and empowerment made on behalf of educational policies such as teacher-led codeswitching; a policy that seeks to empower students from racially marginalised groups by facilitating their proficiency in the language and cultural expressions of societally dominant groups. I set out to evaluate such claims by first sketching two competing formulations of autonomy; namely, (a) liberal autonomy concomitant to political power, and (b) autonomy that arises out of the practice of critical self-reflection. I proceed by testing codeswitching within each formulation to reveal how – in this case – these two conceptualisations of autonomy are educationally incompatible with each other. I conclude by suggesting that educational interventions such as codeswitching may ultimately be complicit in the longer term processes of racialisation and marginalisation that they seek to diminish, not only because they carry the potential to damage minority students' self-integrity, but also because they limit possibilities for both majority and minority students to engage in dialectical encounters that may open avenues to new principles of social and political organisation.

If civic empowerment is our goal, then educators need to teach minority students to 'codeswitch': to represent and express themselves in ways that members of the majority group – those with political privilege and power – will naturally understand and respect. Students should learn that in every community there is a language and culture of power. If one wants to be effective through political dialogue … one must master and use that language and those cultural expressions. (Levinson 2012, 87)

Introduction

This paper takes the above pedagogical prescription as its starting point, seeking to trace and test the veracity of the claim to civic empowerment made within it.

Educational prescriptions such as those above explicitly aim to redress structural disadvantages faced by students from marginalised, racialised minority-groups, by facilitating such students' performative competency within the 'language and cultural expressions' of dominant communities. The rationale underpinning such prescriptions is that minority students who have been taught to successfully perform dominant-group cultural signifiers, gain some form of recognition or respect from that dominant group. As a result of such recognition, minority students are then granted access by the dominant group to public forums in which claims to the equal distribution of political and economic power are negotiated, so that minority students are then afforded greater levels of civic empowerment. Concomitantly, minority groups are then in a better position to advocate on behalf of political efforts to amend and rebalance previous structural disadvantages that would have once impacted their community.

However, I demonstrate that a closer analysis of such prescriptions reveals a strong potential for such interventions to instead – ultimately – exacerbate the mechanisms of social and political exclusion, misrecognition, and silencing, that they seek to allay. This is not only because the internalisation of norms which – by varying degrees – are heteronomous to minority students has the potential to damage such students' sense of self-esteem and self-integrity, but also because such educational interventions limit possibilities for genuine dialectical encounters in education for both minority and dominant-group students alike. That is, dialectical encounters that – epistemologically – are likely to provide dominant-group students with the necessary conceptual material to see beyond the confines of the tacit, racially hierarchised, Eurocentric narratives through which they may initiate and/or perpetuate processes of racialisation and marginalisation.

In the first part of this paper, I briefly work to sketch two different formulations of autonomy; that is (a) liberal autonomy concomitant to political power, and (b) critical autonomy that arises out of the practice of critical self-reflection. This is so as to prefigure this paper's second section in which I evaluate teacher-led code switching against the criteria for autonomy set out in theories supporting formulations (a) and (b). Through the comparison that I draw as a result, I demonstrate that the two formulations of autonomy outlined are not educationally compatible with each other; indeed, policies such as teacher-led code switching – which draw on liberal formulation (a) – are themselves complicit in the ongoing processes of racialised hierarchisation that they seek to dismantle.

Sketching two conceptions of autonomy

In this first section of the paper, I intend to trace and compare two alternative formulations of autonomy. This is so as to prefigure this paper's second section, in which I seek to evaluate a specific example of an educational policy and/or intervention that has as its main aim the cultivation of *empowering* qualities necessary for students originating from groups traditionally considered as societally marginalised; that is, qualities required for such students to gain access to main-stream public and political forums so as to advocate on behalf of, and justify, political and (concomitant) social justice.

Such ideas about education, and by extension wider societal diversity, argue that part of education's proper function is an initiation into, and/or a distribution of the necessary cultural and educational capital that will ultimately allow learners to develop into citizens capable of economic and political functionality and inde-pendence. According to one strand of this line of thought (see Levinson 2012), both an access to, and an ambition towards students' functionality within mainstream aesthetic and political modes of *thinking* and *being* are essential components of educational efforts to justly transform students originating from groups unfairly disadvantaged in the distribution/accumulation of economic and political power. While not denying wider structural barriers and societal prejudices, such an access to 'appropriate' modes of thinking and being – so the argument goes – provides students with the necessary human capital to be deemed worthy of admittance to both the professional jobs market and political forums.

As a result, education for autonomy – on this dominant account – might (roughly) be formulated as a preparation to exercise a freedom and ability to accumulate, negotiate, and then exercise economic and political power so as to be afforded the opportunity – as far as is democratically possible – to determine the course of one's own life, as well as that of one's family and local community. Or, as Rawls puts it; 'to rationally pursue … a conception of what we regard for us as a worthwhile human life' (Rawls 1993, 302). I argue that such assumptions lie behind many theories regarding liberal education and education for participation in liberal democracies.

Alternatively, in his 2004 paper 'What Might Education Mean After Abu Ghraib', Henry Giroux sketches a different form of autonomy, as part of his work to explore the kind of *human reasoning* functional in the collective minds of the American soldiers responsible for the human rights violations that occurred at the Abu Ghraib prison in Iraq in 2003. Taking a lead from Frankfurt School critical theory, he instead suggests that the cultivation or facilitation of conceptual reflexivity is the central concern for the facilitation of autonomy within education. Giroux writes of the Abu Ghraib abuses and, moreover, the public discussions that followed in the US and other Western countries, suggesting that,

> What is often ignored in the debates about Abu Ghraib, both in terms of its causes and what can be done about it, are questions that foreground the relevance of critical edu-cation to the debate. Such questions would clearly focus, at the very least, on what ped-agogical conditions need to be in place to enable people to view the images of abuse at Abu Ghraib prison not as a voyeuristic, even pornographic, reception, but through a vari-ety of discourses that enable them to ask critical and probing questions that get at the heart of how people learn to participate in sadistic acts of abuse and torture, internalise racist assumptions that make it easier to dehumanise people different from themselves, accept commands that violate basic human rights, become indifferent to the suffering and hardships of others, and view dissent as fundamentally unpatriotic. (Giroux 2004, 11)

Autonomy, in this sense, can be formulated as a kind of freedom through which the individual thinker is afforded the opportunity to work their way to seeing through the combined conceptual totalities that are presented to them, so as to (1) question established norms and received narratives, and therefore (2) develop something of a conscious and critical agency when both formulating a conception of the good and then acting within the principles established and then re-established within such a conception.

To this ultimate end, Giroux is advocating for an education that would have originally provided the US soldiers with a critical facility with which to insulate themselves from specific, fierce and almost *total,* ethnic, national and religious narratives emanating from mainstream American and Western media, as well as general, tacit, Eurocentric narratives regarding white supremacy. That is, an insulation from narratives which – when left unchallenged – functioned to prevent the soldiers (1) from acknowledging the *humanness* of their victims, and (2) from having the critical awareness and/or reason(s) to recognise the *untruth* of the narratives with which they were being supplied, and which therefore led them to such a disconnection from those men and women to whom they wilfully did harm.

Adorno similarly writes, in regard to the mass persecution of the European Jewish population perpetrated by the German state in the 1930s and 1940s:

> When men are forbidden to think, thinking sanctions what simply exists. The genuinely critical need of thought to awaken from the cultural phantasmagoria is trapped, channelled, steered into the wrong consciousness. The culture of the habit has broken thought of the habit to ask what all this may be, and to what end. (Adorno [1966] 1973, 5)

Adorno suggests that the forbiddance of thinking and the acceptance of *what simply exists* (reified consciousness), leads to the kind of conceptual and cognitive complacency that Giroux suggests prevents us from asking 'critical and probing questions', and which, by extension, prevented the American soldiers at Abu Ghraib from recognising the untruth of the narratives supplied to them. Adorno – recasting a much altered version of Hegelian dialectics – suggests that in order for the *untruth* of a conceptual system to become apparent to a thinker (an 'awakening from the cultural phantasmagoria'), a thinker must – as an initial step – have the opportunity to encounter *difference*; namely, examples of alternative conceptualisations and systems of thought that provide a contradiction when held up against the received or dominant narrative. Under the right conditions, such an encounter with difference places the thinker within a disorientating, conscious space of conceptual tension that initiates a process of questioning; namely, dialectically thinking through this tension, as opposed to falling into the habit of not asking 'what all this might be and to what end'. (ibid, 6).

However, Adorno suggests that dominant social and political forms of (liberal) organisation are inimical to such a process as they require conformity in citizens through the establishment of dominant cultural norms; these norms create a general ultimatum via which the individual must either conform or be excluded, and they therefore function as a mechanism that erodes away at wider societal variance and, as a result, at the opportunity for each thinker to encounter a contradictory conceptual system that opposes their own. The individual is therefore discouraged – or even *forbidden* – from thinking, and is instead encouraged *to identify*.

If we are to take the respective educational claims – that is the Rawlsian claim and the critical-theory-inspired claim – for the exercise of liberal political autonomy and critical/conceptual autonomy seriously, and if at the same time such claims can be considered as being exclusive of each other, then evaluative questions need to be asked as to which of the two approaches – or a synthesis of both – will genuinely facilitate the kind of democratic ideals that they both make claim to; and which, as a result, may be judged as most appropriate in the formulation of an education system that contributes to wider human and social justice, equality, and diversity. In the following section I attempt to evaluate an example of educational policy (namely, teacher led code-switching) that explicitly arises from the first of these two conceptions of autonomy, hoping to use a critical theory based conceptual framework to further elucidate where the two approaches might depart from each other, and the educational implications that follow.

Adorno, Levinson and the case of code-switching

By means of framing such an evaluation, it is worth noting two passages in 'Education After Auschwitz' in which Adorno describes 'reified consciousness' as,

> a disastrous state of conscious and unconscious thought [that] includes the erroneous idea that one's own particular way of being – that one is just so and not otherwise – is nature, an unalterable given, and not a historical evolution … a consciousness blinded to all historical past, all insight into one's own conditionedness, and posits as absolute what exists contingently. If this coercive mechanism were once ruptured, then, I think, something would be gained. (Adorno 1967, 7)

A large part of Adorno's project within the 1966 radio broadcast, 'Education After Auschwitz', is to lay the foundations of a claim that education should aim towards facilitating a mode of cognition that is both concept-critical and, as a result, open to difference; namely, a form of rationality that is antithetical to both the objectifying mentality and what Adorno here refers to as 'reified consciousness'. In a similar vein Adorno suggests that,

> people who blindly slot themselves into the collective already make themselves some-thing like inert material, extinguish themselves as self-determined beings. With this comes the willingness to treat others as an amorphous mass … people of such a nature have, as it were, assimilated themselves to things. And then, when possible, they assim-ilate others to things. (Adorno 1967, 6)

Code-switching

As an example of an educational policy that aims towards emancipatory educa-tional outcomes, but which instead – despite the best of intentions – contributes to a widespread facilitation of a form of cognition unable to support such aims, I turn to Levinson's 2012 book *No Citizen Left Behind*. A veteran of education work among low-income, African American communities, Levinson draws on the work of African-American educationalists (including Prudence Carter 2005 and Lisa Delpit 1995) to suggest that:

> If civic empowerment is our goal, then educators need to teach minority students to 'codeswitch': to represent and express themselves in ways that members of the majority group – those with political privilege and power – will naturally understand and respect. Students should learn that in every community there is a language and culture of power. If one wants to be effective through political dialogue, as opposed solely through direct action, boycotts, or radical street theatre, say, one must master and use that language and those cultural expressions. (Levinson 2012, 87)

This prescription forms part of a larger and much more nuanced book in which Levinson sets out to justify educational interventions that cultivate the correct qualities necessary for minority students to functionally engage (1) within political forums (namely, to take formal democratic action of various kinds), and (2) within professional spaces (namely, to gain employment). To this end, and particularly in the case of code-switching, Levinson argues that African-American students – especially those from low-income areas – should be taught to speak and 'act' like members of the societally dominant group; namely, white, middle-class Americans. By means of demonstrating wider support for such an approach, Levinson quotes another African-American educationalist, Prudence Carter, who similarly suggests that 'education is as much about being inculcated with the ways of the 'culture of power' as it is about learning to read, count and think critically' (Carter 2005, 47).

In order to try to do proper justice to Levinson's text within limited space, it is important to make clear that Levinson's justification of an educational imperative to code-switch is accompanied by a strong condition that the 'language of power' should be taught alongside a student's own 'home-language' and 'cultural forms of knowledge' so as to ensure that students' home cultures are not erased. This, Levinson suggests, is to be achieved through translation exercises such as 'contrastive analysis', in which students 'not only translate Black English (or whatever the local language or dialect is) into Standard American English, but also translate SAE texts into their home dialect'. (Levinson 2012, 88).

As a result, rather than being encouraged into a 'wholesale abandonment of their own ways of being in the world' (89), African-American students are instead educated to be bilingual, swapping their manner of expression away from their original mode of talk, to conform to the expectations of the respective mainstream forums in which they may wish to operate when making any democratic claim to active citizenship. In this way, Levinson stresses that students should not be taught to think of themselves as necessarily excluded from the wider civic community, as neither should they be taught 'one more way in which they are deficient and will never gain power' (90). However, teachers should make it clear that as members of a minority community such students are indeed 'outsiders in the sense of having to learn and use a language of power that is initially not their own' (90), so as to become 'strategic movers across cultural spheres' (88).

Such interventions do, of course, have the best of liberal, inclusive and democratic intentions at their core. Indeed, the second formulation of autonomy that I outlined on page 2 above, becomes pertinent here: that is, 'providing students with sufficient dominant social, cultural, and educational capital in this way, resonates with a definition of education for autonomy formulated as a preparation to exercise the freedom and ability to accumulate, negotiate, and then exercise economic and political power so as to be afforded the opportunity – as far as is democratically possible – to determine/negotiate the course of one's own life, as well as that of one's family and local community'. An education that is pursuant of these aims would, I argue, advocate for classroom practices that provide students with 'correct' cultural and educational goods in the manner that Levinson suggests, so as to gain access to streams of political and economic power or capital. Such political and economic power or capital, so the argument goes, is synonymous with (or at least prior to) the civic empowerment that Levinson outlines.

Such a definition also resonates with wider liberal and liberal education theory. Indeed, it is apparent in one formulation of autonomy offered by Levinson in an earlier book, *The Demands of Liberal Education*. On page 15, Levinson sketches a perfectionist liberal version of autonomy as being

> the capacity to form a conception of the good, to evaluate one's values and ends with the genuine possibility of revising them should they be found wanting, and then to realise one's revised ends. (Levinson 1999, 15)

My working definition/characterisation of liberal autonomy (as outlined in the paragraph above) nestles into the third aspect of what Levinson offers here; namely, that in order to bring about or realise one's revised ends, an individual must have garnered the requisite political or other capital in order to effectively make and negotiate changes to their circumstances. This requires an (educational) initiation into the language and etiquette of expression necessary to be both heard and recognised by the dominant group.

However, drawing on Adorno's work, in the next section, I argue that policies such as code-switching are detrimental to the second (and potentially the first) component of this Rawlsian formulation. That is, such policies limit any genuine development of autonomy through a stifling of a student's capacity to 'evaluate their own values and ends with the genuine possibility of revising them should they be found wanting.'

Code-switching as alienation through the commodification of self

I suggest that the imperative to code-switch involves a tacit, and therefore unnoticed, move towards commodification in education.

Marx writes that a commodity is:

a mysterious thing, simply because in it the social character of men's labour appears to them as an objective character stamped upon the product of that labor; because the relation of the producers to the sum total of their own labour is presented to them as a social relation, existing not between themselves, but between the products of their labour. This is the reason why the products of labour become commodities, social things whose qualities are at the same time perceptible and imperceptible by the senses. (Marx 1995, 43)

In this way, Marx directs our attention to the manner in which the products of labour have both a 'use value' (namely, an object's utility arising out of the object's being in itself), and an 'exchange value' (a level of worth attached to an object that, rather than arising out of either the identity or the unique constitution of the object itself, is instead comparatively generated from within a market of tradable objects).

The imperative to code-switch marks a move towards commodification within education in the sense that rather than directing educational labour towards a cultivation of educational products understood as objects that inhabit their own space of being, such policies arguably encourage educational labourers to instead value the products of their work in terms of those products' exchange value when weighed against other products/objects within a comparative and competitive political market.

Here, educational labour is the work done by both teachers and, more importantly, by students. The products of that labour are the students themselves, as education acts upon and within the person to bring about a transformation of some sort. We might, then, imagine that an education that privileges the creation of use value would focus itself toward a responsiveness to the needs of the student in their own being; namely, a responsiveness to the uniquely constituted subject who both perceives the world, and functions within the world as framed by their own experience – an experience that is partly shared with their near neighbours and other members of their local community.

Conversely, an education that focuses itself towards the cultivation of the exchange value of the products of educational labour, would not be able to achieve such a responsiveness. Instead, such an education represents a commodification of the products of such labour, where such a product is the future student themselves at some end-point along their educational journey. In other words, the student is invited to envision the worth of their later, educated and therefore transformed self that they are working towards, as being dependent on the comparative value bestowed upon that future self by market forces; namely, a value deemed appropriate within an established political economy of identity that is heteronomous to the student themselves.

To step back from educational labour for a moment, it stands to reason that producers of general products for any market may, once the logic and configuration of that market has been revealed to them, seek to alter the process of production as well as the ultimate nature of their products, so as to optimise the value – that is, the exchange value – of those products.

Returning to education, and to code-switching in particular, we can see an intervention through which the logic of the current system of social and political organisation is revealed to students in such a way that they become aware of an interconnected past, present and future reality in which certain cultural modes of thinking and being are hierarchised as being more valuable (in regard to their exchange value) than others. Exchange value, here, is the measure of any product of educational labour (the educationally transformed student) when compared to established dominant norms and expectations. An appropriate set of cultural signifiers (such as the white, middle class norms in Levinson's example) are recognised and enacted as worthy tokens to provide entrance into prestigious positions within, say, the jobs market and mainstream political forums. Less worthy cultural signifiers (read, African American modes of cultural expression) are deemed indicative of less appropriate educational labour and, therefore, do not transact entrance to such forums.

Teachers work with such students to facilitate the adaptation of their educational labour so as to appropriately assimilate the end product of such labour (viz. the student) to the social, political and aesthetic imperatives that govern the particular market and/or political economy in which that product – the students themselves – will finally be both released and assessed. Such an adjustment, or transformation, is (incorrectly) deemed liberatory in the sense that by increasing the value of a student's profile within the current and given system of social, political and aesthetic conditions, such a student then has greater access to the kind of economic and political power necessary for them to gain recognition and, as a result, negotiate a path to fulfilling their life as befits their own conception of the good.

However, as I have suggested, such a mechanism of transformation instead risks a limitation of a student's capacity to 'evaluate their own values and ends with the genuine possibility of revising them should they be found wanting' (Levinson 1999, 15). This is because, despite Levinson's attempts to maintain a parity of esteem between a (minority) student's home-culture and schooled culture through techniques such as contrastive analysis, and despite any 'bilingualism' that might result, the students are additionally initiated into and immersed within an understanding and acceptance of a hierarchy of cultural signifiers and their respective, associated conceptual content. Indeed, at an early stage in such a student's critical development, they are taught to make glib, short-cut self-adjustments in order to gain recognition, without necessarily being taught about the underlying structural mechanisms underpinning the establishment and maintenance of such a hierarchisation.

To return to Marx, 'the relation of the producers to the sum total of their own labour is presented to them [the students] as a social relation, existing not between themselves, but between the products of their labour'. We might therefore suggest that students are encouraged to view the transition from their current selves to the selves that they will become, not as something that might arise out of their own situatedness or subjectivity as such, but instead as a process that is sourced, driven and guided by forces external to themselves; forces which take on the appearance of an objective character, and to which they must capitulate. There is therefore a tacit imperative targeted at the students, through which they are not encouraged to speak and develop their voice as their true selves, but are instead encouraged to speak and therefore develop in a manner that is optimally appropriate. Students are incentivised to excise those aspects of their selves that do not fit the ideal image of the human being that is sanctioned by the market. As Sara Ahmed writes, 'the pressure not to 'assert one's culture' is lived as a demand to pass and integrate, not necessarily by becoming white but by being more alike' (Ahmed 2012, 158).

Minority students cannot bring their *whole* selves to this process of development: under these circumstances, students from minority communities are permitted to bring only a portion of their subjectivity into the classroom. In other words, such students may be asked to leave many aspects of their personalities at the classroom door, as such conceptual content will have no traction within those public forums in which such knowledge is not *recognised*. This is a disadvantage in comparison to their more 'mainstream' peers. Those minority students who struggle to internalise mainstream manners of expression and any accompanying conceptual content, may become alienated from both educational content, as well as from the difficult educational process through which they are being asked to become more norm-laden. Conversely, for those students who are more successful, the language that such students will develop in order to articulate their experience of the world, will not be a language that can fully reflect their lived experience, but will instead leave a disjuncture between their fully experienced selves, and the self that they are able to articulate.

To return to the Adorno quotation at the top of this chapter,

> People who blindly slot themselves into the collective already make themselves something like inert material, extinguish themselves as self-determined beings. With this comes the willingness to treat others as an amorphous mass ... people of such a nature have, as it were, assimilated themselves to things. And then, when possible, they assimilate others to things. (Adorno 1967, 6)

The inert nature of the students who are able to code-switch, and who therefore 'slot themselves into the collective', resides in the fact that as soon as they come to both perform, internalise, and *become* those sanctioned modes of thinking and being, they cease to act as examples of a contradiction. The important educational point here is that non-minority students can benefit, as outlined in the chapter above, from the presence of conceptual and cultural contradiction (namely minority students), particularly when they meet such difference in a relation of equal dignity so that such difference, dialectically, comes to reveal the constructed and therefore fallible nature of their own conceptual system. If this was the case, rather than re-making minority students to fit dominant norms and expectations (and often failing to do so), teachers might instead take the opportunity that the lived substance of the lives of *different* students offer; that is, teachers should facilitate genuine dialogue between themselves and between *different* students, so as to reveal the interesting similarities, differences, and inadequacies across each conceptual regime, thereby similarly revealing the situatedness or conditionedness of each cultural standpoint. Such an intervention would truly represent an education that chases after genuine liberal ideals by allowing all students to be different, while at the same time open to the authentic (rather than the altered) voice of their respective others. In this vein Adorno writes that;

> If public life has reached a state in which thought is being turned inescapably into a commodity and language into a celebration of the commodity, the attempt to trace the sources of this degradation must refuse obedience to the current linguistic and intellectual demands, before it is rendered entirely futile by the consequence of those demands. (Adorno [1944] 1972, xiv)

Instead, the remaking of minority students, and the quietening of their authentic voices, represents a perhaps accidental, and well intentioned, requisitioning of those students to support the social and political status quo; that is, to create future citizens who, rather than being in a position to criticise a conceptual system that pours scorn on their own cultural origins, are instead – along with their non-minority peers – robbed of the opportunity to see through the 'cultural phantasmagoria' as a result of having been crudely enmeshed within it. Minority and non-minority students alike are encouraged to 'make sense of the 'here and now' in terms of the 'there and then', i.e., to ideas of what is *supposed* (by actors) *to be*' (de Nora 2003, 6); that is, rather than enter into a process of constructing new ways of thinking and being in order make sense of the world, they instead rely on inherited, and sometimes tainted, categories of knowledge that carry – among other things – racial hierarchisation within them. As a result they fall victim to a reified consciousness. Simon Jarvis writes of Adorno and this process:

> What Marx is thus able to uncover is the way in which a discourse with apparently exemplary liberal and enlightened credentials … in fact keeps relying on archaic and mythical categories which it cannot afford to question. It does this, not because it has simply got the facts wrong, but because it reproduces a logic of misidentification which is already present in capitalist exchange and production itself. An outstanding instance of this, and one of central importance for Adorno, is provided by Marx's analysis 'the fetishism of the commodity and its secret'. (Jarvis 2004, 88)

In conclusion, educational interventions that seek to promote empowerment through the provision of centrally sanctioned social, cultural and educational goods, where access to such goods is deemed advantageous in regard to acceptance within mainstream public and political forums, have an effect that is in practical and conceptual tension with a genuinely robust notion of civic empowerment. Indeed, such interventions might be read as the provision of sets of performed signifiers (e.g. linguistic or behavioural norms) that elicit trust from dominant groups, while also reframing the pre-existing competency of non-dominant individuals within the language and expectations of those more dominant groups. In this way, as revealed through the above analysis, students who embody and signify difference through the lived substance of their lives, are encouraged to abandon such qualities in such a way that not only jeopardises an integral sense of self, but also precludes the possibility of genuine dialectical encounters in otherwise one-dimensional educational spaces.

Therefore, in this paper, I hope to have laid out the case for an increased capacity for conceptual and cultural diversity in educational spaces. I have also advocated on behalf of, and pointed towards, educational policies that facilitate a kind genuine dialectical engagement; that is, a dialectical engagement that – through the development of a kind of critical conceptual autonomy – can advance the agenda of civic empowerment by providing the epistemological conditions for both majority and minority students alike to see beyond their current conceptual regimes, and think towards new possibilities in regard to principles of social and political (and racial) organisation. Or as Adorno writes:

> An emancipated society … would not be a unitary state, but the realisation of universality in the reconciliation of differences. Politics that are still seriously concerned with such a society ought not, therefore, propound the abstract equality of men even as an idea. Instead they should point to the bad equality today … and conceive the better state as one in which people could be different without fear. (Adorno [1974] 2005, 103)

Disclosure statement

No potential conflict of interest was reported by the author.

Funding

This work was supported by the Arts and Humanities Research Council.

ORCID

Jack Bicker (iD) http://orcid.org/0000-0002-1390-2770

References

Adorno, T. [1944] 1972. *Dialectic of Enlightenment*. London: Verso.
Adorno, T. [1966] 1973. *Negative Dialectics*. New York: Continuum.
Adorno, T. [1967] 2005. 'Education After Auschwitz'. In: *Critical Models: Interventions and Catchwords*, 191–204. New York: Columbia University Press. ISBN 9780231135054.
Adorno, T. [1974] 2005. *Minima Moralia*. London: Verso.
Ahmed, S. 2012. *On Being Included*. Durham, NC: Duke University Press.
Carter, P. 2005. *Keepin' It Real: School Success Beyond Black and White*. New York: Oxford University Press.
Delpit, L. 1995. *Other People's Children*. New York: The New Press.
Giroux, H. 2004. "What Might Education Mean After Abu Ghraib: Revisiting Adorno's Politics of Education." *Comparative Studies of South Asia, Africa and the Middle East* 24 (1): 3–22.

Jarvis, S. 2004. "Adorno, Marx, Materialism." In *The Cambridge Companion to Adorno*, edited by T. Huhn, 79–100. Cambridge: Cambridge University Press.

Levinson, M. 2012. *No Citizen Left Behind*. Boston MA: Harvard University Press.

Levinson, M. 1999. *The Demands of Liberal Education*. Oxford: Oxford University Press.

Marx, K. 1995. *Captial: An Abridged Edition*. Oxford: Oxford University Press.

de Nora, T. 2003. *After Adorno: Rethinking Music Sociology*. Cambridge: Cambridge University Press.

Rawls, J. 1993. *Political Liberalism: Expanded Edition*. New York: Columbia University Press.

6   Affect, race, and white discomfort in schooling

Decolonial strategies for 'pedagogies of discomfort'

Michalinos Zembylas

ABSTRACT

The present paper theorises white discomfort as not an individual psychologised emotion, but rather as a social and political affect that is part of the production and maintenance of white colonial structures and practices. Therefore, it is suggested that white discomfort cannot be critically addressed merely in pedagogic terms and conditions within schools and universities. By foregrounding white discomfort in broader terms, the aim of the paper is to provide a more holistic and dynamic account which opens up a realm that situates the pedagogisation of white discomfort within the broader decolonising project of disrupting white colonial structures and practices. The paper calls for *both* a decolonising *and* a critical affective approach to pedagogies of discomfort that would focus on examining and addressing strategically how white discomfort comes to be experienced and dismantled within broader affective, material and discursive assemblages of race, racism and whiteness.

Introduction

While it is difficult to pin down a definition of *whiteness* (Roediger 1991), there is widespread agreement that whiteness is a socially constructed category that is normalized within a system that privileges Whites. Through the lens of Critical Whiteness Studies in particular, whiteness is understood to be not only about skin color, but intimately related to the construction of race, and particularly the invisible structures that (re)produce white supremacy and privilege (Applebaum 2016).[1] Perhaps not surprisingly, recent scholarship in Critical Whiteness Studies and critical race pedagogy shows that Whites express emotional resistance when they are asked to confront their whiteness as supremacy and privilege; these discomforting emotions raise insurmountable obstacles toward racial understanding and the undoing of racism (Leonardo and Porter 2010; Matias 2016a; Matias and

Mackey 2016; Matias and Zembylas 2014; Zembylas 2015b). To account for Whites' discomforting feelings (e.g. anger, fear, denial, and guilt) to address issues of race, racism and whiteness, the term *white discomfort* has been coined.[2] White discomfort has been primarily explained in terms of Whites' unwillingness to scrutinize their personal advantages and privileges, demanding that race dialogue takes place in a 'safe space.' To address discomfort pedagogically, it has been suggested that 'pedagogies of discomfort' (Boler and Zembylas 2003; Cutri and Whiting 2015, Leibowitz et al. 2010; Zembylas and Boler 2002; Zembylas 2015a, 2017b; Zembylas and Papamichael 2017) offer a framework through which educators may provide a relatively safe space to challenge individuals' comfort zones and transform the emotionality of Whites.

Yet, despite advancements in both theory and empirical investigation in this field of research, one central problem remains when it comes to challenging and transforming white discomfort. Attributing white discomfort to *individuals* – e.g. Whites' disinclination to scrutinise their personal advantages and privileges – and urging Whites to 'deal with' their discomforting feelings do not necessarily interrogate the wider structures and practices of race, racism and whiteness that trigger such feelings in the first place. Such an approach maintains a reductionist account of white resistance, because it frames white discomfort as merely a reluctance to grapple with the emotionally 'difficult knowledge' (Britzman 1998) of race, racism and whiteness. More importantly, in conceptualizing white discomfort as a matter that can somehow be 'addressed' pedagogically in schools and universities, there is the risk of *pedagogising* the – much broader and far more complex – political project of *decolonising* white colonial structures and practices both within and beyond the education sector.

According to Bernstein (2001), we live in a totally pedagogised society, that is, a society in which the social relations we develop in its various domains operate by specific forms of pedagogical regulation. Bernstein's notion of 'pedagogisation' denotes the establishment of a certain type of social relation which involves attempts to modify the social, affective, and epistemological frameworks of social agents engaged in specific practices (Stavrou 2016). In this manner, the concept of pedagogisation can be valuable in providing a description of how social control operates through specific pedagogic relations in educational and social institutions – schools, universities, workplaces and so on. In this paper, I want to take a step further and suggest a distinction between *schooling pedagogisation,* that is, forms of pedagogisation that take places in schools and educational institutions, and *societal pedagogisation*, which goes beyond educational institutions. I argue that this distinction can be useful in rethinking the relation between pedagogisation and white discomfort. In particular, the pedagogisation of white discomfort in schools and universities – which is a case of schooling pedagogisation – takes place, for example, when pedagogies of discomfort are used to modify the emotionally difficult knowledge of white students and teachers through specific curricular and instructional activities.[3] However, it should not be taken for granted that schooling pedagogisation necessarily translates into or leads to societal pedagogisation; this 'leap' which might often be assumed – namely, that white discomfort can be modified through pedagogic work conducted in schools and universities and that this work will be somehow transferred beyond schools and universities – entails two traps that need to be theoretically scrutinised: first, the taken-for-grantedness of 'white discomfort' and 'white emotionality', and second, the essentialisation of pedagogies of discomfort in schools and universities – what I call the *schooling of white discomfort* – as a radical means of modifying white discomfort beyond schools and universities.

With these concerns in mind, the present paper theorises white discomfort as not an individual psychologised emotion, but rather as embedded in broader affective, material and discursive assemblages (Deleuze and Guattari 1987) of race, racism and whiteness. Without engaging in the simultaneous deconstruction of these assemblages, I suggest that white discomfort cannot be critically addressed merely in pedagogic terms and conditions within schools and universities. Hence, by foregrounding white discomfort as a social and political affect that is part of the production and maintenance of white colonial structures and practices, my aim is to provide a more holistic and dynamic account of white discomfort – an account which opens up a realm that situates the pedagogisation of white discomfort within the broader decolonising project of disrupting white colonial structures and practices. I argue, therefore, that pedagogies of discomfort, as a means of schooling white discomfort, entail risks as much as they offer opportunities. This argument essentially amounts to a call for *both* a decolonising *and* a critical affective approach to pedagogies of discomfort that goes beyond the boundaries of educational institutions. Such an approach would focus on examining and addressing strategically how white discomfort comes to be experienced and dismantled within broader affective, material and discursive assemblages of race, racism and whiteness.

To develop my argument, I will begin with a discussion of the Deleuzian notion of 'assemblage' and how it can be useful in understanding race, racism and whiteness. Then I briefly review research on the emotionality of whiteness and white discomfort to show the complexity and nuance of the notion of white discomfort. This is followed by an analysis of the Bernsteinian concept of 'pedagogisation' applied to the notion of white discomfort and a discussion of the risks involved in using pedagogies of discomfort to pedagogise white discomfort in schools and universities. The last part of the paper suggests decolonial strategies for a critical affective approach that confronts white discomfort within broader affective, material and discursive assemblages of race, racism and whiteness. In particular, I explore more fully how educators can utilise moments of white discomfort to generate possibilities of participation in the wider unmaking of white colonial structures and practices.

Affective, material and discursive assemblages of race, racism and whiteness

The dominant frameworks in which race has been conceived so far tend to be grounded either in biological terms (i.e. races are fixed) or sociological ones (i.e. there are no races; there is only culture/language) (Saldanha 2006, 2010; see also Mills 1997; Yancy 2008). The former has been rendered obsolete by contemporary science, so the latter has become the prevalent notion, namely, race is perceived as a social construction. However, there have been critiques of the tendency to present race as a social construct, because it is argued that it pays attention to people's 'representations' rather than to 'people themselves' (Saldanha 2006, 9). As it is suggested, the notion of race as a social construct fails to capture how bodies, spaces, events and encounters become racialised, that is, how they constitute *assemblages* of material, discursive and affective forces, intensities and encounters that are irreducible to a timeless essence (Nayak 2010; see also Mills 2014; Yancy 2014).

Deleuze and Guattari's (1987) notion of assemblage refers to networks of forces, intensities and encounters that produce agency, capacities and events (Braidotti 2006). The body, for example, is an assemblage of 'relations of movement and rest between molecules or particles, capacities to affect and be affected' (Deleuze and Guattari 1987, 261). Bodies, material elements, emotions, discourses, and other 'things' come together and form relations that are fluid, impermanent and non-hierarchical (Deleuze 2007). In this framework, racialisation constitutes a specific type of assemblage through which bodies comes together, producing certain affects that circulate and attach to other bodies (Ahmed 2004). As Ahmed suggests, this economy of affect functions through an intensity of attachment that aligns bodies with social space. Thus the approach that looks at race as assemblage shifts the locus of attention to what bodies *do* rather than what bodies (supposedly) 'are' (Lim 2010).

The notion of assemblage, then, changes how we understand race, racism and whiteness. Race, for example, is understood as being constituted through relational networks that include heterogeneous materialities of bodies and spaces leading to racial differences (Swanton 2010). Also, thinking about racism in these terms involves analysing the affective mobilisations, material effects, and discursive formation of race; all of these elements come together inflicting different forms of enduring racism (Tarc 2013). Finally, whiteness is understood as a set of affective investments, practices, discourses, power relations, and material wealth that constitute white supremacy (Leonardo and Zembylas 2013; Matias 2016a). All in all, viewing race, racism, and whiteness as assemblages captures the complex ways in which flows of affect, material elements and discourses coalesce to form social phenomena that are beyond the individual subjective responses, feelings, and sensibilities (Tolia and Crang 2010). As assemblages, race, racism and whiteness exceed the binary logics of fixed identities that dominate conventional under-standings, focusing instead on what race, racism and whiteness *do* in the everyday.

In particular, I want to highlight two important theoretical implications of view-ing race, racism and whiteness as affective, material and discursive assemblages. First, theorising these notions as assemblages approaches race, racism and white-ness as *events* rather than as socially constructed categories (Lim 2010; Saldanha 2006). In this theoretical framework, race, racism and whiteness are situated within a broader network of forces, intensities and encounters that entail specific affective, material and discursive elements. These elements might include, for example, skin colour, segregation practices, colonial structures, laws, and so on, but they are all entangled in processes of racial differentiation, taking an indeterminate direction each time and in each different setting (Swanton 2010).

Theorising race, racism and whiteness as events alerts educators to approach 'white resistance' (Rodriguez 2009) as not an essentialised concept, because the emphasis is on the ways in which affective, material and discursive assemblages are manifest within a certain context as not pre-determined by social structures or fixed identities, but rather as continually emerging in an open-ended process. This 'ontological' understanding of race, racism and whiteness is important, because it allows educators to trace the specific practices through which multifaceted affects such as white discomfort are constituted, circulated and perpetuated. Given that there is a multiplicity of ways with which discomforting feelings could be pro-duced, the indeterminacy of white discomfort disrupts conventional understand-ings of discomforting feelings as fixed, but rather looks at discomfort within the particular assemblages in which it emerges. Theoretically and methodologically, then, nothing is taken for granted, as pre-existing, or essentialising, but the entan-glement of affective, material and discursive elements hints at the inventiveness of race, racism, and whiteness that come to mean and feel differently to different people and settings.

Second, viewing race, racism and whiteness as affective, material and discur-sive assemblages creates openings for new theorisations of bodies and affects in schools and universities. Thus, white discomfort, for example, is understood as an effect of specific affective, material and discursive elements that are pres-ent not only at the micro-political level of the school or university, but also at the macro-level of white colonial structures and practices. This is why addressing white discomfort at the micro-level of the school or the university is not enough, because it individualises a much broader political phenomenon that is aligned with coloniality (Leonardo 2009; Matias 2016a). Consequently, to understand white discomfort, it is important to pay attention to (white) affective practices in action and their harmful effects in terms of circumscribing what a body is capable of at particular times and places (Saldanha 2006). For example, an understanding of white discomfort as an affective practice shows how racialized relations between bodies might be perpetuated, not because of any essence in these relations but because of the ways in which certain emotions (e.g. fear, anger, repulsion) 'stick' to certain bodies (Ahmed 2004), fixating Whites and Others into exclusive subject categories. Every time Whites enact a particular performance of proximity or distance with other bodies, there is a set of affective, material and discursive investments of some sort. From this perspective, to engage white discomfort productively and strategically, educators will need to scrutinise how certain assemblages diminish or increase Whites' bodily capacities to be with 'others'. In the next part of the paper, I briefly review research on the emotionality of whiteness and white discomfort to further show the complexity and nuance of the notion of white discomfort.

The emotionality of whiteness and white discomfort

Literature in critical race pedagogy and critical whiteness studies suggests that there is a prevalence of white resistance in white students and teachers' involvement with issues of race, racism and whiteness (Matias 2016a; Ringrose 2007; Rodriguez 2009). For example, white resistance manifests itself in the form of white guilt or ambivalence (Leonardo 2011), white shame (Thandeka 1999), or white anger (Godfrey 2004). These different manifestations suggest that the emotionality of whiteness is rather nuanced (Matias, Montoya, and Nishi 2016) and includes both unconscious and repressed issues as well as socio-political ones. As Matias suggests, understanding the emotionality of whiteness 'must include the identification of emotions, processes of how these emotions are expressed, repressed, and projected, and theorisations as to why they are expressed in regard to the power structure of race' (2016b, 226). In other words, the emotionality of whiteness should not be simply limited to the unconscious or innate feelings of white discomfort; rather, white emotionality needs to be also understood as socially and politically produced within the material, affective and discursive assemblages of whiteness and white supremacy. In what follows, I discuss some examples from the literature to show how these assemblages take different forms and help us understand the multifaceted manifestations of white discomfort.

In one of the early examples of research on white students' resistance to engage with issues of race and racism, Tatum (1992, 1994) documented how white college students denied raced readings of social and political reality in the United States. Tatum argued that the discomfort of white college students to talk about race could be traced to their childhood and was reproduced through their denial to accept any complicity in perpetuating racism. Other scholars, like Gonsalves (2008) also documented the discomfort of white preservice teachers to talk about race as an indication of how white emotionality functioned at a subconscious level. Gonsalves theorised white resistance in psychoanalytic terms, suggesting that white denial works as a defence mechanism to ensure that whiteness ideologies and structures are well defended and replicated. Along similar lines, Thandeka (1999) provided a psychoanalytic interpretation of white racial trauma that is associated with the repression of racial awareness.

In her extensive research on white emotionality in education, Matias (2016a, 2016b; see also Matias and Mackey 2016; Matias, Montoya, and Nishi 2016; Matias and Zembylas 2014) provides rich accounts of the challenges that emerge from the emotionality of Whites. Matias highlights that an important risk in pedagogical responses to the emotionality of whiteness is sentimentalisation: 'racialised sentimentalisation is a process where Whites can profess one emotion as a way to suppress those emotions that may indict them for being a racist' (Matias, Montoya, and Nishi 2016, 9). For example, white preservice teachers express pity (the socially acceptable emotional display) to people of colour, rather than displaying anger or resentment out of concern that they might be called racists (Matias and Zembylas 2014). Sentimentalisation, then, is an indication of the worry that the very focus – at a theoretical and classroom pedagogy level – on the emotions of Whites can recentre white emotional states and thus block critical race work (Matias, Montoya, and Nishi 2016). In showing how the emotionality of whiteness leaves an imprint in the everyday life of schools and universities, Matias suggests that emotions are not simply innate or psychoanalytic, but are in fact embedded within white supremacist power relations and structures. Her research indicates that white teachers are emotionally unprepared and uncomfortable to undertake antiracist teaching practices, because they have internalised whiteness ideology for the purpose of surviving a white world; thus it is emotionally difficult for white teachers to become secure enough to engage in racial justice in their teaching.

In their own contribution to this field of study, Leonardo and Zembylas (2013) have theorised whiteness as a technology of affect, aiming to capture the mental, emotional, and bodily dimensions of whiteness in the context of racial dialogue. Affective technologies, explain Leonardo and Zembylas, include the mechanisms through which affects and emotions come to be instrumentalised, containing certain social norms and dynamics of inclusion/exclusion with respect to one's self and an Other. For example, one of the affective technologies of whiteness is its ability to project itself as its own alibi; that is, Whites have built anti-racist understandings that construct the racist as always someone else, the problem residing elsewhere in other Whites or, in some instances, this alibi is a white subject's former self. This analysis shows once again the nuanced ways with which emotions like white discomfort manifest and organise the material, affective and discursive space of encounters, creating powerful borders between Whites and others.

In summary, there are three important lessons from research on the emotionality of whiteness and white discomfort:

(1) First, there will always be emotional discomfort when engaging white students and teachers with issues of race, racism and whiteness, because Whites' cherished beliefs and taken-for-granted assumptions are challenged (Boler 1999, 2004; de Freitas and McAuley 2008; Leibowitz et al. 2010; Matias 2016a).

(2) Second, White discomfort might be performed explicitly or implicitly as evading questions, dismissing counter arguments, expressing shame, remaining silent, interrupting others in anger, withdrawing from conversations, avoiding non-Whites and so on. A significant step toward analysing white discomfort, therefore, is identifying and examining how discomforting feelings are manifest in different settings, how they are 'attached to things, people, ideas, sensations, relations, activities, ambitions, institutions, and any number of other things, including other affects' (Sedgwick 2003, 19).

(3) Finally, it is important to understand that different affective, material and discursive assemblages of white discomfort are entangled with white supremacy (Leonardo 2009; Matias 2016a).

The above lessons raise a renewed set of challenging questions for educators:

- If white discomfort is not only an unconscious or innate feeling but also an emotion and affect that is partly constituted by social and political reality, what can we realistically expect educators to do at the micro-political level of classroom to pedagogically address white discomfort?
- As Whites continue to be complicit in the violence of white coloniality and participate in its reproduction, how can educators ethically address Whites' affective responses, such as guilt, shame, denial, and anger at the loss of privilege, status, and security without sentimentalising their pedagogical approach, but rather contributing to dismantling white supremacist power relations and structures?

Elements of these questions, especially in relation to discomforting feelings, have been previously explored, yet in the following I want to focus on the risks and possibilities of pedagogies of discomfort.

Pedagogies of discomfort and the risks of pedagogising white discomfort

The notion of *pedagogies of discomfort* (Boler 1999; Boler and Zembylas 2003; Zembylas and Boler 2002) has been proposed as a pedagogical means by which learners – especially those who are privileged – are encouraged 'to engage in critical inquiry regarding values and cherished beliefs, and to examine constructed self-images in relation to how one has learned to perceive others' (Boler 1999, 176, 177). This notion is grounded in theoretical ideas of critical pedagogy (e.g. emancipation, critical inquiry, dialogue) and particularly the assumption that discomforting feelings can be the point of departure to challenge dominant beliefs, social habits and normative practices that sustain social inequities, thus creating openings for individual and social transformation (see also Boler 2004; Faulkner and Crowhurst 2014; Ohito 2016; Zembylas 2015a; Zembylas and McGlynn 2012).

As Zembylas and Boler further explain: 'Pedagogy of discomfort… offers direction for emancipatory education through its recognition that effective analysis of ideology requires not only rational inquiry and dialogue but also excavation of the emotional investments that underlie any ideological commitments' (2002, 2).

However, in light of the complex affective, material and discursive assemblages in which white discomfort is constituted and reproduced, one wonders how radical are the affordances of pedagogies of discomfort. As it has been suggested, pedagogies of discomfort should not be assumed to be always already transformative or beyond ethical concerns (Zembylas 2015b; Zembylas and McGlynn 2012). Discomforting learning can be harmful, because there seems to be always some sort of violence done in the name of some ethical idea/principle against those who do not conform to certain ideas/principles. Similarly, Leonardo and Porter (2010) suggest that the procedural rule in race dialogue for 'safe space' essentially maintains white comfort zones and becomes a symbolic form of violence experienced by people of colour. For this reason, Leonardo and Porter argue that we need pedagogies of disruption that may constitute themselves as forms of violence, yet humanising versions that build intellectual solidarity rather than intellectualising racism and reducing it to an idea, as whites often do to confront their discomfort. 'Our main criticism for safe space,' write Leonardo and Porter, 'is that it is laced with a narcissism that designates safety for individuals in already dominant positions of power, which is not safe at all but perpetuates a systematic relation of violence' (2010, 148). This argument confirms the position that it is political work that needs to be done to confront the consequences of white supremacy rather than the narcissistic and sentimentalised illusion of constructing emotionally safe spaces for Whites. A similar argument, from a slightly different angle, has been recently made by Applebaum (2017) who points out that the pedagogical practice of 'comforting discomfort in the social justice classroom' (862) is dangerous. Applebaum mentions, for example, the case of white feminists, suggesting that 'Instead of focusing on organizational change, the self-centred strategies of white feminists comforting one another serve to preserve white moral self-image and to deflect attention away from the concerns and emotions of feminists of colour' (865). Comforting discomfort, then, is dangerous because it does not only constitute a form of violence that allows for the suffering of students of colour to go unnoticed; it also perpetuates the possibility that white privilege may remain unchallenged, both individually and collectively, because Whites are relieved from their emotional pain.[4]

Therefore, what I want to emphasise here is the need to explore the political consequences of schooling white discomfort through pedagogies of discomfort. What risks might be involved? The point of departure for my discussion is Bernstein's (2001) idea that we live in a 'totally pedagogised society.' A 'totally pedagogised society' is a society characterised by 'a seamless coordination of meanings, activities, and practices' that involve 'continuous pedagogical re-formations' in order for individuals to cope with the requirements of life and work (Bernstein 2001,

365). In other words, there is a proliferation of pedagogic discourses in all facets and aspects of everyday life that aim at 'governance by pedagogic means' (Singh 2015, 379). As Singh explains, all pedagogic discourses promote certain rules or principles of power with which they select and organise knowledge for pedagogic purposes. Even the most 'noble' pedagogic discourses – e.g. pedagogies of discomfort – aim at shaping communication and controlling pedagogic relations according to certain principles, so there is always an element of regulation or control in what is selected as valid knowledge. For this reason, Singh (2015) argues that there is ambivalence in the pedagogisation of knowledge; in other words, pedagogic discourses do not only 'liberate' or renew knowledge, but they are also bound up with politicisation and moralisation processes as they intend to frame social relations in particular ways.

Similarly, Stavrou (2016) argues that pedagogisation is a deliberative act that aims at changing someone's cognitive, emotional and practical categories of action. This has a twofold interpretation, suggests Stavrou, oscillating between the belief in the rhetoric of improvement, on the one hand, and the element of regulating or constraining what is selected as valid knowledge, on the other. The first interpretation – the most commonly identified in the literature – is observed, for instance, when pedagogic agents consider themselves as missionaries for addressing and modifying white teachers' and students' discomforting feelings so that some sort of individual transformation is achieved. Based on ideas of social justice, critical race, and anti-racist education, these agents perceive it as their personal mission to change the mentalities of white teachers and students and separate themselves from those who are regarded as 'resistant' or 'lacking awareness' (cf. Stavrou 2016, 797).

The second interpretation alludes to the possibility that a pedagogic discourse or practice might work against the rhetoric of improvement or change itself by framing white discomfort as if it is a matter that can somehow be addressed in pedagogic terms and conditions. In other words, pedagogic agents and others are *pedagogising* white discomfort, when they assume that new social relations are established and white supremacy is somehow 'addressed' through specific pedagogic activities. For this reason, I want to distinguish between *schooling pedagogisation* that limits itself to the schooling of white discomfort (i.e. schools and universities), and *societal pedagogisation* in which the process of pedagogisation is extended to the society. This distinction enables us to raise concerns for the claims made about the 'radical affordances of discomfort vis-à-vis pedagogical subversion in learning spaces' (Ohito 2016x, 797), particularly in light of the prevalence of white colonial structures and practices (Matias 2016a).

What seems important in this conversation is less the issue of 'who is to be pedagogised' than the issue of 'how' the pedagogisation (cf. Stavrou 2016) of white discomfort operates not only within the education sector but also beyond schools and universities and most importantly, whether it really challenges white colonial structures and practices rather than merely comforting white emotionality. One of the risks of pedagogies of discomfort that functions in ways that school white discomfort is its sentimentalisation. As noted earlier, sentimentalising white discomfort reappropriates the language of race, racism and whiteness by recentering discourse and pedagogical practice to the emotional needs of Whites (Matias, Montoya, and Nishi 2016). Therefore, unless white discomfort in schools and universities is recontextualised within the broader affective, material and discursive assemblages of race, racism and whiteness, pedagogies of discomfort risk remaining framed within very limited pedagogical terms and conditions.

The sort of reading of pedagogising white discomfort that I offer here makes a contribution by suggesting two theoretical breaks to understanding pedagogies of discomfort. First, it builds on the idea that both white discomfort and pedagogies of discomfort need to be theorised as elements of wider and ambivalent processes of pedagogisation. The use of the concept of pedagogisation in interpreting empirical data in various contexts enables us to shed light on the complex and nuanced notion of white discomfort, showing how it is reproduced in a variety of ways in different settings. The second theoretical break is that the concept of pedagogisation can offer new perspectives that enrich pedagogies of discomfort by situating them within the broader project of decolonisation. Thus, acknowledging the ambivalent processes of pedagogisation suggests that pedagogies of discomfort are theoretically and practically enriched with decolonial theory and praxis. The last part of the essay makes an attempt to bring together decolonial thought and pedagogies of discomfort.

Decolonial strategies for 'pedagogies of discomfort'

It has been recently argued that decolonial, anti-colonial or postcolonial perspectives are not necessarily equivalent, complementary or even supplementary to critical theory and pedagogy projects (Gaztambide-Fernandez 2012; Tuck and Yang 2012). As noted earlier, pedagogies of discomfort draw on critical pedagogy ideas to promote social justice-oriented agendas. However, Tuck and Yang (2012) argue, there are significant differences between critical pedagogies and decolonial projects. Critical pedagogies situate the work of liberation in the minds of the oppressed, whereas decolonial projects position the work of liberation in the structures of colonisation that need to be dismantled. Hence, As Tuck and Yang emphasize,

> Decolonisation, which we assert as a distinct project from other civil and human rights-based social justice projects, is far too often subsumed into the directives of these projects, with no regard for how decolonisation wants something different than those forms of justice. (2012, 2)

In other words, although there may be convergences between the aims of social justice projects and those of decolonial projects, it would be a mistake to subsume the latter under the former, as the two projects might be grounded in different epistemological and ontological frameworks. For example, there might be limitations in the Eurocentric modernist framework that undergirds critical theory and pedagogy and thus it is important to confront the possibility that critical pedagogies might be implicated in modernity and coloniality (cf. Deutscher and Lafont 2017).

A decolonial framework, then, is an appropriate conduit for enriching critical pedagogy's framework of pedagogies of discomfort so that it confronts white discomfort on a renewed basis. A decolonial framework not only exposes the roots of white discomfort – that is, white colonial structures and practices – but also enables pedagogic agents to engage in theoretically inflected actions toward anti- and decolonial ends that offer alternative ways of being in the world (Gaztambide-Fernandez 2012; Smith 1999; Tuck and Yang 2012). The renewal of pedagogies of discomfort with decolonial perspectives will provide productive possibilities for revitalizing the transformative orientation of pedagogies of discomfort. My goal, then, in bringing into conversation decolonizing pedagogies and pedagogies of discomfort is to open possibilities for a decolonising pedagogical praxis in addressing white discomfort.

Pedagogies of discomfort that confront white discomfort as part of broader affective, material and discursive assemblages of race, racism and whiteness are inevitably part of the wider project of decolonisation; therefore, they will function as decolonising pedagogies only when they adopt a decolonial praxis. As Tejeda, Espinoza and Gutierrez have argued, decolonising pedagogy is a practice that

> must be guided by a conceptually dynamic worldview and a set of values that make it anticapitalist, antiracist, antisexist, and antihomophobic. It is informed by a theoretical heteroglossia that strategically utilizes theorizations and understandings from various fields and conceptual frameworks to unmask the logics, workings, and effects of [...] colonial domination, oppression, and exploitation in our contemporary contexts. (2003, 21)

Tejeda and his colleagues note that 'there is a direct and material relation between the political processes and social structures of colonialism on the one hand, and Western regimes of knowledge and representation on the other' (ibid., 24). For pedagogies of discomfort to become decolonising pedagogies, then, they need to develop practices and accounts of knowledge that force Whites to confront their complicity in coloniality, without sentimentalising the terms and conditions of doing so.

Unless Whites admit their everyday complicity in coloniality, which means 'to open oneself to features of one's social world and one's way of inhabiting that world that are discomfiting' (Gilson 2011, 319; added emphasis), then pedagogies of discomfort run the risk of becoming a sentimental education aimed merely at modifying the way individuals feel by cultivating moral feelings. Pedagogies of discomfort without the decolonial injunction may easily fall into the trap of psychologizing solidarity and sympathy, while neglecting material/structural conditions of inequality. For this reason, I will end by suggesting three strategies – inspired by Barreto (2012) – that offer possibilities to enrich pedagogies of discomfort in order to confront white discomfort with a decolonial lens.

The first decolonial strategy calls for a re-contextualisation of white discomfort and pedagogies of discomfort in the affective, material and discursive assemblages that extend beyond schools and universities. This means that white discomfort is not viewed as ahistorical or situated in no context at all, but rather as a set of affects whose properties are contextually contingent, the result of specific affective, cultural and political processes. Therefore, to address white discomfort, educators will have to examine how white discomfort is constituted and reproduced within a specific social and political context and then offer pedagogies of discomfort that decolonise white discomfort and create alternative affects. For example, 'de-colonial love' (Sandoval 2000) could be such an example of an alternative affect; it entails breaking away from classifications of humans in essentialised categories.[5] Decolonial love is imagined and lived in a world in which ethical relationships are built beyond taken for granted social categories and colonial structures (Zembylas 2017a).

The second decolonial strategy suggests a critique of critical theory and pedagogy and its enrichment with decolonial thinking and praxis. As Jansen (2009) maintains, critical theory and critical pedagogy receive and construct the world as divided (e.g. black/white, oppressors/oppressed) and then take sides to free the oppressed. However, the rhetoric of critical pedagogy as we know it might prove inadequate, because it remains too firmly grounded in such binary pairings as oppressor/oppressed, master/slave, and power/freedom (Albrecht-Crane 2005; Ellsworth 1989; Yoon 2005; Zembylas 2013). As Yang (2015) suggests, decolonising pedagogy is an alternative to critical pedagogy precisely because the latter remains deeply humanist when it comes to liberation, whereas for pedagogies of discomfort to become decolonising, they have to dismantle any binary divisions that unknowingly may contribute to the perpetuation of white colonial knowledge structures. For this to happen, for example, educators will need to adopt an antiessentialist approach to knowledge and learning or promote an ethics of solidarity that is not psychologised (Subedi 2013). Decolonised pedagogies of discomfort entail making subjugated knowledges key points of reference in the curriculum and engendering pedagogies of solidarity that reject racial essentialisms, while confronting how white supremacy continues to inform what legitimate knowledge is in schools, in academia and in everyday life (Gaztambide-Fernandez 2012).

Finally, the last decolonial strategy calls for the adoption of an ethics of critical affect as an ethics of pedagogising white discomfort. The affective turn in the social sciences and humanities (Clough 2007) offers important insights towards establishing a link between colonialism and affects, especially in relation to how white discomfort is entangled with colonialism. Failing to understand how white discomfort is strongly entangled with white racial trauma will undermine and limit educators' pedagogical interventions. Working from the assumption that decolonising pedagogy must engage this terrain of difficult emotional knowledge in ways that have not been sufficiently addressed by critical pedagogy so far, decolonising pedagogies of discomfort need to pay attention to the difficult knowledge of white discomfort as a source of fruitful and critical sentimental practices rather than naive sentimental ones (Zembylas 2016). This implies moving away from moralised and sentimentalised approaches toward practices that actively promote solidarity and critical empathy with those who suffer from coloniality – including Whites as both victims and victimisers of white colonial structures. For example, decolonising pedagogies of discomfort could encourage 'implicit activisms', that is, actions which are 'small-scale' and proceed 'with little fanfare' (Horton and Kraftl 2009, 14) such as showing solidarity for those who suffer through modest everyday acts or standing up for those who are discriminated in the public sphere through supportive words and gestures. These modest forms of activism may not leave much (representational) trace but extend the field of activism and solidarity and open more transformative possibilities for Whites to get involved with pragmatic everyday actions that make a contribution to social justice causes and challenge white colonial structures in the everyday. The point, suggest Martin, Hanson, and Fontaine (2007), is 'not to identify every daily act as activist, but to theorize how small acts transform social relations in ways that have the potential to foster social change' (79). The difference from other social justice approaches is that implicit activisms are used as systematic tools of challenging the structures of colonisation in everyday encounters.

Conclusion

In this article, I have attempted to lay out some of the key differences between pedagogies of discomfort that engage in schooling white discomfort and decolonising pedagogies that recontextualise white discomfort in broader terms. I have acknowledged the debt we owe to pedagogies of discomfort, framed in critical pedagogy ideas, for addressing white emotionality and white discomfort. Yet, I have identified some risks that are associated with the undertheorisation of pedagogies of discomfort and the schooling of white discomfort in that schooling pedagogisation fails to take into consideration broader affective, material and discursive assemblages of race, racism and whiteness. Rethinking white discomfort and pedagogies of discomfort in terms of these broader affective, material and discursive assemblages can be the starting point for paying attention to the complexities and nuances of white discomfort more critically and strategically.

There is no doubt that it takes time and much discomfort for white teachers and students to discover how they can engage their emotions and affects as critical and transformative forces in schools and universities without sentimentalising them. A decolonising approach towards white discomfort and pedagogies of discomfort acknowledges the emotional damage to Whites *themselves* caused by colonisation and recontextualises the pedagogisation of white discomfort to facilitate a critical affective engagement of love, solidarity and empathy – all of which need to be redefined (Leonardo and Porter 2010). Continuing to explore and address the varied, subtle and unpredictable ways with which white discomfort is entangled with race, racism and whiteness in schools, universities and beyond can help us produce a more robust theory and pedagogical practice to confront white discomfort.

Notes

1. There are various accounts of 'whiteness' in the literature on Critical Whiteness Studies, Critical Race Theory and Critical Philosophy of Race. Critical Whiteness Studies, for example, pay particular attention to the invisible cultural practices that perpetuate white privilege and supremacy. Critical Race Theory focuses on the notion that racism is pervasive and systemic, not merely an individual pathology. Critical Philosophy of Race looks at how race is understood through various philosophical traditions (e.g. epistemology, phenomenology etc.). It is beyond the scope of this article to compare and contrast these accounts in terms of their understanding of 'whiteness', although it is important to recognise that there might be conflicting accounts (e.g. how critical philosophy of race retains the concept of race). My interest here is in highlighting the existence of structures of white supremacy and privilege in the broader society that are created and maintained through institutions, relationships and practices; this is why I draw mainly from Critical Whiteness Studies in this paper.
2. A related term in the literature is DiAngelo's (2011) notion of 'white fragility', which has been used to explain the tendency of Whites to avoid any discomfort, triggering a range of defensive moves (e.g. argumentation, silence, avoidance). Although there are similarities between 'white fragility' and 'white discomfort', I prefer the latter term in this paper for two reasons. First, the notion of discomfort is directly relevant to the term 'pedagogies of discomfort' that constitutes the focus of my analysis. Second, the notion of discomfort emphasizes more specifically the manifestations of anxiety and stress, whereas fragility is a more general term for the state of vulnerability. Given that my interest is on racial anxiety and stress as affective/emotional practices, I find that the notion of discomfort captures more precisely what I want to highlight.
3. For example, reading a novel or watching a movie and discussing how empathising with some of the characters' suffering can lead to a more critical understanding of the invisible white privilege and the sustained oppression of people of colour.
4. Applebaum (2017) suggests that educators' 'strategic empathy' (Zembylas 2015a) with white students in the classroom 'may be problematic,' because 'it might function as a form of comforting the white student' (864). The questions emerging from this claim are: Under which circumstances strategic empathy might function in this manner? Is there something 'endemic' in the function of strategic empathy that makes it susceptible to the practice of comforting? I find it somewhat troublesome that strategic empathy may be confused with the practice of comforting. The fact that an educator chooses to empathise with white students – that is, to understand their perspectives and imagine how they might feel, working against his or her own emotions – does not imply that he or she condones their perspectives nor does it suggest that empathy is automatically translated into some sort of comforting practice. Sometimes in our virtuous efforts to confront white discomfort, we (social-justice educators) may be compelled into the position of dismissing the function of strategic empathy out of fear that it might provide comfort to white students. Although I agree that comforting white discomfort

might be problematic, it would be equally problematic to dismiss empathy as a strategic response to concerns that white students might be treated 'too hard'.

5. Decolonial love, according to Sandoval (2000), is a process of social and political transformation that promotes a new ethics of relationality that is grounded in reparative practices of love towards the Other; thus, decolonial love re-imagines human relationships on a different ethical basis. The recognition of the violence of dehumanization as a result of coloniality is necessary for forging ethical relationships based on love (Figueroa 2015).

Acknowledgement

I am deeply grateful to Cheryl Matias for reading an earlier version of this paper and offering generous and encouraging feedback.

Disclosure statement

No potential conflict of interest was reported by the author.

References

Ahmed, S. 2004. *The Cultural Politics of Emotion*. Edinburgh: University of Edinburgh Press.
Albrecht-Crane, C. 2005. "Pedagogy as Friendship: Identity and Affect in the Conservative Classroom." *Cultural Studies* 19 (4): 491–514.
Applebaum, B. 2016. "Critical Whiteness Studies." In *Oxford Encyclopaedia of Education*, edited by G. W. Noblit, 1–25. Oxford: Oxford University Press, doi: 10.1093/acrefore/9780190264093.013.5
Applebaum, B. 2017. "Comforting Discomfort as Complicity: White Fragility and the Pursuit of Invulnerability." *Hypatia* 32 (4): 862–875.
Barreto, J.-M. 2012. "Decolonial Strategies and Dialogue in the Human Rights Field: A Manifesto." *Transnational Legal Theory* 3 (1): 1–29.
Bernstein, B. 2001. "From Pedagogies to Knowledges." In *Towards a Sociology of Pedagogy. The Contribution of Basil Bernstein to Research*, edited by A. Morais, I. Neves, B. Davies and H. Daniels, 363–368. New York: Peter Lang.
Boler, M. 1999. *Feeling Power: Emotions and Education*. New York: Routledge.

Boler, M. 2004. "Teaching for Hope: The Ethics of Shattering World Views." In *Teaching, Learning and Loving: Reclaiming Passion in Educational Practice*, edited by D. Liston and J. Garrison, 117–131. New York: RoutledgeFalmer.

Boler, M., and M. Zembylas. 2003. "Discomforting Truths: The Emotional Terrain of Understanding Differences." In *Pedagogies of Difference: Rethinking Education for Social Justice*, edited by P. Trifonas, 110–136. New York: Routledge.

Braidotti, R. 2006. *Transpositions: Nomadic Ethics*. Cambridge: Polity Press.

Britzman, D. P. 1998. *Lost Subjects, Contested Objects: Toward a Psychoanalytic Inquiry of Learning*. Albany: State University of New York Press.

Clough, P. 2007. "Introduction." In *The Affective Turn: Theorizing the Social*, edited by P. Clough with J. Halley, 1–33. Durham: Duke University Press.

Cutri, R., and E. Whiting. 2015. "The Emotional Work of Discomfort and Vulnerability in Multicultural Teacher Education." *Teachers and Teaching: Theory and Practice* 21 (8): 1010–1025.

Deleuze, G. 2007. "Eight Years Later: 1980 Interview." In *Two Regimes of Madness: Texts and Interviews, 1975–1995*, translated by A. Hodges and M. Taormina, 175–180. New York: Semiotext(e).

Deleuze, G., and F. Guattari. 1987. *A Thousand Plateaus: Capitalism and Schizophrenia*. Minneapolis: University of Minnesota Press.

Deutscher, P., and C. Lafont, eds. 2017. *Critical Theory in Critical Times: Transforming the Global Political and Economic Order*. New York: Columbia University Press.

DiAngelo, R. 2011. "White Fragility." *International Journal of Critical Pedagogy* 3 (3): 54–70.

Ellsworth, E. 1989. "Why Doesn't this Feel Empowering? Working Through the Repressive Myths of Critical Pedagogy." *Harvard Educational Review* 59: 297–324.

Faulkner, J., and M. Crowhurst. 2014. ""So far Multicultural that She is Racist to Australians": Discomfort as a Pedagogy for Change." *Pedagogy, Culture & Society* 22 (3): 389–403.

Figueroa, Y. 2015. "Reparations as Transformation: Radical Literary (re)imaginings of Futurities through Decolonial Love." *Decolonization: Indigeneity Education & Society* 4 (1): 41–58.

de Freitas, E., and A. McAuley. 2008. "Teaching for Diversity by Troubling Whiteness: Strategies for Classrooms in Isolated white Communities." *Race Ethnicity and Education* 11 (4): 429–442.

Gaztambide-Fernandez, R. 2012. "Decolonization and the Pedagogy of Solidarity." *Decolonization: Indigeneity Education & Society* 1 (1): 41–67.

Gilson, E. 2011. "Vulnerability, Ignorance, and Oppression." *Hypatia* 26 (2): 308–332.

Godfrey, P. 2004. ""Sweet Little (White) Girls"? Sex and Fantasy Across the Color Line and the Contestation of Patriarchal White Supremacy." *Equity & Excellence in Education* 37: 204–218.

Gonsalves, R. 2008. "Hysterical Blindness and the Ideology of Denial: Preservice Teachers' Resistance to Multicultural Education." In *Ideologies in Education: Unmasking the Trap of Teacher Neutrality*, edited by L. Bartolomé, 3–27. New York: Peter Lang.

Horton, J., and P. Kraftl. 2009. "Small Acts, Kind Words and "not too Much Fuss": Implicit Activisms." *Emotion, Space and Society* 2 (1): 14–23.

Jansen, J. 2009. *Knowledge in the Blood: Confronting Race and the Apartheid Past*. Stanford, CA: Stanford University Press.

Leibowitz, B., V. Bozalek, P. Rohleder, R. Carolissen, and L. Swartz. 2010. ""Ah, but the Whiteys Love to Talk about Themselves": Discomfort as a Pedagogy for Change." *Race Ethnicity and Education* 13 (1): 83–100.

Leonardo, Z. 2009. *Race, Whiteness, and Education*. New York: Routledge.

Leonardo, Z. 2011. "After the Glow: Race Ambivalence and other Educational Prognoses." *Educational Philosophy and Theory* 43: 675–698.

Leonardo, Z., and R. Porter. 2010. "Pedagogy of Fear: Toward a Fanonian Theory of 'Safety' in Race Dialogue." *Race Ethnicity and Education* 13 (2): 139–157.

Leonardo, Z., and M. Zembylas. 2013. "Whiteness as Technology of Affect: Implications for Educational Theory and Praxis." *Equity and Excellence in Education* 46 (1): 150–165.

Lim, J. 2010. "Immanent Politics: Thinking Race and Ethnicity through Affect and Machinism." *Environment and Planning A* 42 (10): 2393–2409.

Martin, D., S. Hanson, and D. Fontaine. 2007. "What Counts as Activism? The Role of Individuals in Creating Change." *Women's Studies Quarterly* 35 (3/4): 78–94.

Matias, C. 2016a. *Feeling White: Whiteness, Emotionality, and Education*. Rotterdam: Sense Publishers.

Matias, C. 2016b. "White Skin, Black Friend. A Fanonian Application to Theorise Racial Fetish in Teacher Education." *Educational Philosophy and Theory* 48 (3): 221–236.

Matias, C., and J. Mackey. 2016. "Breaking' Down Whiteness in Antiracist Teaching: Introducing Critical Whiteness Pedagogy." *Urban Review* 48: 32–50.

Matias, C., and M. Zembylas. 2014. ""When Saying you Care is not really Caring": Emotions of Disgust, Whiteness Ideology and Teacher Education." *Critical Studies in Education* 55 (3): 319–337.

Matias, C., R. Montoya, and N. Nishi. 2016. "Blocking CRT: How the Emotionality of Whiteness Blocks CRT in Urban Teacher Education." *Educational Studies* 52 (1): 1–19.

Mills, C. 1997. *The Racial Contract*. Ithaca, NY: Cornell University Press.

Mills, C. 2014. "Materializing Race." In *Living Alterities: Phenomenology, Embodiment, Race*, edited by E. S. Lee, 19–42. Albany, NY: SUNY Press.

Nayak, A. 2010. "Race, Affect, and Emotion: Young People, Racism, and Graffiti in the Postcolonial English Suburbs." *Environment and Planning A* 42 (10): 2370–2392.

Ohito, E. 2016. "Making the Emperor's New Clothes Visible in Anti-racist Teacher Education: Enacting a Pedagogy of Discomfort with White Preservice Teachers." *Equity & Excellence in Education* 49 (4): 454–467.

Ringrose, J. 2007. "Rethinking White Resistance: Exploring the Discursive Practices and Psychical Negotiations of 'Whiteness' in Feminist, Anti-racist Education." *Race Ethnicity and Education* 10 (3): 323–344.

Rodriguez, D. 2009. "The Usual Suspect: Negotiating White Student Resistance and Teacher Authority in a Predominantly White Classroom." *Cultural Studies <-> Critical Methodologies* 9 (4): 483–508.

Roediger, D. 1991. *The Wages of Whiteness: Race and the Making of the American Working Class*. New York: Verso.

Saldanha, A. 2006. "Reontologising Race: The Machine Geography of Phenotype." *Environment and Planning D: Society and Space* 24: 9–24.

Saldanha, A. 2010. "Skin, Affect, Aggregation: Guattarian Variations on Fanon." *Environment and Planning A* 42 (10): 2410–2427.

Sandoval, C. 2000. *Methodology of the Oppressed*. Minneapolis: University of Minnesota Press.

Sedgwick, E. 2003. *Touching Feeling: Affect, Pedagogy, Performativity*. Durham, NC: Duke University Press.

Singh, P. 2015. "Performativity and Pedagogising Knowledge: Globalising Educational Policy Formation, Dissemination and Enactment." *Journal of Education Policy* 30 (3): 363–384.

Smith, L. 1999. *Decolonising Methodologies: Research and Indigenous Peoples*. London: Zed Books.

Stavrou, S. 2016. "Pedagogising the University: On Higher Education Policy Implementation and its Effects on Social Relations." *Journal of Educational Policy* 31 (6): 789–804.

Subedi, B. 2013. "Decolonising the Curriculum from Global Perspectives." *Educational Theory* 63 (6): 621–638.

Swanton, S. 2010. "Sorting Bodies: Race, Affect, and Everyday Multiculture in a Mill Town in Northern England." *Environment and Planning A* 42 (10): 2332–2350.

Tarc, A. M. 2013. "Race Moves: Following Global Manifestations of New Racisms in Intimate Space." *Race Ethnicity and Education* 16 (3): 365–385.

Tatum, B. 1992. "Talking about Race, Learning about Racism: The Application of Racial Identity Development Theory in the Classroom." *Harvard Educational Review* 62 (1): 1–25.

Tatum, B. 1994. "Teaching White Students about Racism: The Search for White Allies and the Restoration of Hope." *Teachers College Record* 95: 462–476.

Tejeda, C., M. Espinoza, and K. Gutierrez. 2003. "Toward a Decolonising Pedagogy: Social Justice Reconsidered." In *Pedagogies of Difference: Rethinking Education for Social Justice*, edited by P. Trifonas, 10–40. New York: RoutledgeFalmer.

Thandeka. 1999. *Learning to be White: Money, Race and God in America*. New York: Continuum International.

Tolia, D. P., and M. Crang. 2010. "Guest Editorial: Affect, Race and Identities." *Environment and Planning A* 42 (10): 2309–2314.

Tuck, E., and K. W. Yang. 2012. "Decolonisation is not a Metaphor." *Decolonisation Indigeneity Education & Society* 1 (1): 1–40.

Yancy, G. 2008. *Black Bodies, White Gazes: The Continuing Significance of Race*. Lanham, MD: Rowman & Littlefield.

Yancy, G. 2014. "White Gazes: What it Feels like to be an Essence." In *Living Alterities: Phenomenology, Embodiment, Race*, edited by E. S. Lee, 43–64. Albany, NY: SUNY Press.

Yang, K. W. 2015. "Afterword: Will human Rights Education be Decolonizing?" In *Bringing Human Rights Education to US Classrooms: Exemplary Models from Elementary Grades to University*, edited by S. R. Katz and A. McEvoy Spero, 225–235. New York: Palgrave Macmillan.

Yoon, K. H. 2005. "Affecting the Transformative Intellectual: Questioning "Noble" Sentiments in Critical Pedagogy and Composition." *JAC: A Journal of Rhetoric, Culture & Politics* 25(4): 717-759.

Zembylas, M. 2013. "Critical Pedagogy and Emotion: Working through Troubled Knowledge in Posttraumatic Societies." *Critical Studies in Education* 54 (2): 176–189.

Zembylas, M. 2015a. "'Pedagogy of Discomfort' and its Ethical Implications: The Tensions of Ethical Violence in Social Justice Education." *Ethics and Education* 10 (2): 1–12.

Zembylas, M. 2015b. "Rethinking Race and Racism as Technologies of Affect: Theorizing the Implications for Antiracist Politics and Practice in Education." *Race Ethnicity and Education* 18 (2): 145–162.

Zembylas, M. 2016. "Toward a Critical-sentimental Orientation in Human Rights Education." *Educational Philosophy and Theory* 48 (11): 1151–1167.

Zembylas, M. 2017a. "Love as Ethico-Political Practice: Inventing Reparative Pedagogies of Aimance in "Disjointed" Times." *Journal of Curriculum and Pedagogy* 14 (1): 23–38.

Zembylas, M. 2017b. "Practicing an Ethic of Discomfort as an Ethic of Care in Higher Education Teaching." *Critical Studies in Teaching and Learning* 5 (1): 1–17.

Zembylas, M., and M. Boler. 2002. "On the Spirit of Patriotism: Challenges of a "Pedagogy of Discomfort"." Special issue on *Education and September 11. Teachers College Record On-line*, Accessed http://tcrecord.org

Zembylas, M., and C. McGlynn. 2012. "Discomforting Pedagogies: Emotional Tensions, Ethical Dilemmas and Transformative Possibilities." *British Educational Research Journal* 38 (1): 41–60.

Zembylas, M., and E. Papamichael. 2017. "Teaching for Anti-racism by Troubling Teachers' Comfort Zones: Discomfort and Empathy as Pedagogies in Teacher Professional Development." *Intercultural Education* 28 (1): 1–19.

7 Race, pre-college philosophy, and the pursuit of a critical race pedagogy for higher education

Melissa Fitzpatrick 🄳 and Amy Reed-Sandoval

ABSTRACT

This article seeks to explore ways in which pre-college pedagogical resources – particularly Critical Race Pedagogy (CPR) developed for high school students, as well as Philosophy for Children (P4C) – can be helpfully employed by college level instructors who wish to dialogue with students about the nature of race and racial oppression. More specifically, we wish to explore (a) how P4C can both learn from, and be put to the service of, CRP, and (b) how this provides a useful framework for philosophical conversations about race at the college and pre-college levels. Our arguments are interwoven with narratives of our personal experiences utilising these pre-college pedagogical resources in conversations about race, so as to illustrate and provide context for our claims. We ultimately contend that these resources can help pedagogues in both higher and lower education work toward unmuting the voices of undervalued and underserved students in the United States.

Introduction

Attempting to engage undergraduate students in philosophical dialogues about the nature of race, the nature of racism, and how to enact anti-racist practices in one's life and society can pose unexpected challenges for instructors. For instance, one might find that one's carefully tailored and painstakingly planned syllabus does not contain resources that directly enable one to address the questions that one's current students find most urgent and intriguing. Or one might find that while philosophy classes often do an excellent job of dealing with race and racism at an abstract level, they may come up short in terms of clearly connecting such abstract theories to students' lived experiences of race and racism. Finally, and perhaps most obviously, conversations about race and racism can be charged and uncomfortable. Philosophy instructors at the university level do not often receive training in dealing with the attendant discomfort.

To better illustrate these challenges, we offer two narratives from the personal, place-based pedagogical experiences of the authors:

(1) Amy Reed-Sandoval taught a Philosophies of Race and Racism seminar in 2016 at the University of Texas at El Paso. This was an undergraduate and graduate 'hybrid seminar' cross-listed in the Department of Philosophy and the African-American Studies Program. UTEP is a Hispanic Serving Institution located right at the US-Mexico border, and the majority of students in the class were self-identified Latina/o/xs and Chicanxs ('Chicano/Chicanx' is a term of self-identification for Mexican-Americans who wish to emphasise their Indigenous heritage and a corresponding political orientation). Given the topic, and the fact that the class was cross-listed in African-American Studies, a group of self-identified African-American undergraduate students at UTEP were also enrolled in the class. There were about two self-identified white students in the class of 30, and the instructor self-identifies as white.

Bearing in mind that the majority of students enrolled in this course would likely self-identify as Latinx and African-American, the instructor included readings in the syllabus that she hoped would speak to the experiences of racialised students in both groups.[1]

While students in the class were generally receptive to the literature, the instructor quickly found that there were other relevant questions that students urgently wanted to discuss – questions that she simply had not anticipated in designing her syllabus. First, students eagerly wanted to explore the ethics of inter-racial dating. Though Sandoval had considered including Mills (1996) 'Do Black Men Have a Moral Duty to Marry Black Women?' on the syllabus, she had decided against it, incorrectly assuming that young millennials – particularly those who live in El Paso, where inter-racial couplings are relatively common – would not be particularly interested in this question. However, this theme regularly came up, and many students wrote in their in-class 'free-write' assignment that they wanted ethical guidance on how to navigate challenges associated with inter-racial dating in their own lives.

Second – and even more challenging, from the perspective of the instructor – both African-American and Latina/o/x students sought opportunities to engage in philosophical dialogue about perceived race-based tensions between African-Americans and Latina/o/xs in El Paso and beyond. This posed a challenge to the instructor who, as a self-identified white woman, was particularly concerned (and felt particularly obligated) to explicitly address issues of white supremacy during class-time. Feeling influenced by the 'prejudice-plus-power' view of racism as described by Taylor (2013, 35), she was therefore often uncertain, pedagogically and philosophically, of the best way to navigate claims from students that Latina/o/xs were racist against African-Americans, or *vice versa*.[2] This challenge was deepened by the fact that there is scant literature in more 'mainstream' Philosophy of

Race on black-Latina/o/x relations. The dissonance between the content of her syllabus and the questions her students wanted to explore – augmented by her positionality as a self-identified white women – generated discomfort for the philosophy instructor.

(2) Melissa Fitzpatrick also encountered such challenges, albeit in a slightly different context. During the summer of 2017, Melissa designed and taught a college-level Intro to Ethics course, 'The Good Life', to high school students in the Mississippi Delta, participating in the Freedom Summer Collegiate Fellowship program, which, paying homage to the 1964 Mississippi Freedom Schools,[3] sends PhD candidates in various disciplines to teach their areas of specialisation to underserved and under-resourced students in the United States.

The class met for two hours each day in the Eudora, Arkansas courthouse, and the students (ranging from rising freshman rising seniors) were almost all African-American, except for three Mexican-Americans who were also enrolled in the class. Because Melissa self-identifies as both white and Mexican-American/Chicana, she assumed she would often serve as the white voice in the classroom; however, given the color of her skin and texture of her hair, the students quickly identified her as 'mixed' – not fully grouping her into their understanding of 'whiteness'. Within the first few minutes of meeting the students, the students told her which parts of the town were 'black', which parts of the town were 'white', which churches 'served which race', and what it is like to be a teenager of color in the Delta.

Because of severe economic turmoil, the Eudora school district closed in 2008, forcing its students (almost 100% of which were African-American) to take an (at minimum) hour-long bus ride to Lakeside High School (at the time, roughly 50% black and 50% white). Although desegregation in Chicot Country took place in the 1970s, segregation and its negative repercussions still permeate Lakeside High School. The consolidation of school districts provoked a major wave of 'white flight' and racially charged community disputes, ultimately preserving prejudices and racial disparity. As a result of all this, the students Melissa taught understand themselves to be degraded through the eyes of school administration and the 'powers-that-be', as they consistently find themselves lacking transportation, resources, funding, afterschool activities, and most significantly, teachers.[4] This self-understanding was evidenced by all of the students, unanimously, during various classroom discussions in which racial oppression came up.

While hoping to give her students a taste of the history of ethics in Western philosophy (including excerpts from thinkers like Plato, Aristotle, Epictetus, and Kant), the instructor assumed, after what was conveyed in the Freedom Summer teacher-training, that she would have to theoretically problematise the 'whiteness'[5] of the canon as often as possible – potentially incorporating key texts from Feminist Theory and Critical Race Theory. However, before committing to those syllabus modifications, both she and the other PhD candidate teaching in Eudora realised within the first week of teaching that the students did not appear – at least not in those early interactions – to be interested in contemplating their oppression, or discussing racial disparity in abstract terms.

With challenges such as these in mind, this article seeks to explore ways in which pre- college pedagogical resources – particularly Critical Race Pedagogy (CPR) developed for high school students, as well as Philosophy for Children (P4C) – can be helpfully employed at the college level by instructors who wish to dialogue with students about the nature of race and racial oppression. More specifically, we wish to explore (a) how P4C can both learn from, and be put to the service of, CRP, and (b) how this provides a useful framework for philosophical conversations about race at the college and pre-college levels. Both authors have experienced challenging philosophical dialogues about race in college and pre-college classrooms, and both have employed the pre-college pedagogical techniques we shall explore below at the university level. Our arguments are interwoven with narratives of our personal experiences, utilising these techniques in conversations about race; we do this in hopes of illustrating and providing context for our claims.

Our paper is structured as follows. We begin by providing an overview of Critical Race Pedagogy (CRP) for the pre-college classroom. Second, we provide a general overview of Philosophy for Children (P4C). Third, we indicate ways in which P4C's methods can be put to the service of CRP – at both the pre-college and college levels Fourth, we turn to the question of what P4C might be able to learn from CRP. We conclude by indicating ways in which these pre-college resources – CRP and P4C, understood to be complementary to one another – can be useful to college-level instructors who want to address issues of racial oppression in the classroom.

The quest for a critical race pedagogy

We begin by outlining some of the key tenets of Critical Race Pedagogy, which we shall consider in the context of both pre-college and college classes.

Marvin Lynn's 'Toward A Critical Race Pedagogy' begins by echoing Carter G. Woodson, asking: *At what point will all of our children have access to quality educa-tion? When will the miseducation of Africans end? And what can we do to ameliorate this exigency?* (1999, 606–607). Drawing from the testimonies of African American teachers in lower education, Lynn probes how schools might be able to help end racial, gender, and ethnic subordination, and how critical race theory can be con-nected to broader discussions on pedagogy – especially emancipatory teaching practices of people of color, attempting to counteract the devaluation of racially oppressed students (1999, 611).

Grounded in Critical Race Theory's commitment to tackling questions and prob-lems in education through the lens of women and men of color, Lynn defines Critical Race Pedagogy as 'an analysis of race, ethnicity, and gender subordination that relies on the perceptions, experiences, and counterhegemonic practices of educators of color' that lends itself to 'an articulation of emancipatory pedagogical strategies and techniques that are proved to be successful with racially and cultur-ally subordinated students' (1999, 615). Practitioners of CRP are thus committed to unmuting the voices of undervalued and therefore underserved students by confronting 'the endemic nature of racism in the United States; the importance of cultural identity; the necessary interaction of race, class, and gender; and the practice of liberation pedagogy' (Lynn 1999, 615).

By Lynn's account, CRP advocates the encouragement of inquiry and dialogue in the classroom, so as to foster communities in which students actively participate in the co-construction of knowledge. Part of this involves celebrating each student's individuality, and underscoring the importance of their respective cultures. As Lynn points out, unique to CRP is the fact that it considers 'all of the facets of our multilayered identities while arguing that race should be utilized as the primary unit of analysis in critical discussions of schooling in the United States – a former slave society' (1999, 622). The crucial first step in CRP is bearing witness to the nec-essarily racialised context in the United States – a country founded on the notion that some groups of people are intrinsically inferior to others.

Another crucial aspect of CRP is its pedagogues reminding themselves that 'all teaching and learning are political' (Lynn 1999, 620),[6] and that the process of building a more democratic state begins with the education of our youth, and educating that youth in a way that grants credence to each of their unique voices and perspectives. This practice simultaneously gives students 'control over their own learning', while actively addressing issues of racial, ethnic, and gender inequal-ity by perpetually working to recognise the gifts that every person, community, culture, race, ethnicity, gender, etc. have to offer (Lynn 1999, 622).

Some of the major challenges to CRP that Lynn draws out include: (1) securing the epistemic specificity that is required for tailoring discourse to marginalised audiences; (2) confronting the ways in which racism is deeply embedded in almost all of our country's social structures and practices (it is 'a normal and fixed part of the American social landscape') (Lynn 1999, 616); (3) the spiritual and emo-tional drain that teachers of colour feel in attempting to combat the status quo in education in the United States; (4) the lack of adequate cultural training for white teachers serving students of colour, so as to build more culturally relevant curriculums; and (5) the consequences teachers face for challenging advocates of hegemonic, counter-emancipatory practices (Lynn 1999, 619).

Although Lynn focuses on challenges specific to high school teachers of col-our, we wish to highlight that the challenges he raises also resonate with college professors of all racialised identities conducting philosophical dialogue about race. Paralleling the need for high school instructors to stick to the required high school curriculum/Common Core State Standards, college professors have the added pressure to stick to 'relevant' literature, or 'stick to the text' in a way that potentially forsakes the existential context from which the text, professor, and students speak – and, as Claire Katz puts it, 'what it means for our everyday life'

(2004, 532).[7]Academia protects a certain level of specialisation and expertise that respects and preserves the work done in a given discipline, and often for good reasons. The trouble with this, however, is that the prioritisation of expertise and specialisation can foster somewhat 'isolated, self-indulgent practices' (Katz 2012, 150) that can lead professors to fixate on the text and/or 'relevant' literature, and lose sight of the moral and intellectual development of their students. Over time, they may also unwittingly lose sight of the fact that their students have meaningful things to contribute.[8]

In regards to college-level philosophy (of race, ethics, etc.) in particular, the rise of the modern institution has arguably led to the prioritisation of the knowledge of objects over active thinking with, or participation in, the content at hand.[9] As Robert Frodeman and Adam Briggle contend in their recent *New York Times* piece, 'When Philosophy Lost its Way' (2016), philosophy, in its attempt to emulate the method of the natural and social sciences in the modern university, began operating under the modus operandi of knowledge production, prioritising 'knowledge of the good over doing the good'. Frodeman and Briggle argue that philosophy has lost its way in the sense that it has strayed from valuing philosophy as therapy for the soul in favour of valuing philosophy as a rigorous science – again, pushing professors to prioritise getting through a certain amount of 'seminal' peer-reviewed content, often at the expense of fruitful in-class discussions. College-level professors may, therefore, be disincentivised from granting their students any degree of control over, or *authentic engagement with*, their learning.

A lack of student input or involvement in college-level philosophy courses is often the consequence of employing a 'one-way' or 'asymmetrical' or 'top-down' model of learning, in which the professor is tasked to bestow their students with knowledge, and the students, insofar as they are willing, are there to receive what the professor provides. It seems reasonable to suggest that this is the norm in undergraduate college classrooms. Implicit in this 'top-down' approach is the idea that the professor is at least in some sense superior to the students, and that it is the professor *qua* single source of authority in the room, who pours knowledge into what would otherwise be an 'empty vessel'. This is not to say that attributing expertise to professors implies that students are *necessarily* understood to be empty vessels, but rather that a 'top-down' classroom dynamic can be such that students' vital perspectives – especially in regard to race and racism – can all too easily be overlooked.

With this in mind, the challenges that college-level philosophy professors face seem to mirror many of the challenges that CRP practitioners in lower education face. In both cases, institutional pressures – that is, pressures from institutions that are deeply embedded with racism (as part of the necessarily racialised context in the United States) – can inhibit instructors from effectively *unmuting* the voices of students who speak from within cultures that have failed to be represented or served in education. Beyond this, the need to stick to 'seminal' texts and debates within the 'expert'-defined parameters of a given discipline (or in the case of high school teachers, the need to stick within the parameters as defined by the Common Core State Standards) can stifle efforts to work toward the epistemic specificity required to respect, ignite, and inspire students that come from radically different walks of life than the authors of 'key' texts and governing debates. Or in other words, these institutional pressures can (and do) stifle both high school teachers' and college professors' efforts to actualise liberation pedagogy.[10]

Race and pre-college philosophy

Having explored core features of Critical Race Pedagogy and the challenges its pedagogues face – which, we have argued, is highly relevant at both the college and pre-college levels – we now turn to pre-college philosophy. In this section, we explore the ways in which P4C can support at least some of the aforementioned goals of a Critical Race Pedagogy.

Philosophy for Children (P4C) or 'pre-college philosophy' classes take many ped-agogical forms, but they are usually organised around the goal of providing young people with the opportunity to ask and explore the philosophical questions that are most meaningful to them. They are generally based on two assumptions: (1) that children (including very young children) are capable of philosophising *and* (2) this often goes problematically unnoticed in our society. As Gareth B. Matthews rather poignantly argued, '…once children become well settled into school, they learn only "useful" questioning is expected of them. Philosophy then either goes underground, to be pursued privately, perhaps, and not shared with others, or else becomes totally dormant' (1994, 5). Philosophy for Children classes therefore aim to 'break the mold' of an educational system that, for a variety of complicated reasons, renders dormant the philosophical impulse in young children.

In pursuit of this aim, many pre-college philosophy instructors employ what Matthew Lipman called a 'Community of Inquiry' (CoI) model to facilitate philo-sophical discussions with young people.[11] In a CoI, the P4C facilitator will often read a children's book that is understood to inspire philosophical discussion – like *The Giving Tree*, to name just one popular example. Then, rather than 'direct' a philosophical discussion the main questions of which have been identified by the facilitator in advance, the facilitator will ask the children/youth in the classroom to identify the questions that the text has inspired for them. As the children/youth articulate these philosophical questions, the facilitator lists them on a chalkboard (when available). The facilitator then asks the young people in the room to vote for their favourite question, rendering the P4C classroom more democratic than many 'traditional' education spaces.[12]

Finally, the children/youth – who are generally seated in a circle, along with the facilitator – participate in an open dialogue in which they collectively aim to respond to the question for which they have voted. Maughn Rollins Gregory has identified a six-stage framework of 'dialogical inquiry' that, when employed by Philosophy for Children instructors, can serve to enhance this process. These stages include: (1) the identification of 'issues relevant to purposes'; (2) the formulation and organisation of relevant questions; (3) the formulation and organisation of hypotheses in response to questions; (4) clarification and testing of hypotheses in dialogue – and possible confirming, testing, and abandoning of hypothesis; (5) experimentation of hypotheses 'in experience' and possible warranting, revising or abandoning of the hypotheses: and (6) the implementation of a warranted hypotheses (Gregory 2007, 62).

Students are encouraged both to disagree with one another (when appropriate), and to identify common themes that have emerged in the group discussion. It is important that the P4C classroom be, at least as much as possible, a free and open exchange of ideas. It can be challenging to achieve and pursue this, however, for reasons that we shall discuss at the end of the paper. While CoI is certainly one of the most popular methods of facilitating philosophical discussions with young people, facilitators of pre-college philosophy classes often employ a variety of games, thought experiments, and artistic activities to inspire young people to engage philosophically – to 'tap into' their philosophical impulse, despite over-whelming social and institutional pressure to do otherwise.[13]

We submit that in light of the challenges outlined above, there are a variety of ways in which P4C's methods, in tandem with pre-college level CRP's aims, might be able to benefit the development of college-level CRP. We will focus on four.

First, perhaps most distinct to P4C is that its methodologies attempt to dis-mantle the more traditional model of authority in the classroom. Contrary to the asymmetrical/'top-down' model of teaching often employed at the college-level, P4C's model of teaching is almost exclusively 'bottom-up'. Student contribution is not only vital in P4C classrooms, but is actually the *centerpiece* of each lesson plan. This directly relates to CRP's aim to grant students more agency in and engage-ment with their learning. Although the teacher in P4C spaces guides the classroom discourse in the sense of choosing a topic, theme, or initial warm up question, and then immersing the students in a given account of that theme (e.g. *The Giving Tree*, or a game illustrating Rawls's notion of 'the veil of ignorance'), where the students go from there is ultimately up to them.

For example, after describing philosophy as a way of critically examining and engaging our lives, Melissa realised that it would be beneficial for her students to practice constructing arguments at the beginning of every class: choosing a conviction that they hold dear (starting simple, e.g. arguing why cats make bet-ter pets than dogs) and providing three to five premises supporting that convic-tion. Once everyone finished building their arguments, each student would share their argument, and the class as a whole would critically engage it by evaluating its premises and providing counter-arguments. The instructor noted that after employing such an open-ended activity, her students suddenly wanted to explore issues of racial oppression (even though, as noted in the introduction, they had originally been resistant to such topics when she presented them in a more 'top down' fashion). Notable examples include: one black[14] student arguing for why

Lakeside High School should care more about education than the way (black) students are dressed; another black student arguing for why students should not be served spoiled milk at lunch; and a Mexican-American student arguing for why 'gays' should be 'left alone', which was an especially controversial topic considering the often intense religious impulses/presuppositions in the room.

These argument-evaluating conversations – often incorporating, but by no means limited to, the content presented by the instructor – made the practical dimension of philosophy more palpable for the students, provoking their hunger for careful introspection and the critique of systems of oppression. What was immediately apparent to the instructor was that her students were not afraid to discuss race on their terms: to own the space from which they spoke, and to utilise philosophy's resources to empower their stance in that space, as they saw fit. Crucially, however, it was only through giving students the space for free argumentation that they warmed up to the idea of discussing their oppression.

Reed-Sandoval experienced something similar when attempting to engage in a philosophical dialogue about immigration justice with a group of Mexican and Mexican- American elementary children in a P4C class in El Paso. She quickly learned that some of the children in her class had/have family members that work for the Border Patrol and US Customs and Border Enforcement. Possibly because of this, her young students did not immediately want to talk about possible injustices associated with excluding immigrants at the border; this, however, is what the instructor had anticipated discussing that day. Rather, the students revealed – over the course of a CoI – that they wanted to explore the question of why law enforcement officials carry weapons, and whether it was just for them to do so. Some of the children had seen their family members in law enforcement carrying guns, and they wondered philosophically about this. The instructor allowed the philosophical dialogue to go in this direction, and suspected that her plans to discuss immigration justice that day had been fully derailed. However, the students soon turned to the question of whether it is 'OK for police to target immigrants with weapons'. The students grasped the importance of questions of immigration justice – but they wanted to approach it on their terms. The philosophical questions emerged from lived experiences that could only be known by the teacher by first listening to the students.

Furthermore, as mentioned in the previous section, a key facet of teaching within a particular discipline at the college-level is framing one's syllabus with a certain set of expert/peer-approved texts and questions (as it is ultimately by way of these authors and debates that one develops and gains esteem within their area of expertise). The potential trouble with this is that the specific framing of a question is itself *political*, as it directly or indirectly leads students toward anticipated answers and conversations, rather than fostering the sort of free thinking that is required to give students more control over their learning, and the ability to embrace (and further understand) the contexts from which they speak. To foster democracy in the classroom is to accept that students might not find certain questions pertinent – especially in regard to race (or a lack of regard to race).[15]

Thus, second, P4C offers a helpful open format. Rather than requiring instructors to cover specific philosophical content, the chief aim is to safeguard an alternative space in which, echoing Lynn, the instructor can celebrate each student's individuality, underscore the importance of their respective cultures and contexts, and facilitate honest conversations. This pedagogical approach of letting the students determine the course of conversation in the classroom speaks to CRP's encouragement of inquiry and dialogue, and is also one way of beginning to address the difficulty of providing the epistemic specificity required to adequately make space for the insights of marginalised students. Insofar as students are, at least to a certain extent, in control of the topic of conversation and pertinent guiding questions, they are able to express what it is that they value *and why*. By focusing on student values (and really hearing those values, even if they are to be challenged), teachers are given insight into what matters to the their students, and are granted an important degree of access into the epistemic space from which they speak.

Third, and in the same vein, P4C's CoI model and constant facilitation of open collaborative conversation also begin to address the lack of cultural training that teachers are given in preparation for serving students of colour, so as to build more culturally relevant curriculums. A key aim in P4C spaces is empowering students to respond to the questions they deem pertinent by sharing what they think *and why*, receiving and giving input from the instructor and the other students. Fostering this sort of open collaborative conversation, in which students share and justify their convictions about a particular topic, theme, or claim, is related to, albeit distinct from building a CoI.

It is distinct in the sense that rather than denoting the process of students literally voting on which questions they deem most important, it denotes the activity of students working together to dig deeper into, and further unravel, the topic, theme, or claim at hand. Much like constructing a CoI, facilitating open collaborative conversation is distinct from 'cold-calling' in that it is 'warm' invitation to contribute rather than a 'cold' demand for answers.

It seems clear that the best way to cultivate openness among students and a general willingness to contribute in in-class discussions is to, as the instructor, exemplify what it means to do this well. On the part of the instructor, this involves: (1) actively responding to every student in class, (2) being willing to weigh-in/contribute, (3) not judging anyone's conviction or ideas as 'good', 'bad', 'right', or 'wrong' (full stop), but instead habituating the process of dissecting those convictions, unpacking the reasons behind them, and then working together to figure out if they stand on solid ground. Is it therefore through these processes (of building CoIs and fostering open collaborative conversation) that P4C supports CRP's aim to recognise the gifts that every person, community, culture, race, ethnicity, gender, etc. have to offer, while concomitantly furthering it own aim of teaching students how to *critically think*.

We argue that understanding the spaces from which each student speaks allows teachers to craft effective lesson plans that incorporate a blend of both what the teacher deems important and what the students care about/find philosophically captivating. This of course *does not* provide all of the training that is required to for (particularly white) teachers to sufficiently connect with students whose experiences are incommensurable to that of the teacher, but it can provide a window into their worlds by celebrating each of their respective perspectives, and subsequently building a circle of trust in the classroom. If this level of trust is established, then when it is time for students to share their convictions, and more importantly, their reasons for those convictions based on the context from which they speak, students are not only willing to share, but are eager for the conversation itself: eager for the challenges they might receive from the instructor and other students, eager for the opportunity to think something new.

In her article, 'Witnessing Education', Katz – who is both a professor at Texas A&M, and active advocate and practitioner of P4C – analyses the significance and responsibility of the 'messenger' in education, i.e. the teacher who is conveying content to her students. Among other questions, she probes: *what are we doing when we teach philosophy? Are our students' concerns really the same as ours? Do we not have as much to learn from our students than by learning how to hear their voices and respond to them?* Crucial, by Katz's account, is understanding teaching as a relation, which involves (1) understanding that our students' concerns are *not* always the same as ours, and (2) understanding that the art of listening to consenting and dissenting voices in the classroom is vital (Katz 2003, 122–130).

Fourth (and finally), this notion of 'active listening' is essential to P4C pedagogy, and represents one aspect of P4C's commitment to promoting Socratic dialogue.[16] The instructor's role in a P4C classroom is to be a present interlocutor, and to (much like Socrates) hear what each student has to say, and actively push their thoughts to new spaces by provoking them, and asking them *why*. It seems clear that this sort of listening is the defining feature of true conversation; active listening is what connects one's perspective to the perspective of another by *hosting*,[17] and therefore granting credence to, their ideas, ultimately in hopes of working together to collectively come to new levels of understanding. Active listening involves humility on the part of the instructor, recognising that they, too, are a learner in the classroom, and that their students are valid sources of knowledge. And again, this emphasis on active listening-humility directly speaks to CRP's call for inquiry and dialogue in the classroom, so as to foster communities in which students actively participate in the co-construction of knowledge. To truly co-construct knowledge, and therefore *think together* both actively and openly, there needs to be attentive exchange among all members of the classroom.

The other aspect of P4C's commitment to promoting Socratic dialogue in the classroom is its understanding and practice of philosophy as *provocation*. This is to say that P4C understands philosophy as a discipline that does not hesitate to offer disquieting suggestions, that is not afraid to 'offend' its participants, and that serves as an occasion to playfully bring students into the business of *knowing thyself* in all of that self's multiplicity.[18] Along these lines, P4C actively questions the 'politically correct' *qua* things that 'should' or 'should not' be said out loud, recognising that it can sometimes be more problematic to cover up or avoid addressing prejudices for the sake of preventing accidental 'offense' than it is to offend or provoke, albeit in an open/non-prejudiced/hospitable way. With Lynn's remarks about the need to bear witness to the way in which racism permeates all of our country's social structures and practices, it seems clear that political correctness, too, *qua* common social practice in the United States, is deeply embedded with racism.

During one of Melissa's classes, a black student made a remark about where white people go in town, and ended by saying, 'no offense'. Melissa asked, 'Why would I be offended?!' The student was quiet. Melissa encouraged the student to explain herself, lightheartedly asking 'what' the student thought she was, and the student eventually said, 'You are mixed'. Somewhat shocked by how candid the conversation was – recognising that her privilege was being made explicit, placed on the table for discussion – Melissa used the student's remarks as an occasion to discuss race in relation to positions of power and socio-economic status, lightening the conversation by letting the students work through their understanding of different stereotypes (including their impressions about her, e.g. her being white enough to share in white privilege, and what those impressions were based on, e.g. her ability to travel by plane, her living in Boston, her studying philosophy, her getting a PhD, her being able to *temporarily* teach in the Delta, etc.), reminding them that philosophy, as a practice, works to probe generalisations and their corresponding phenomena.

It is important to note that the instructor was not trying to correct her students' thinking (as their social-identification of her was not inaccurate), but was instead trying to celebrate the open/honest conversation, giving the students space to make their understandings of privilege, whiteness, and oppression manifest, while welcoming the opportunity for herself to reflect on the often complicated relationship between self-identification and social-identification – specifically the variety of ways in which our assumptions about ourselves can be called into question in different social contexts. The crucial take away from this case is that regardless of the age group, when race comes up in the classroom (as it almost inevitably does), we should not hesitate to unload our presuppositions and talk about them, asking ourselves (instructor included): what, if anything, are we missing? The way in which P4C methods challenge 'political correctness' not only warrants these conversations, but understands them as part of the process of dismantling prejudices and de-tabooing the other – no matter *who* that other is.

In sum, although P4C cannot address all of the issues that CRP practitioners face, we have argued for some of the ways in which it supports CRP's goals, and might be able to aid in CRP's development at the college-level, including P4C's: (1) attempt to dismantle the more traditional 'top-down' model of authority in the classroom, potentially replacing the power of the teacher with the power of the respective voices of students in the classroom; (2) emphasis on maintaining an open format that safeguards an alternative space for students to share their lived experiences/offer epistemic specificity; (3) prioritisation of building a community of inquiry and fostering open collaborative conversation; and (4) commitment to promoting Socratic dialogue by insisting on active listening- humility in the classroom, and on understanding and practicing philosophy as provocation.

With these points in mind, we can turn to the question of how CRP can assist in the development of P4C, and how the two methodologies can not only comple- ment each other, but can work together to construct a more democratic approach to education.

How CRP can aid in the development of P4C

Throughout this paper, we have been arguing that Philosophy for Children/pre-col- lege philosophy pedagogical techniques can be useful to college-level instructors who aim to adopt a Critical Race Pedagogy in their classroom, particularly when teaching courses about race and racism. Our claims have focused on the ways in which P4C classes employ a 'bottom up' philosophical approach – sometimes, but not always, through the creation of a Community of Inquiry (CoI) in the classroom – that takes as a philosophical and dialectical starting point the questions and concerns of students in the classroom.

We do not wish, however, to overstate uncritically the extent to which Philosophy for Children methods currently support a Critical Race Pedagogy. In fact, in this final section we explore some lessons that Philosophy for Children/pre-college philosophy instructors can and should learn from the tools of CRP and Critical Race Theory (CRT).

Chetty (2014) has compellingly argued that CoI methodology, when employed uncritically (in terms of the goals of CRP) in the Philosophy for Children classroom, can, in fact, serve to marginalise the voices of students of colour. Chetty's article indicates that this is particularly likely to transpire when P4C classes (a) explore issues of race and racism when (b) students of color are in the classroom minority. In such cases, children and youth of color are often expected to raise the most critical questions pertaining to race and racism. As discussed earlier, the philo- sophical questions are generated by the students, not the teacher – and people of colour are often (rightfully) understood to have greater epistemic access to the realities of structural racism.[19] However, Chetty argues that it is unrealistic – and perhaps even irresponsible – to expect children of colour in white- majority classroom to take on the burden of raising critical questions about race and racism in a CoI. Furthermore, when children of colour feel reluctant to raise such critical questions in a white- majority classroom, white supremacy in the classroom may go unacknowledged.

Rainville (2000, 11–38) has also called into question the so-called neutrality of the CoI in Philosophy for Children classes in .She problematises ways in which

P4C has often been presented as a purely democratic and philosophically neutral pedagogy in the context of settler colonial societies. That is, Rainville contends that when P4C classes are presented and enacted as though they were politically 'neutral' in the settler state, they actually can serve to obscure the realities of, and thereby reinforce, settler colonialism and its attendant epistemologies. Rainville argues that children and youth in such P4C classes can come to feel that they are participating in a simulation of an 'ideal democratic process' without having to consider the fact that their 'fair and democratic' dialogue is actually occurring on stolen Indigenous land. Not only can this contribute to the perpetuation of 'white ignorance' (Mills 2007) on the part of white students, Rainville argues, it can also deeply alienate Native students in a CoI.

While we believe, and have argued throughout this paper, that pre-college philosophy techniques can support the objectives of Critical Race Pedagogy at the pre-college and college levels, we also submit that Chetty's and Rainville's respective critiques indicate ways in which Philosophy for Children practitioners should learn lessons from Critical Race Pedagogy. We suggest that facilitators of pre-college philosophy – and also college-level instructors who wish to use P4C methods to dialogue about race and racism in the classroom – should: (1) find ways to secure the *epistemic specificity* that is required to 'tailor discourse to marginalized audiences' (e.g. offering an open classroom format in which students are, at least to a certain extent, in control of the topic of conversation and pertinent guiding questions,); (2) work with the goal of confronting racism in the American, not to mention global, social landscape (e.g. when lesson planning, never losing sight of the fact that racism is deeply embedded in almost all of our country's social structures and practices); and (3) discuss and incorporate strategies for addressing the various barriers and burdens that teachers of colour and teachers committed to adopting anti-racist practices in the classroom regularly face. Furthermore, we believe that it is possible for P4C practitioners to work toward these goals of Critical Race Pedagogy without sacrificing the 'bottom up', comparatively free and open-ended nature of pre-college philosophy pedagogical techniques.

Several strategies for achieving this goal have been articulated by Amy Reed-Sandoval and Alain Carmen Sykes in 'Who Talks? Who Listens? Taking Positionality Seriously in Philosophy for Children' (Reed-Sandoval and Sykes 2017, 219–226). First, they argue practitioners of P4C – and, we would add, university-level instructors who teach on issues of race and racism – should be explicitly attentive to the positionalities of teachers and students in the classroom. Teachers should seek out productive ways to acknowledge their own ethno-racial positionalities in the classroom while empowering students to explicitly acknowledge theirs (when they feel comfortable doing so). If students and teacher can come to acknowledge that the philosophical views they espouse in an open philosophical dialogue/CoI are likely to be affected by their respective positionalities, there is potential for the entire group to be enlisted in the task of interrogating potential white and settler-normativity in the classroom.

Second, Reed-Sandoval and Sykes also argue that Philosophy for Children practitioners should come to regard student *silences* as potentially philosophically suggestive. In Chetty's example of the lone student of colour in an otherwise white classroom who does not feel empowered to raise critical questions about race and racism, the P4C instructor might come to regard that student's silence as a valuable and even philosophically rich contribution to dialogue in question. For instance, that silence might be interpreted as a potential rejection of the way in which a topic is being presented, or as a suggestion that it might be better to pursue the topic in a different way. Finally, they argue that pre-college philosophy instructors should strive to support ethno-racial diversity among Philosophy for Children teachers. Note that all of these strategies can be employed at both the college and pre-college levels, and both are consistent with the pedagogical methods we have been outlining throughout this essay.

Conclusion

We began this paper by sharing two stories from our personal experiences of challenges associated with dialoguing, or attempting to dialogue, about race and racism in the college-level and pre-college classroom. We noted that instructors, particularly at the college level, may feel uncomfortable talking about race. They may find that their syllabus for the semester or lesson plan for the day does not contain resources that address what students truly wish (and perhaps need) to discuss – particularly at the outset of a philosophical dialogue about race. Furthermore, instructors may struggle to connect, in the eyes of the students, abstract philosophical theories with the lived realities of their unique experiences.

We have attempted to show that pre-college pedagogical resources – including Critical Race Pedagogy as it has been developed for the pre-college classroom, and Philosophy for Children, which can learn from and be put to the service of CRP – can potentially help instructors dealing with such challenges. These resources include: (1) the attempt to dismantle the more traditional 'top-down' model of authority in the classroom; (2) the emphasis on maintaining an open format that safeguards an alternative space for students to share their lived experiences/offer epistemic specificity; (3) the prioritisation of building a community of inquiry and fostering open collaborative conversation; and (4) the commitment to promoting Socratic dialogue by insisting on active listening-humility in the classroom, and on understanding and practicing philosophy as provocation.

At the risk of sounding overly optimistic, we submit that these practices help to give credence to the voices of *all* of our youth. They can help us actively work to hear the unique and often complex positionalities from which they speak, and to empower them to challenge what is *and what should not be* a normal and fixed part of the American social landscape.

Notes

1. The syllabus can be accessed here [https://www.academia.edu/20317528/Syllabus_ Philosophies_of_Race_and_Racism_Spring_2016] The syllabus and corresponding course materials included course readings on the history of the concept of race, competing approaches to defining and understanding race, ethnicity and racism, intersectionality, the philosophical 'problems' of mixed-race identity, particularities of anti-Black racisms and anti-Latinxs racisms, and how the 'black-white binary' serves to render invisible the experiences of other racialised minority groups.

2. This is not to say, of course, that white supremacy is not a (the?) root cause of such inter-racial tensions; rather, it is to say that white supremacy was not always the most intuitive philosophical starting point for many students in the class.

3. The '1964 Mississippi Freedom Schools' refers to a group of alternative schools that were created in Mississippi during the 'Freedom Summer' (a key moment during the civil rights movement in the United States) in response to the miseducation of the black youth in the Mississippi Delta. Volunteers from various institutions in the United States came to Mississippi to provide black students with an intellectually stimulating and politically/culturally relevant education that the public schools simply would not provide. For an excellent overview of the Mississippi Freedom Schools, the unique pedagogies they employed, and the challenges they faced, see Perlstein (1990).

4. These statistics/overview of the situation in Eudora were provided during the pre-teaching training that the Freedom Summer Collegiates received just before heading off to teach at their respective sites in the Mississippi Delta.

5. 'Whiteness' here refers to the disproportionate amount of 'white' voices in the Western philosophical canon.

6. It is worth noting that this assumption that 'all teaching and learning are political', as well as the concomitant commitment to the co-construction of knowledge in the classroom, are key dimensions of CRP that CRP shares with the tradition of Critical Pedagogy associated with Paolo Freire.

7. It is here that Katz provides an illuminating account of the separation in (contemporary) philosophy of *reading the text* and *reading ourselves*.

8. Katz's *Levinas and the Crisis of Humanism* (2012) does a beautiful job analysing this problematic, and, in reference to Emmanuel Levinas's work on subjectivity and Jewish education, she provides a variety of ways in which we might be able to effectively move past this 'crisis', and re-imagine the way we educate our youth – focusing instead on *inflaming their minds*, and nourishing a sense of co-responsibility in the classroom, and (even beyond the classroom) responsibility for the other.

9. See the final chapter of Katz (2012) for a pertinent analysis of this issue and potential remedies.

10. Here we have in mind Freire's (1970).

11. For further discussion, see Lipman (1980), particularly Chapter 7, 'Guiding a Philosophical Conversation'.

12. Of course, voting may lead to a reduced amount of attention given to minority interests in the classroom (a 'tyranny of the majority' situation) – particularly in contrast to a course in which a social justice educator selects topics that engage issues of race and racism. We return to these concerns later in the paper. For further information about ways in which Philosophy for Children founder Matthew Lipman was influenced by Dewey's writing on democracy, see Lipman (2003).

13. Examples of activities other than CoI that can be used in pre-college philosophy classes can be found in texts such as Shapiro (2008) and Lone and Burroughs (2016).

14. Students in the class referred to themselves as 'black', rather than 'African-American', so we follow their preferred term in this paper.
15. We will address some of the potential problems with this democratic process below.
16. That is, 'Socratic dialogue' as practiced by Plato's Socrates in the Platonic dialogues.
17. 'Hosting' in the Levinasian sense of the term. For Levinas, to host 'the stranger' is to welcome, in radical humility and hospitality, that which is otherwise than oneself (the Other). This involves striving to preserve/respect/appreciate difference, and seeking to listen, rather than dictate.
18. Katz (2003 and elsewhere) Katz underscores the centrality of the Delphic order to know thyself in the project of philosophy – philosophy's 'original, powerful aim' (531) – and describe the way in which the discipline has suffered in the de-centering of that order, including its loss of interest in education.
19. On this, see Mills (2007).

Disclosure statement

No potential conflict of interest was reported by the authors.

ORCID

Melissa Fitzpatrick ⓘ http://orcid.org/0000-0003-0723-3993

References

Chetty, D. 2014. "The Elephant in the Room: Picturebooks, Philosophy for Children, and Racism." *Childhood & Philosophy* 10 (19): 11–31.
Freire, Paolo. 1970. *Pedagogy of the Oppressed*. New York: Continuum.
Frodeman, R., and A. Briggle. 2016. "When Philosophy Lost its Way." *New York Times*, January 11. https://opinionator.blogs.nytimes.com/2016/01/11/when-philosophy-lost-its-way/
Gregory, M. 2007. "A Framework for Facilitating Classroom Dialogue." *Teaching Philosophy* 30 (1): 59–84.
Katz, C. 2003. "Witnessing Education." *Studies in Practical Philosophy: A Journal of Ethical and Political Philosophy* 3 (2): 107–131.
Katz, C. 2004. "Teaching Our Children Well: Pedagogy, Religion and the Future of Philosophy." *Crosscurrents* 53 (4): 530–545.
Katz, C. 2012. *Levinas and the Crisis of Humanism*. Bloomington: Indiana University Press.
Lipman, M. 1980. *Philosophy in the Classroom*. Philadelphia, PA: Temple University Press.
Lipman, M. 2003. *Thinking in Education*. Cambridge: Cambridge University Press.
Lone, J. M., and M. D. Burroughs. 2016. *Philosophy and the Young Child: Questioning and Dialogue in Schools*. Lanham, MD: Rowman & Littlefield.
Lynn, M. 1999. "Toward a Critical Race Pedagogy." *Urban Education* 33 (5): 606–626.
Matthews, G. B. 1994. *The Philosophy of Childhood*. Cambridge, MA: Harvard University Press.
Mills, Charles W. 1996. "Do Black Men Have a Moral Duty to Marry Black Women?" In *Rethinking Masculinities: Philosophical Explorations in Light of Feminism*, edited by Larry May, Robert Strikwerda and Patrick D. Hopkins, 135–160. London: Rowman & Littlefield.
Mills, Charles W. 2007. "White Ignorance." In *Race and Epistemologies of Ignorance*, edited by Shannon Sullivan and Nancy Tuana, 11–38. Albany: State University of New York Press.

Perlstein, D. 1990. "Teaching Freedom: SNCC and the Creation of the Mississippi Freedom Schools." *History of Education Quarterly* 30 (3): 297–324.

Rainville, N. 2000. "Philosophy for Children in Native America: A Post-Colonial Critique." *Analytic Teaching* 21 (1): 65–77.

Reed-Sandoval, A., and A. C. Sykes. 2017. "Who Talks? Who Listens? Taking Positionality Seriously in Philosophy for Children." In *The Routledge International Handbook for Philosophy for Children*, edited by Maughn Gregory, Joanna Haynes and Karen Murris, 219–226. New York: Routledge.

Shapiro, D. 2008. *Plato Was Wrong! Footnotes on Philosophy for Young People*. Plymouth: Rowman and Littlefield.

Taylor, P. 2013. *Race: A Philosophical Introduction*. Cambridge: Polity Press.

8 On intellectual diversity and differences that may not make a difference

Kristie Dotson

ABSTRACT

Calls for diversity in higher education have been ongoing for, at least, a century. Today, the diversity movement in higher education is in danger of being co-opted in the US by a move to make 'intellectual diversity,' i.e. the diversity of political opinion, on par with the cultural and historical diversity that one finds within differently racialized populations. Intellectual diversity is thought to track different modes of thinking between conservatives and progressives that need policy interventions to promote and protect. Here I offer an account of a mode of thinking to probe what conservative, libertarian, progressive, and critical theory orientations, as modes of thinking, should show in order to present themselves as tokens of 'intellectual diversity.' Ultimately, I gesture to the conclusion that intellectual diversity as a mode of thinking degrades into either infinite particularity or impossible singularity that do little establish a call for policy intervention.

An introduction

The call to diversify US professional philosophy has been intensifying for, at least, four decades. This is primarily because what has constituted 'the' philosophical canon, what questions seem to be unapologetically philosophical, and the orientations professional philosophy expects mastery of and/or acquaintance with are almost primarily generated from work produced by persons racialized as white and cis-privileged males.[1] As a result, the call for diversity in professional philosophy has been a fairly constant mantra. Yet, it took years of publishing, advocacy, and plain agitation to make diversity a part of professional philosophy's conversation about itself in the US.[2] This almost half a century of work in US professional philosophy, and beyond, has made the call for diversity heard in US professional philosophy (even if it hasn't been evenly heeded or accepted).

Diversity in professional philosophy is part of a larger movement for diversity in higher education that has been ongoing for, at least, a century.[3] However, today, the diversity movement in higher education is in danger of being co-opted by a move to make 'intellectual diversity,' e.g. the diversity of political opinion primarily among people racialized as white, the same as the cultural and historical diversity that one finds within differently racialized populations. To be clear, the intellectual diversity movement in the US, which essentially argues that there needs to be an 'affirmative action' plan in US colleges and universities for conservatives, attempts to portend at the kind of diversity that, they claim, is the same as the kind of diversity that has been advocated for in the past century by marginalized populations in the US (Roth 2017c, 2017b, 2017a).

The move to shift conversations on diversity in the US away from excluded racialized minorities and other historically marginalized populations, for example, to, primarily, white conservatives is not altogether new. The intellectual diversity movement, which started with David Horowitz's 'Academic Bill of Rights' (2004a) is part of a cause that champions requiring colleges and universities to 'retain political pluralism and diversity' with target efforts to oversee and ensure such inclusion (Freedom 2003).[4] This move, to identify diversity among people racialized as white and label that a kind of 'diversity' that needs to be preserved is not a particularly new phenomenon. It is not unusual to encounter all white (and mostly cis-gendered male) philosophy departments citing their 'diversity,' by highlighting differences of opinion among the, otherwise, similarly situated faculty. Today, however, we see a return (or a doubling down) on the notion that differences among populations largely racialized as white and cis-gendered male constitutes 'genuine' diversity in the form of intellectual diversity.[5] Of significant concern, then, is the question: to what does the 'diversity' in 'intellectual diversity' refer?

As the call to ensure 'intellectual diversity' continues to gain steam in the US, it would behoove us to get a sense of what generates the 'diversity' in intellectual diversity. Michael Roth, a self-identified progressive, who advocates for 'affirmative action' for conservatives, understands 'intellectual diversity' to refer to different modes of thinking (Roth 2017d). He lists 'conservative, religious and libertarian modes of thinking,' alongside 'progressivism and critical theory' as modes of thinking that college campuses need specific programs to promote and sustain (Roth 2017c). Here I offer an account of a mode of thinking, i.e. Toni Morrison's notion of creative imagination, so as to probe what conservative, religious, libertarian, progressive, and critical theory orientations, as modes of thinking, have to show in order to present themselves as tokens of 'intellectual diversity.' That is to say, one needs an account of (1) what enables the mode of thinking, (2) how that mode functions, and (3) to what end(s) that mode operates. Ultimately, I gesture to the conclusion that intellectual diversity, if taken as a mode of thinking, degrades into infinite particularity or impossible singularity that does little to help establish a call for special policy interventions for conservative political thought.

This paper will proceed in three parts. First, I execute a theoretical archeology of Toni Morrison's various writings on her own creative process in writing *Beloved*, to generate an understanding of creative imagination that points to what a 'mode of thinking' might entail.[6] Specifically, *creative imagination* here refers to the utilisation of imaginative pathways, which are produced by cathected proximity, that are aimed at generative, embedded futurities. This understanding includes, (1) how creative imagination, as a mode of thinking, is enabled, i.e. *cathected proximity*, (2) how creative imagination functions *imaginative pathways*, and (3) what purpose(s) creative imagination serves, i.e. *embedded, generative futurities*. Second, I briefly narrate Denver's character in *Beloved* to offer an example of creative imagination as it is articulated here. *Third*, and finally, I discuss how this notion of creative imagination indicates that 'intellectual diversity' is far more difficult to establish than may first appear.

A what, how, and why of Morrison's creative imagination

Toni Morrison can be said to outline an understanding of creative imagination that can take us far to understanding how deep diversity can be in our creative and intellectual endeavours. On my account, Morrison articulates creative imagination via *literary archaeology* that utilises images and memory in order to aim for the *future of time*. My own rendition of Morrison's notion of creative imagination is as follows: *creative imagination* can be identified according to the utilization of imaginative pathways catalysed by cathected proximity that leans towards embedded futurities. *Imaginative pathways*, here, are what I am calling the intergenerational 'images' Morrison uses for her literary archaeologies. *Cathected proximity* refers to spatial, historical, and genealogical relations that generate imaginative pathways. *Embedded futurities* refers to leanings that extend from a given location with an aim to reach beyond the possibilities of that location, where the 'beyond' is, in part, shaped by the givenness in question, even while the resulting imagined possibilities extend beyond that givenness. In what follows, I articulate and explain all of the key terms presented here. What emerges is an understanding of creative imagination (and a genesis) that can aid in deciphering the 'diversity' in 'intellectual diversity'.

Fragments for Toni Morrison's creative imagination

Morrison begins her articulation of her creative process in writing *Beloved* by emphasising the importance of autobiography, in her essay, 'The Site of Memory'. *Beloved*, Morrison writes, is an attempt to reconstruct the interior lives of enslaved people that begins, in part, as a supplement to slave narratives. Authors of slave narratives record their 'singular and representative' lives for one purpose, 'to change things,' according to Morrison (2008b, 67). However, in pursuing that goal, as

Morrison believes, 'there was no mention of an interior life' (70). Her desire 'to find and expose a truth about the interior lives of people who didn't write it' (72) pushes Morrison to consider her approach, the material that will aid such a project, and what such a project contributes to literary production. According to Morrison, she conducts a literary archeology in order to reconstruct the interior lives of Black people enslaved during US slavery. This kind of archeology is performed 'on the basis of some information and a little bit of guesswork, [sic] you journey to a site to see what remains were left behind and to reconstruct the world that these remains imply' (Morrison 2008b, 71).

The specific archaeology outlined is a 'recollection that moves from image to text' (72) that, Morrison writes, becomes fiction due to 'the nature of the imaginative act: … [her own] reliance on the image – on the remains – in addition to recollection, to yield up a kind of truth' (71). Morrison's reliance on image follows from her impression that pictures have 'feelings that accompany' them and that, in her estimation, is what she is on the hunt for, i.e. feelings, emotions – in general, the stuff of interior lives' (71). What is important to note here is, for Morrison, the ingredients for her creative imagination are images and recollection that can generate 'a kind of truth.'[7] In what follows, I flesh out these fragments with another kind of archeology, a theoretical archeology, so as to offer a conceptual story about an understanding of creative imagination that might support these fragments.

Enabling a mode of thinking: imaginative pathways for reconstruction

Images may have the ability to generate feelings that become avenues for creative reconstruction precisely because of their connection to beings other than ourselves. They do not emerge from (and within) a vacuum. They require sense and sensibilities that are constructed with and by other people, for example, and, as such, provide access to sites rife for reconstruction. Morrison explains:

> People are my access to me; they are my entrance into my own interior life. Which is why the images that float around them- the remains, so to speak, at the archeological site – surface first, and they surface so vividly and so compellingly that I acknowledge them as my route to a reconstruction of a world, to an exploration of an interior life that was not written and to the revelation of a kind of truth. (2008b, 74)

It would seem that there are a great many aspects of our lives that are conditioned upon the existence of other people that might serve in the place of images. Any manifestation that is generated by a kind of visceral, other-facing constitution can serve in the place of image. As long as that manifestation, like images for Morrison, offers a 'route to a reconstruction of a world,' then it can serve as an ingredient for the notion of creative imagination I am building here. So, though image is definitely important for Morrison, what is a key ingredient for her understanding of creative imagination are visceral pathways that can propel reconstruction and exploration. I call these pathways, imaginative pathways.

Imaginative pathways, here, refers to visceral sites of creative and/or intellectual exploration and reconstruction that are opened up by our relations to others. Through imaginative pathways, we exercise our imaginations towards reconstruction and exploration of precisely those parts of our worlds that are other-facing. I will return to this point shortly. What is important to note is that these imaginative pathways are generated, in large part, by others in our lives. But not just anyone or anything else; beings that can prompt the kind of emotional response needed to turn the manifestation in question into a pathway for exploration. That is to say, beings that can take us beyond proximity to image or, in the terms being developed here, from cathected proximity to imaginative pathways.

'How' of creative imagination: cathected proximity and collective memory

Morrison will go onto explain two particularly central images for her writing of *Beloved*. One is of her parents napping in the afternoon and the second is watching her parents walk across the street from their house to attend their household farm (Morrison 2008b, 75, 76). Her close association of these images with emotions like confusion and joy serve as a possible entryway into happenings that exceed her own affective response, but where her affective responses are integral to reaching beyond her own sense of the events in question. The confusion of her parents turning away to nap, for example, to a sphere of engagement (and relationships) she did not share, but was witness to, provide clues for taking fragmentary remains of the observed lives of enslaved peoples in the US and reconstructing them to arrive at 'text and subtext' (2008b, 76). Morrison claims her relationship to her parents' naps and the images of them napping, as an insider and an outsider, generates emotional effects. These affective traces of her encounter with others, even (or maybe especially) encounters with her parents as others, *and* her familiarity with being an 'outsider within,' opened up possibility for archaeological excavation of interior lives that she did not directly experience.[8]

The importance of being an outsider with proximal access to interior lives and relations that one does not share should not go unnoticed. The intimacy of her parents napping, which occasioned emotions like confusion and joy, for Morrison, is an intimacy she shared, but, at once, did not share. The child-Morrison is surely an outsider to the event of her parents napping, while she is an insider to the home that allows her to regularly bear witness to those naps. These 'images,' or one might say imaginative pathways, offer Morrison places to start reconstructing the interior lives of people she is, at once, outside of and, because of her being a descendent of slaves, has a cathected proximity to. *Cathected proximity*, here, is understood as a relation (or set of relations), spatial or otherwise, to others that are invested with emotion. These proximities generate imaginative pathways, which become sites for reconstruction and exploration.

Cathected proximity, on my account, is part of what makes images sites for reconstruction. The investment in the beings who provoke visceral response from us catalyse the kind of pathways that Morrison says she relies upon in her creative writing. In other words, images surrounding people that have affective content, i.e. parts of her parents' lives that she bore witness to, but did not share, and the proximity to the content of the images matter for Morrison's account of creative imagination. It is also a methodology that Morrison calls, literary archeology. *Literary archaeology*, here, considers reconstruction based on affect-laden images and the proximity of being both and insider and an outsider all at once. The outsider within (or insider without) status will become important, as this requires leaps of imagination that may not be needed if one is considered an unapologetic 'insider'. Morrison will go onto highlight tools that are integral to excavating images and the cathected proximity they imply, that become mechanisms for how creative imagination can function, i.e. collective memory.

Collective memory

When outlining what was required to 'remove the veil' around the interior life of Black people who were enslaved in US slavery, Morrison writes, 'moving aside that veil requires … certain things. First of all, I must trust my own recollections. I must also depend on the recollections of others. Thus memory weighs heavily in what I write, in how I begin and in what I find to be significant', (2008b, 71). Morrison goes on to say, 'no matter how "fictional" the account … or how much it was a product of invention, the act of imagination is bound up with memory', (2008b, 76, 77). Memory, one's own and collective recollection, becomes an orienting focus, for Morrison. Not only in terms of what a narrative includes, how it begins, etc., but also in terms of what is made significant. Salience, it would seem, would be driven in large part by collective memory. However, the importance of one's own recollections and the recollections of others concerns not only fodder for a literary archaeology. Morrison also locates collective memory as an integral part of existence. One's own recollections and the recollections of others form the orientations of our lives, but also the beings that we are.

For Morrison, excavating and reconstructing 'memories within' is the 'subsoil' of her work. She explains, perspective has a point of genesis in 'the quality of human habitation within its full span' (Morrison 2008a, 182). The span of human habitation is important, precisely because one's own memories are constructed among and with respect to the recollection of others, the memory of land and water. And one's collective memory, which includes emotional memory, serves as a mode of cathecting proximity that, in turn, opens imaginative pathways (Morrison 2008b, 77). Our memories are longer than our lifespans and that potential reality is a place where imagination is inspired and exercised. There is one more ingredient, however, for creative imagination besides cathected proximity and imaginative pathways, i.e. embedded futurity.

'Why' of creative imagination: embedded futurities

One of the questions left unanswered by identifying imaginative pathways and cathected proximity as sites for the exercise and development of imagination is: what marks the 'creative' in the exercises of imagination outlined thus far? I suppose one answer here could refer to, what Morrison calls, the 'future of time' as opposed to a signature focus on an infinite past. When considering the purpose of contemporary literature, Morrison asks the question, pace Toni Cade Bambara, 'are you *sure* you want to be well?' (2008a, 182). And though this question may seem irrelevant to considerations of literary archaeology and collective memory, I think Morrison might locate it as central to creative imagination. The question of whether one wants to be well is not only about an orientation capable of focusing on a past that is always present, it is also the ability to strive for a potential future that is not present, i.e. a kind of future of time. This invocation of the future of time refers not simply to present possible futures, but rather, and more importantly, to possible futures that the act of imagining futures can detect 'like a tuning fork' (Morrison 2008a, 183). This orientation towards a not-present future can manifest as a kind of sensibility, a kind of beginning again, or a kind of vision (Morrison 2008a, 185).

Morrison's notion of imagination, on my account, seems to become 'creative' when it opens space for that which extends beyond this present world. It opens up an infinite future, as well as an infinite past. Here the manifestation of creative imagination, i.e. the manifest book, poem, concept, painting, etc. is less important than the cultivation of a future of time; a time beyond the 'now,' that could not have been generated in any other place besides this 'now.' Morrison explains, 'I believe I am detecting an informed vision based on harrowing experience that nevertheless gestures towards a redemptive future. And I notice the milieu from which this vision rises. It is race inflected, gendered, colonized, displaced and hunted,' (2008a, 185). Creativity, then, can emerge between

> … divergent imaginaries, between the sadness of no more time, of the poignancy of inverted time – time as only a past – of time itself living on 'borrowed time,' between that imaginary and the other one that has growing expectations of time with a relentless future. (2008a, 185)

This reaching towards futurity is a mode of creativity that is connected to one's intergenerational memory and the cathected proximity that animates that memory even as it leans towards a 'relentless future.' To that end, it is an embedded futurity. *Embedded futurity*, here, refers to leanings that extend from a given location with an aim to reach beyond the possibilities of that location, where the 'beyond' is, in part, shaped by the givenness in question, even while the resulting imagined possibilities extend beyond that givenness.

Creative imagination, then, aims at detecting signs of renewal and displaying those signs as part of a process animated by collective, intergenerational memory, including the relations with each other and the land that these memories imply, that produce imaginative pathways that open sites for reconstruction and exploration of our worlds. There is a generative form of futurism that can be found in Morrison's work that indicate that creativity operates precisely where its results are not utterly exhausted by the past.[9] In the next section, I demonstrate this account of creative imagination in an exploration of Denver, a character from Morrison's *Beloved,* as a paradigmatic example of someone who is required, for her everyday living, to exercise the creative imagination Morrison can be said to extol. I conclude with highlighting that what emerges from Morrison's account of creative imagination is an understanding of a mode of thinking that generates a schedule of intellectual diversity that can exist at, at least, two levels of analysis. They are: (1) diversity in what enables the mode of thinking, which is, in large part, articulated by the mode of thinking itself, e.g. different cathected proximities and imaginative pathways as per Morrison's creative imagination, or (2) diversity in the kind of mode of thinking relied upon, e.g. something other than creative imagination. I conclude by gesturing to the need to construct conservative or liberal leanings within the same tradition of thought to be intellectually diverse according to what enables them as part of a mode of thinking *or* how they are each tokens of distinct modes of thinking.

Denver and creative imagination

In what follows, I offer a brief character analysis of Denver, from Morrison's *Beloved*, in order to further demonstrate the Morrison-inspired notion of creative imagination developed in the previous section. This articulation helps to understand how Morrison's notion of creative imagination points to two types of intellectual diversity, diversity within a mode of thinking and potential diversity across varying modes of thinking.

Beloved begins in 1873 in Cincinnati, Ohio, where Sethe, a black woman who was formerly enslaved, has been living with her seventeen-year-old daughter Denver (Morrison 2004). Sethe, as the Margaret Garner figure of *Beloved*,[10] was pregnant with Denver when she made her attempt to escape slavery. We are told that Sethe's mother-in-law, Baby Suggs, lived with them until her death eight years prior. And just before Baby Suggs's death, Sethe's two sons, Howard and Buglar, ran away. Sethe believes they fled because of the malevolent presence of an abusive 'baby ghost' that continually 'haunted' their house at 124 Bluestone Road. Though the older children are said to see the ghost as a menace, Denver liked the haunting, which we are many times led to believe was the spirit of her long dead older sister or the daughter Sethe killed rather than see her returned to slavery.

Introducing Denver

Denver, the unborn child at the time of Sethe's escape from slavery, is continually influenced by a set of acts and a way of life that she, herself, did not witness or experience. She has the dubious privilege to experience the hauntings of her slain older sister as someone who is both a part and not a part of the events that center the novel, i.e. slavery and infanticide. Whereas her older brothers witness the infanticide, Denver did not and cannot have this relationship to the hauntings that are shaping her present in the novel. Also, as the novel unfolds, one realizes that Denver never experiences a day of slavery. Sethe's attempt to gain freedom is successful, unlike Margaret Garner's actual situation.[11] So though she is relationally connected to the slaying of her sister and the slavery Sethe was running from, her position as an 'outsider within' makes it difficult for her to acquire (and, hence, speak with) experiential authority about those relations and the images they invoke. Denver, then, is an outsider of slavery and Sethe's act of infanticide all the while she is an insider to the impact of slavery and the impact of her mother's killing of her sister. Denver *has to* rely upon imagination just to make sense of what happens around her.

Denver, a character genuinely positioned as an 'outsider within,' in *Beloved*, must rely upon her imagination to make sense of what is happening around her. Denver's relational proximity to the happenings that shape the novel is a catalyst for her own imagination almost precisely *because of* the demands that proximity make on her. She lives at 124 Bluestone Road, the major site of the novel's present conflicts and hauntings. She lives with her mother, who is haunted by slavery and her own act of infanticide. She, herself, also lives with the hauntings of slavery and infanticide that she did not experience. And figuring out 'what happened' to produce that 'present' is not a flight of fancy, it is a matter of survival. But it is only a matter of survival because of her proximity to the past that is shaping the present and the present that she lives within. I have called these kinds of proximate relations, cathected proximities.

Recall, cathected proximity is a key ingredient for Morrison's creative imagination. Cathected proximity, and the imaginative pathways that they produce, do not emerge in a vacuum. They come from living with people and places, where the relations to people and land make demands on us. Denver's Proximity demanded the turn to 'make sense' of what was happening around her (or as Morrison might say, where to begin and what becomes salient), but her relationship with her mother, her family, and the house they lived in invested the demands of proximity with emotion. It *mattered* to her to be able to answer the question, 'what is happening at 124 Bluestone Road?' To this end, Morrison's creative imagination, particularly imaginative pathways, can be seen as the result of every day engagements with people and places central to our lives. This is particularly important where proximity generates and reveals the ability of others to deeply affect us. One starting point for creative imagination, then, can be found in everyday attempts at forging and maintaining intergenerational relations that serve to catalyse, and are enabled by, cathected proximities. And those proximities give rise to imaginative pathways for reconstruction.

The transformation wrought in Denver through *Beloved* attests to movements from admittedly fanciful, imaginative excursions, i.e. in the wooded 'playroom'

(Morrison 2004, 28), to Denver becoming someone whose own opinion on current happenings between Sethe and Beloved takes on considerable narrative force, i.e. her ability to deliver the definitive characterisation of the relationship between Sethe and Beloved (Morrison 2004, 295). This transformation is one aspect of Denver's coming of age story. By the end of the novel, Denver has developed the story she tells of what is happening at 124 Bluestone Road. And it is a story that is no less true for the fact it is a story. In the signature moment where we are allowed, as readers, a great deal of access into the internal dynamics between Sethe and Beloved, the narrator explains of Denver:

> Denver thought she understood the connection between her mother and Beloved: Sethe was trying to make up for the handsaw; Beloved was making her pay for it. But there would never be an end to that, and seeing her mother diminished shamed and infuriated her. Yet she knew Sethe's greatest fear was the same one Denver has in the beginning – that Beloved might leave. That before Sethe could make her understand what it meant – what it took to drag the teeth of the saw under the little chin; to feel the baby blood pump like oil in her hands; to hold her face so her head would stay on; to squeeze her so she could absorb, still, the death spasms that shot through that adored body, plump and sweet with life – Beloved might leave. Leave before Sethe could make her realize that worse than that – far worse – was what Baby Suggs died of, what Ella knew, what Stamp saw and what made Paul D tremble. That anybody white could take your whole self for anything that came to mind. Not just work, kill, or maim you, but dirty you. Dirty you so bad you couldn't like yourself anymore. Dirty you so bad you forgot who you were and couldn't think it up. And though she and others lived through and got over it, she would never let it happen to her own. The best things she was, was her children. Whites might dirty *her* all right, but not her best thing, her beautiful magical best thing – the part of her that was clean … And no one, nobody on this earth, would list her daughter's characteristics on the animal side of the paper. No. Oh no. Maybe Baby Suggs could worry about it, live with the likelihood of it; Sethe had refused – and refused still. (Morrison 2004, 295)

Denver's rendition of the dynamics between Sethe and Beloved is informed by memories; but not by Denver's memories alone. Denver's account was created via imagination with her own memories, her mother's memories, potentially the memories of a long dead sister, and a larger communal memory in order to piece together a story to be told about the hauntings at 124 Bluestone Road. The range of potential imaginative pathways, generated by cathected proximity, along with her relative lack of experience with the events shaping the novel, demonstrate that Denver's ability to speak to the conditions in her own home were largely the result of imagination.

Denver had to imagine multiple worlds just to understand what was happening around her. And these worlds are not someone else's worlds. They are her own. This, it seems to me, is the 'kind of truth' Morrison says follows from literary archaeology. The kind of truth that requires imagination for its construction, even as it is not solely composed of imagination. The kind of truth where personal experience does little to vindicate one's conclusions, but is not wholly irrelevant to those conclusions. Denver had personal experiences with the *impact* of affairs she never directly experienced, from slavery to infanticide. However, those experiences only facilitate her with fragments of a past that is still present. She must, then, engage in a reconstruction to make sense of her present and the people and places in it. Because she must rely on a great deal of 'guess work' and the happenings that shape her life are not directly her own, Denver must, in very large part, rely on her imagination. The limits and possibilities of Denver's imagination are both her challenge and redemption in *Beloved*.

In this way, Denver is an ideal character for outlining the labour of Morrison's creative imagination. Denver's insights, as an 'outsider within,' and the communities she is part of, offer her the ability to imagine not only the worlds she inhabits, but also different modes of existence within those worlds. 'Coming into her own,' with her own opinions, includes her becoming imminently her own within a community. And this 'ownness' isn't a break with history per se. It is a potential emergence of 'divergent imaginaries' (Morrison 2008a, 185), as Sethe might narrate the events happening at 124 Bluestone Road very differently. But that difference does not undermine the potential truth of Denver's narration, it simply demonstrates the near infinite diversity possible within a mode of thinking. I will return to this in the next section.

In Denver, we again see a sign of renewal. She, and her possibilities, can also be seen as in line with Morrison's understanding of the future of time. Morrison writes:

> Perhaps it is the reality of a future as durable and far-reaching as the past, a future that will be shaped by those who have been pressed to the margins, by those who have been dismissed as irrelevant surplus, but those who have been cloaked with the demon's cape; perhaps it is the contemplation of that future that has occasioned the tremble of the latter-day prophets afraid that the current disequilibrium is a stirring and not an erasure. That history is not dead, but that it is about to take its first unfettered breath. (2008a, 186)

Denver is not an 'unfettered breath' of history, but, for Morrison, she may be a hope for such a possibility. A hope for a future that is not present. Morrison is clear that this possibility is a distant one. But she might insist that it is not unimaginable, even if one has to exercise *major feats of creativity* to imagine it. In this way, futurities like the one Denver might represent and exercise towards rendering the present legible and the future possible, require *creative* imagination. Because though they are born of our worlds, they are not of a piece with them.

Intellectual diversity as a mode of thinking?

At this stage, one might ask, how does the above understanding of creative imagination weigh on the question of 'intellectual diversity' as such? The answer, of course, depends on what we mean by 'intellectual diversity.' Is intellectual diversity generated *within* a mode of thinking, e.g. different outputs of creative imagination, or across modes of thinking, i.e. creative imagination vs. analytic imagination (if such a distinction exists at all)? Michael Roth's use of the term 'intellectual diversity' refers to 'modes of thinking organized under … banner[s]' (2017c, 3). He explains:

Our present political circumstances should not prevent us from engaging with a variety of conservative, religious and libertarian modes of thinking, just as they shouldn't prevent us from engaging with modes of thinking organized under the banner of progressivism or critical theory. (Roth 2017c, 3)

It is unclear what a 'mode of thinking' organised under 'banners' or general labels means. I have offered a theory of Morrison's creative imagination because, as it is developed here, it is precisely a mode of thinking that I have organised under the banner of 'creative imagination.' But let us attend to what this mode of thinking entails. It entails a story about how that mode is enabled, e.g. cathected proximity, a story about how the mode operates, e.g. imaginative pathways, and a story about what purpose(s) the mode has, e.g. embedded futurities. How, then, do conservative and liberal political orientations constitute, on their own, modes of thinking that are representative of some form of intellectual diversity?

One has to be very careful here. There are, at least, two paths one can take to establish intellectual diversity. First, one can take intellectual diversity as differences that emerge *within* modes of thinking. But then we may all be so different that we are each tokens of intellectual diversity. That is to say, the claim to diversity within a mode of thinking might be too easy to make. Identifying intellectual diversity within a mode of thinking depends, of course, on the privileged mode of thinking that orients differentiating features. But there is a very real threat, as I will explain below, that those differentiating features render any practitioner so idiosyncratic as to be different one from another in significant ways. And a second way to highlight intellectual diversity is to say it exists across varying modes of thinking. This could easily result in no one, anywhere, being intellectually diverse because the claim to such diversity is too difficult to make. Either of these outcomes would undermine the claim that intellectual diversity requires affirmative action for conservatives to safeguard their existence in the academy.[12]

Option 1: idiosyncratic particularity or how intellectual diversity is for everyone

Again, one way to say progressives and conservatives represent different modes of thinking is to establish them as diverse manifestations of a given mode of thinking. Intellectual diversity, taken as diversity within a mode of thinking, may make every person exercising the mode of thinking so idiosyncratic as to be too particular for targeted policy. That is to say, different expressions within a mode of thinking may reduce to infinite particularity. To detect this possibility, consider Denver's ability to occupy her reconstruction of the happenings at 124 Bluestone Road when she runs into Paul D towards the very end of *Beloved*:

Paul D: Well, if you want my opinion …

Denver: I don't. I have my own. (Morrison 2004, 314)

We saw in Denver someone who relied on imaginative pathways, cathected proximity, and collective recollection to exercise imagination in order to construct a story about what was happening in her own home. But, it is entirely possible, indeed extremely likely, that her rendition of the events shaping the novel will be very different from Paul D's rendition. This potential outcome follows from the different proximities they both have to Sethe, US slavery, 124 Bluestone Road, and the potential differences in what they would utilise as imaginative pathways. This difference would exist even though they arguably share having to live with the impacts of slavery, for example, even if those impacts are not exactly the same.

There is something at once communal and idiosyncratic about the fodder of either Denver or Paul D's potential creative imaginations about what is happening at 124 Bluestone Road. This would mean that within Morrison's creative imagination, as a mode of thinking, there exists a near infinite range of possibilities for the exercise of that imagination and it is very likely no two people's creative imagination produce exactly the same results, even if they are arguably shaped by the same sweeping historical realities. Would this kind of near infinite particularity equate to intellectual diversity? In that case, it would be very difficult to create and execute effective policy, like affirmative action for conservatives, with respect to the kind of particularity that modes of thinking can generate within their own operative folds.[13]

Option 2: impossible singularity or how intellectual diversity is for no one

Another way to think of intellectual diversity is to say that diversity exists across modes of thinking. The trick of this approach would mean that one needs to articulate a mode of thinking, i.e. its whats, hows, and whys, *and* explain how a given manifestation is a product of that mode. It is the latter move that is particularly difficult. One can articulate creative imagination, like the Morrison-inspired account offered here, and still not be able to identify its use in any given practitioner or position. And identifying its use is only one third of what one has to do. After (1) articulating a potentially operative mode(s) of thinking, (2) identifying its manifestation as operative, one must also (3) differentiate it from some other, presumably, significantly different mode of thinking. It is almost impossible to demonstrate what would be required to show that liberalism or conservativism within the same tradition meet this demand. What often remains underdeveloped in calls for intellectual diversity is the claim that a conservative is operating differently, in terms of their mode of thinking, than a progressive, for example. It would seem that this is a very difficult, if not impossible, endeavour for it requires the ability to generate stories of intellectual differentiation that may well be impossible.

Conclusion: why this matters?

I am writing this essay, this way, for two reasons. First, I do not believe we will see the end of calls to monitor colleges and universities for their inclusion of 'conservative' positions in the US. Stanley Fish said it best, 'The left may have won the curricular battle, but it lost the public-relations war' (2004, 1). They lost the war over public opinion of what is taught in classrooms in colleges and universities and, more importantly, why. They also lost the war for inclusion on campus speaker circuits, where the radical right are being offered platforms that the radical left are still left imagining as distant possibilities. This paper is something of a cautionary note on contemporary politics around diversity in higher education in the US. The concern is that the more, mostly white, progressives jump on the 'affirmative action' for conservatives bandwagon, the more people of colour in the US should be concerned. This will not end well for us. The hard fought battle for diversity may well revert to a call for so-called 'intellectual diversity,' where tokens of this kind of diversity are almost solely people who are racialised as white and cis-gendered male, who are still dominantly represented in the US academy.

Second, I hoped to draw attention to the kinds of sophisticated theorising and philosophising it takes to establish something as a mode of thinking and the rather significant tradition of such theorising that exists in the work of Black peoples, using the example of Toni Morrison on creative imagination. There are centuries upon centuries of theorising about modes of thinking in people of colour's work in the US. These are the feats to which we have been pressed to say that we have different ways of understanding the world that result from our differential relationships to it. And these are the feats to which the intellectual diversity advocates must be pressed as well. What is their story, beyond the repetition of the phrase, 'intellectual diversity?' Without a plausible and, indeed, *warranted* story establishing either conservativism or progressivism within the same range of traditions as modes of thinking, then there is no reason to entertain rubbish like affirmative action for conservatives.

Notes

1. I owe the term 'racialized as white' to Nathaniel Coleman's use of the term in his earlier statements of the lack of Black-centered curriculum in higher education in a UK context. (Also, for a brief, but significant, recounting of the dominance of populations racialized as white in professional philosophy, see Coleman 2015).
2. (See, for example, Jones 1977–1978; Harris 1989, 1997; Moulton 1996; Nye 1998; Mills 2005; Walker 2005; Yancy 2007; Haslanger 2008; Salamon 2009; Marcano 2010; Dotson 2012; Alcoff 2013; Erlenbusch forthcoming).
3. Of course, it is important to note that the call for 'diversity in higher education' exists in various national contexts and in many areas of study, interdisciplinary studies, and transdisciplinary contexts besides.
4. The so-called 'Academic Bill of Rights,' started as a call for safeguarding conservative positions in the academy and, early on, found some measure of legislative support.

For example, the House of Representatives in Missouri (Jaschik 2007) and Pennsylvania (Jaschik 2005) attempted to move towards monitoring colleges and university to ensure the protection of conservative views as an outgrowth of protecting 'intellectual diversity.' The intellectual diversity movement in the US has been building for almost 15 years and has finally culminated in so-called 'progressives,' like Michael Roth, adopting the clarion call of 'affirmative action for conservatives' (Roth 2017c). There are dissenters, however (See, for example, Fish 2004; Rees 2017).

5. This charge cuts, at least two ways. First, there is the position, reminiscent of Horowitz, that claims that intellectual diversity refers to diversity existing between conservative and liberal people, for example (Horowitz 2004a, 2004b). The second use of intellectual diversity is deployed by Glenn Geher to refer to the 'intellectual diversity' between 'men' and 'women' (Geher 2017). The difference between these two positions on intellectual diversity is quite wide, though Geher seems to collapse them together. To explain this collapsing will take this paper too far afield. Rather, this paper focuses on the first position. Intellectual diversity, here, refers to significant differences among political orientations, which is a far more pervasive positon today (See Boyers 2017, for an attempt to offer a, presumably, 'balanced' understanding of the call for intellectual diversity on US campuses today.).

6. Theoretical archeology, here, 'refers to a process that takes fragments of concepts and/or theoretical frameworks and reconstructs the philosophical investigations [or conceptualizations] that these remains imply,' (Dotson 2017, 418). For a fuller explanation see, 'Theorizing Jane Crow, Theorizing Unknowability' (Dotson 2017).

7. I owe the use of 'ingredient' here to Xhercis Mendez's work. She writes, 'the word ingredient conjures up the idea of cooking, an activity that is often linked to female bodies and often includes creatively bringing very different things together in order to create something new (a meal) that both contributes to life and is life sustaining,' (Mendez 2015, 49n9). I take the term 'ingredient' to be a closer approximation of how Morrison outlines a theory of creative imagination than other words generally used in the academy.

8. For a fuller exploration of the 'outsider within' as a researcher position, see Patricia Hill Collins' articulation in 'Learning from the Outsider Within,' (1986).

9. I owe these insights about the use and value of future-directed engagements to many conversations with Yomaira Figueroa, a consummate decolonial futurity scholar and friend (See also, Figueroa 2015).

10. Margaret Garner was a runaway, US, black, enslaved woman who, upon imminent recapture, in January 1856, tried to kill her children and herself rather than return to slavery. At least, this is how her story is usually told. The details of Margaret Garner's actions are hazy. What is clear from historical record is that Margaret Garner, succeeded in killing her 2-year old daughter, Mary Garner, in January 1856 by slitting her throat with a carving knife.

11. Margaret Garner was separated from her family and sold further south.

12. It is important to note that affirmative action programs were not created to ensure intellectual diversity (Harris and Narayan 2007). And even relatively conservative people in US professional philosophy understand that reality (Leiter 2017). So, this conclusion does not impact affirmative action programs as they were traditionally conceived in the US.

13. This, of course, can be overcome by warrantedly establishing what types of difference make a difference for intellectual diversity within a mode of thinking. It is unclear whether conservative, libertarian, progressive and critical theory orientations can offer such signposts. In any event, these kinds of arguments need to be made and cannot be simply assumed.

Acknowledgment

Many thanks to the editors of this special issue for their invaluable feedback on several drafts of this paper. Thank you also to the audiences at the 2014 Summer Institute of American Philosophy and NY-SWIP for their feedback and engagement with some of the ideas in this essay.

Disclosure statement

No potential conflict of interest was reported by the author.

ORCID

Kristie Dotson ⓘ http://orcid.org/0000-0002-8055-8228

References

Alcoff, Linda. 2013. "Philosophy's Civil Wars." *Proceedings and Addresses of the APA* 87: 1–28.
Boyers, Robert. 2017. "The Academy's Assauly on Intellectual Diversity." *The Chronicle of Higher Education* 8. https://www.chronicle.com/article/The-Academy-s-Assault-on/239496.
Coleman, Nathaniel. 2015. "How Philosophy Was 'Whitewashed.'" Gender, Race and Philosophy: The Blog. http://sgrp.typepad.com/sgrp/2015/08/how-philosophy-was-whitewashed-an-interview-with-dr-nathaniel-adam-tobias-coleman-by-aaron-salzer-of-scienceorfat-t.html.
Collins, Patricia Hill. 1986. "Learning from the Outsider Within: The Sociological Significance of Black Feminist Thought." *Social Problems* 33 (6): S14–S32.
Dotson, Kristie. 2012. "How is this Paper Philosophy?" *Comparative Philosophy* 3 (1): 3–29.
Dotson, Kristie. 2017. "Theorizing Jane Crow, Theorizing Unknowability." *Social Epistemology* 31 (5): 417–430.
Erlenbusch, Verena. Forthcoming. "Being a Foreigner in Philosophy: A Taxonomy." *Hypatia: A Journal of Feminist Philosophy*: 1–18. doi:10.1111/hypa.12377.
Figueroa, Yomaira C. 2015. "Reparations as Transformation: Radical Literary (re)Imaginings of Futurities through Decolonial Love." *Decolonization: Indigeneity, Education & Society* 4 (1): 41–58.
Fish, Stanley. 2004. "'Intellectual Diversity': The Trojan Horse of a Dark Design." *The Chronicle of Higher Education* 50 (23). http://chronicle.com/free/v50/i23/23b01301.htm.
Freedom, AAUP Committee on Academic. 2003. *Academic Bill of Rights*. American Assoication of University Professors. https://www.aaup.org/report/academic-bill-rights.
Geher, Glenn. 2017. "Diversity Includes Intellctual Diversity." *Psychology Today*. https://www.psychologytoday.com/blog/darwins-subterranean-world/201708/diversity-includes-intellectual-diversity.
Harris, Leonard. 1989. "The Lacuna between Philosophy and History." *Journal of Social Philosophy* 20 (3): 110–114.
Harris, Leonard. 1997. "The Horror of Tradition or How to Burn Babylon and Build Benin While Reading Preface to a Twenty-volume Suicide Note." In *African-American Perspectives and Philosophical Traditions*, edited by John P. Pittman, 94–118. New York: Routledge.
Harris, Luke Charles, and Uma Narayan. 2007. "Affirmative Actions as Equalizing Opportunity: Challeneging the Myth of 'Preferential Treatment.'" In *African American Policy Forum Archive*, edited by Kimberle Crenshaw. https://aapfarchive.wordpress.com/2007/02/25/equalizingopportunity/.

Haslanger, Sally. 2008. "Changing the Ideology and Culture of Philosophy: Not by Reason (Alone)." *Hypatia* 23 (2): 210–223. doi:10.1111/j.1527-2001.2008.tb01195.x.

Horowitz, David. 2004a. *Academic Bill of Rights.* http://la.utexas.edu/users/hcleaver/330T/350kPEEHorowitzAcadBillTable.pdf.

Horowitz, David. 2004b. "In Defense of Intellectual Diversity." *The Chronicle of Higher Education* 50 (23). http://chronicle.com/free/v50/i23/23b01201.htm.

Jaschik, Scott. 2005. "A Win for 'Academic Bill of rights.'" *Inside Higher Education.* https://www.insidehighered.com/news/2005/07/07/tabor.

Jaschik, Scott. 2007. "Intellectual Diversity or Intellectual Insult." *Inside Higher Education* 3. https://www.insidehighered.com/news/2007/04/16/missouri.

Jones, William R. 1977–1978. "The Legitimacy and Necessity of Black Philosophy: Some Preliminary Considerations." *The Philosophical Forum* 9 (2–3): 149–160.

Leiter, Brian. 2017. "Academic Ethics: Is 'Diversity' the Best Reason for Affirmative Action." *The Chronicle of Higher Education.* https://www.chronicle.com/article/Academic-Ethics-Is/241249.

Marcano, Donna-Dale L. 2010. "The Difference that Difference Makes: Black Feminism and Philosophy." In *Convergences: Black Feminism and Continental Philosophy*, edited by Maria del Guadalupe Davidson, Kathryn T. Gines, and Donna-Dale L. Marcano, 53–65. Albany, NY: SUNY Press.

Mendez, Xhercis. 2015. "Notes Toward a Decolonial Feminist Methodology: Revisiting the Race/Gender Matrix." *Trans-scripts* 5: 41–59.

Mills, Charles W. 2005. "'Ideal Theory' as Ideology." *Hypatia* 20 (3): 165–183. doi:10.1111/j.1527-2001.2005.tb00493.x.

Morrison, Toni. 2004. *Beloved.* New York: Vintage Books.

Morrison, Toni. 2008a. "The Future of Time: Literature and Diminished Expectations." In *What Moves at the Margins: Selected Nonfiction*, edited by Carolyn C. Denard, 170–186. Jackson: University Press of Mississippi.

Morrison, Toni. 2008b. "The Site of Memory." In *What Moves at the Margins: Selected Nonfiction*, edited by Carolyn C. Denard, 65–80. Jackson: University Press of Mississippi.

Moulton, Janice. 1996. "A Paradigm of Philosophy: The Adversary Method." In *Women, Knowledge, and Reality: Explorations in Feminist Philosophy*, edited by Ann Garry and Marilyn Pearsall, 11–25. New York: Routledge.

Nye, Andrea. 1998. "'It's Not Philosophy.'" *Hypatia* 13 (2): 107–115. doi:10.1111/j.1527-2001.1998.tb01228.x.

Rees, Jonathan. 2017. "Losing Perspective: The Importacne of Demographic Diversity to Intellectual Diversity, and How Academic Freedom Requires it." *Amaerican Association of University Professors – Colorado* 6. https://aaupcolorado.org/2017/05/03/losing-perspectives-the-importance-of-demographic-diversity-to-intellectual-diversity-and-how-academic-freedom-requires-it/.

Roth, Michael. 2017a. "Against Demonization: Intellectual Diversity and Liberal Education." *HuffPost.* https://www.huffingtonpost.com/entry/against-demonization-intellectual-diversity-and-liberal_us_59e4b792e4b09e31db975ae0.

Roth, Michael. 2017b. "Campus Intellectual Diversity in the Age of Polarization." *Inside Higher Education.* https://www.insidehighered.com/views/2017/07/17/campus-intellectual-diversity-age-polarization-essay.

Roth, Michael. 2017c. "On Intellectual Diversity." In *Roth on Wesleyan.* Wesleyan.edu. http://roth.blogs.wesleyan.edu/2017/05/19/on-intellectual-diversity/.

Roth, Michael. 2017d. "The Opening of the Liberal Mind." *Wall Street Journal.* https://www.wsj.com/articles/the-opening-of-the-liberal-mind-1494515186.

Salamon, Gayle. 2009. "Justification and Queer Method, or Leaving Philosophy." *Hypatia* 24 (1): 225–230. doi:10.1111/j.1527-2001.2009.00015.x.

Walker, Margaret Urban. 2005. "Diotima's Ghost: The Uncertain Place of Feminist Philosophy in Professional Philosophy." *Hypatia* 20 (3): 153–164. doi:10.1111/j.1527-2001.2005.tb00492.x.
Yancy, George. 2007. *Philosophy in Multiple Voices*. Lanham: Rowman & Littlefield.

9 Whiteliness and institutional racism

Hiding behind (un)conscious bias

Shirley Anne Tate ⓘD and Damien Page

ABSTRACT

'Unconscious bias happens by our brains making incredibly quick judgements and assessments without us realising. Biases are influenced by background, cultural environment and experiences and we may not be aware of these views and opinions, or of their full impact and implications. This article opposes this point of view by arguing that bias is not unconscious but is (un)conscious and linked to Charles Mills' 'Racial Contract' and its 'epistemologies of ignorance'. These epistemologies emerge from what the Equality Challenge Unit (ECU) calls 'our background, cultural environment and personal experience'. Asserting that racism stems from 'unconscious bias' diminishes white supremacy and maintains white innocence as a 'will to forget' institutional racism. In equality and diversity training 'unconscious bias' has become a performative act to move beyond racism through training to participate in a constructed 'post-racial' reality. The article argues that through decolonizing 'unconscious bias', 'white fragility' and 'self-forgiveness' we can begin to see hidden institutional whiteliness at the base of (un)conscious bias.

Introduction

'Unconscious bias' has ceased to be just a phrase, a gesture towards so-called 'unwitting racism' and a call to anti-racist forgiveness of individual and institutional racism. 'Unconscious bias' has become ever more prevalent within institutions, transmogrified into corporate training as an essential accoutrement to an organization's equality and diversity mission and institutional anti-racist transformation at the levels of culture, process and systems. With roots in social psychology (see for example Dovidio et al. 1997), unconscious bias has become the magic bullet for organizations, including universities, in the face of the continued occurrence of racism. Despite protestations of egalitarianism and meritocracy, UK universities remain largely white institutions with the rarity of senior academics of colour rivalling the corporate sector. Such is the cognitive dissonance between racism and egalitarianism, universities – like their corporate counterparts – have sought a means of addressing whiteliness that avoids an acknowledgement of structural and systemic racism. Thus, unconscious bias has emerged within the equality, diversity and inclusion environment in UK Higher Education Institutions (HEIs) as an explanation for statistical racial disparities. Unconscious bias is the acceptable face of racism, the phrase that a majority white sector feels comfortable with using and discussing to describe itself. Unconscious bias is neatly addressed by a 10-minute online training course with a multiple-choice assessment offered to all new start-ers in universities across the UK which embrace equality, diversity and inclusion. Unconscious bias training demonstrates universities' good faith and willingness to address racism and offers a re-take should participants fail the first time. No-one is left behind or outside the unconscious bias community because it is regarded as the principal vehicle for institutional culture change. Participants pass the training course if they learn the language, acceptable behaviours and moral psychology of unconscious bias, if they learn to be able to recognise when it is appropriate to assert that an event is the result of unconscious bias. Such events can range from issues of strategic direction, recruitment and selection, promotion processes, curriculum, admissions as well as student experience and outcomes, for example. Unconscious bias pervades all aspects of institutional life.

Jennifer Saul's (2013, 40) work on implicit bias and stereotype threat and their impact on women in Philosophy states that 'implicit biases … are unconscious biases that affect the way we perceive, evaluate or interact with people from the groups that our biases target'. Further:

> psychological research over the last decades has shown that most people – even those who explicitly and sincerely avow egalitarian views-hold …. implicit biases against such groups as blacks, women, gay people and so on. This is even true of the targeted group. So … women can be biased against women. (Saul 2013, 40)

The Equality Challenge Unit (ECU, 2013, 2017) has entered the discussion on uncon-scious bias in academia. The ECU is a registered charity in the UK funded by the Scottish Funding Council, HEFC for Wales, Universities UK and from subscriptions from universities in England and Northern Ireland. Its mission is providing support for 'equality and diversity for staff and students in higher education institutions … [It provides] a central resource and advice to the sector' (https://www.ecu.ac.uk/about-us/ accessed 15 December 2017). The ECU's report on Unconscious Bias and Higher Education (2013) uses a similar definition to Saul's:

> Unconscious bias is a term used to describe the associations that we hold which, despite being outside our conscious awareness, can have a significant influence on our attitudes and behaviour. Regardless of how fair minded we believe ourselves to be, most people have some degree of unconscious bias. This means that we automatically respond to others (e.g. people from different racial or ethnic groups) in positive or negative ways. These associations are difficult to override, regardless of whether we recognise them to be wrong, because they are deeply ingrained into our thinking and emotions (http://www.ecu.ac.uk/publications/unconscious-bias-in-higher-education/ accessed 15 September 2017).

Thus, 'unconscious bias happens by our brains making incredibly quick judgements and assessments of people and situations without us realising. Our biases are influenced by our background, cultural environment and personal experiences. We may not even be aware of these views and opinions, or be aware of their full impact and implications' (www.ecu.ac.uk/guidance-resources/employment-and-careers/staff-recruitment/unconscious-bias/ accessed 4 May 2017). The ECU has also developed training materials to help us to uncover unconscious bias and act to counter it. However, if they are deeply ingrained into our thinking and emotions they must be resistant to change. Notwithstanding this, unconscious bias has initiated a resurgence in equality, inclusion and diversity training within a background of continuing racism, sexism, homophobia, ableism, transphobia, class discrimination and rampant cis-gender politics within UK universities. The concern in this article will be to unravel the continued workings of anti-Black and people of colour racism and white supremacy within 'unconscious bias' as an equality, diversity and inclusion mantra within the UK HEI context. Viewing unconscious bias as one aspect of the institutionalisation of racial liberalism (Mills 2017), the analysis will show that unconscious bias is a technology of racialised governmentality which keeps the status quo of whiteliness in place within the libidinal economy of racism. This is all the more pernicious because whiteliness continues to be enabled within universities which claim to be 'post-racial' (Goldberg 2015) spaces. This article will begin by framing unconscious bias within its social psychological roots which becomes expressed within equality, diversity and inclusion training. It then argues that unconscious bias is an alibi to diminish the recognition, analysis and salience of white supremacy in order to maintain it. This alibi is a wilful silencing which as a political act maintains white innocence at the same time as it enables a white 'will to forget' anti-Black and people of colour racism. The final part of the argument will be focused on the question of who gains from clinging to the idea of 'unconscious bias' as something that can't be helped. This will be done by decolonising 'white fragility' and the 'self-forgiveness' which 'unconscious bias' installs as the institutional approach to anti-racism until 'we all know better'. Let us now move to thinking about unconscious bias and maintaining whiteliness through ignorance.

Framing unconscious bias in equality, diversity and inclusion training

Let us pause for a moment and dwell on 'un', the prefix in 'unconscious'. 'Un' is significant because this is where the denial of anti-Black and people of colour racism is maintained. 'Un' denotes an absence of a quality or state, a reverse of, a lack of and gives a negative force to conscious bias. It denies the possibility of racist bias and erases the possibility of racism. In contradistinction to this, we have another inscription of 'unconscious bias' which becomes (un)conscious bias to point to its very conscious basis and the fact that 'un' as prefix is an alibi for continuing white supremacy.

Notwithstanding this critique, the making of unconscious bias into a magic bullet means that there is no shortage of research on unconscious bias. For example,

Wood et al. (2009) found that applicants with British sounding names were more often shortlisted for jobs; Steinpreis, Anders, and Ritzke (1999) discovered both male and female psychologists were more likely to employ male early career researchers; McConnell and Leibold (2001) found research participants exhibited more defensive body language with black researchers than white researchers; Green et al. (2007) found doctors were more likely to prescribe effective drugs to white rather than black patients. A survey of the literature on unconscious bias reveals that in the vast majority of cases, proceeding from a social psychological perspective, organisational approaches to unconscious bias begin with the idea that bias is inevitable, that it is ingrained within us within the flight-or-fight response, our unconscious "danger detector" that determines if something or someone is safe before we can even begin to consciously make a determination (Easterly and Ricard 2011). From this social psychological perspective which prevails within the equality, diversity and inclusion mission statements of most institutions, the elimination of bias is articulated as an impossibility, inscribed as it is at the 'genetic' and 'instinctual' levels. Racism and ethnocentrism also fall within the inscriptive hard-wiring of bias as, 'ethnic and racial stereotypes are learned as part of normal socialisation and consistent among many populations across time' (Moule 2009).

For social psychologists (and Equality, Diversity and Inclusion training designers and administrators), not only is unconscious bias inevitable at the individual level. It is inevitable and, indeed, normal at the societal level. Racism – a word rarely used in the unconscious bias semantic field, which is revealing in itself – is therefore not an active choice. Instead, it is part of being human, an inescapable product of being a member of society. This approach offers a solution to the organisational cognitive dissonance created by a lack of diversity by removing it from being an active choice to representing it as one over which the individual has no power. Racism from this perspective becomes 'aversive' (Dovidio and Gaertner 1991), a means of characterising the 'racial attitudes of many Whites who endorse egalitarian values, who regard themselves as non-prejudiced, but who discriminate in subtle, rationalisable ways' (Dovidio et al. 1997). In aversively racist organisations – like universities – built on foundations of equality, overt forms of racism are often said to have been eliminated. Other forms, aversive forms, can be explained as the product of inevitable, unconscious bias.

Indeed, most unconscious bias training begins from this basis of inevitability and normality, that prejudice is intrinsically within us, and here is its first inherent weakness. As well as being a weakness it is also a problematic barrier for much needed anti-racist institutional transformation. An example will suffice here by way of illustration. Duguid and Thomas-Hunt (2015) conducted an experiment with managers in which they told one group that stereotypes are rare and told the other group that stereotypes were common. Both groups were then given a job interview transcript where candidates asked for more money and were described as either male or female. The group that were told that stereotypes are common were found to be 28% less likely to hire the female candidate and judged her as 27% less likeable. The findings suggest that when unconscious bias and its inherent stereotyping is normalised, the normalisation process may exacerbate discrimination rather than challenging it: if everyone is biased, it's okay if I am too. In a follow-up experiment, Duguid and Thomas-Hunt (ibid.) changed tack. Instead of just informing managers that stereotypes are common, they added that the majority of people 'try to overcome their stereotypic preconceptions'. The difference in result was stark as discrimination was eliminated. The managers in the experiment were 28% more interested in hiring the female candidate and judged her as 25% more likeable. The implication is clear. To overcome bias, an awareness of normalisation is insufficient; instead, what is needed is a more active process.

The task for those engaged in the equality, diversity and inclusion mission is not just to make individuals aware of their inevitable and 'normal' bias in the belief that such awareness will alchemically reduce racism. The task moves past an awareness of our unconscious bias, to a requirement that we move beyond our 'instinctual nature' and base our judgements and actions on a rational basis. As Easterly and Ricard (2011) argue, most human decisions are made emotionally, and subsequently we collect or generate the facts to justify them. The aim of unconscious bias training is therefore to address the 'dual attitudes' (Wilson, Lindsey, and Schooler 2000) which govern our actions and behaviours. First, the implicit attitudes that 'are automatically activated by the mere presence (actual symbolic) of the attitude object and commonly function without a person's full awareness or control' (Dovidio, Kawakami, and Gaertner 2002). Second, there are the explicit attitudes which 'shape deliberative, well-considered responses for which people have the motivation and opportunity to weigh the costs and benefits of various courses of action' (ibid.). Successfully overcoming unconscious bias is therefore a matter of individuals ensuring their explicit attitudes are sufficiently free of bias so that they can overcome their inevitably biased implicit attitudes. For Dovidio, Kawakami, and Gaertner (2002), this can only be accomplished when individuals have the opportunity and motivation to assess the consequences of their actions. With these two factors – opportunity and motivation – the assumption is that rational, egalitarian, bias-free, explicit attitudes will be allowed to prevail. This is the basis and outcome of unconscious bias training within the academy where the massive under-representation of Black academics and academics of colour is seen as a result of individuals succumbing to inevitable and normalised bias. It is this focus that highlights the inherent weakness of contemporary approaches: the foregrounding of the individual that ignores the institutional and the systemic and positions unconscious bias as an enabler of whiteliness through assertions of ignorance.

Unconscious bias and maintaining whiteliness through ignorance

Yancy (2015) describes whiteliness as a social, psychological and phenomenological racial reality for white people constructed by an intersubjective matrix whereby white people enact a common being-*raced*-in-the world which is seen as utterly benign in its naturalness, but which is 'nefariously oppressive'. Thus, we cannot only label acts committed by openly self-ascribed racists as racist because racism is not just about believing in the existence of biological 'races' (Yancy 2015). Getting people racialised as white to let go of such a false ontology, or to understand that racism is immoral, has been shown not to ring the death-knell for anti-Black and people of colour racism. The coloniality of white power keeps being re-centred because there is no interrogation of whiteliness, of its political, economic, social, imaginative, epistemic and affective boundaries. This is even the case in contexts in which we are asked to look at our unconscious biases. The problem is that such asking does not commit us to de-legitimising those White normative practices, systems of thought and affective regimes that maintain and recycle anti-Black and people of colour racism. Part of what keeps whiteliness in place as legitimate is the 'epistemologies of ignorance' of racism (Mills 1997) where racism and white supremacy do not exist or, in a spectacular denial of white supremacy, if racism exists then Black people can be racist too. Drawing from Charles Mills (1997), Sullivan and Tuana (2007, 2) assert that racism's epistemologies of ignorance entail that the anti-racist task remains:

> [...] tracing what is not known and the politics of such ignorance should be a key element of epistemological and social and political analyses, for it has the potential to reveal the role of power in the construction of what is known and provide a lens for the political values at work in our knowledge practices. [...] [We should pay attention to] the epistemically complex processes of the production and maintenance of ignorance.

We start here thinking about the interweaving of power and a knowing racist ignorance precisely because it enables us to notice that (un)conscious bias is linked to power. As such, (un)conscious bias is also part of the epistemic processes of the production of white supremacy and its concomitant 'white fragility' through its claim to ignorance. Robin DiAngelo (2011, 54) asserts that:

> White people in North America live in a social environment that protects and insulates them from race-based stress. This insulated environment of racial protection builds white expectations for racial comfort while at the same time lowering the ability to tolerate racial stress, leading to what I refer to as White Fragility. White Fragility is a state in which even a minimum amount of racial stress becomes intolerable, triggering a range of defensive moves. These moves include the outward display of emotions such as anger, fear, guilt and behaviors such as argumentation, silence, and leaving the stress-inducing situation. These behaviors, in turn, function to reinstate white racial equilibrium.

The institutionalisation of unconscious bias as alibi for white supremacy is part of white fragility and, thereby, unconscious bias reinstates white racial equilibrium. The inevitability of (un)conscious bias, the very notion providing palatability to discussions of racial discrimination within organisations, facilitates this ignorance. A discussion of anti-Black and people of colour racism is rarely held in majority-white institutions as claiming to be (un)aware of racism would be exposed as not being about a lack of knowledge or information but rather as ignoring racism, a wilful and intentional turning away from what whiteliness has produced. This wilful ignoring is reflected in the way, for example, discussions around the under-attainment of Black students and students of colour become focused on their deficit in the form of an interrogation of whether they are 'commuting students' or dispropor-tionately working alongside full-time study. This is how universities continue to maintain a claim to ignorance of how they continue to fail students because of racism. It simply becomes the fault of students themselves. Similarly, discussions around the curriculum argue for the seminal nature of white, male, western texts that couldn't possibly be replaced, whilst data showing that Black applicants and applicants of colour receive fewer offers of a place than white students provoke further analysis of the impact of socio-economic status instead of race and racism. In this emergence of racism's denial, the inevitability of (un)conscious bias provides the citational context of equality, diversity and inclusion, a performative act that professes an organisational will to challenge racism yet simultaneously avoids engagement with racism via the emphasis on inevitability and normalisation.

(Un)conscious bias in institutional contexts diverts our attention from white power, societies structured through racial dominance and the coloniality of power, being, knowledge and affect (Tate and Bagguley 2017) which it drags into the twenty-first century. Much like epistemologies of ignorance, the continuous pro-duction and tenacious fixation on and maintenance of unconscious bias as part of equality, diversity and inclusion, mean that we go from institutional to personal knowledge, focusing on individual practices rather than ideological values and their imbrication with white institutional power.

The ECU (2013) report asserts that there is a business case for dealing with unconscious bias as well as a moral responsibility on the part of both individuals and institutions to deal with an issue that so pervades every aspect of their/its work:

> People and institutions not only have a moral responsibility for their implicit biases, but a business responsibility; institutions need to be efficient and effective, and deci-sions and actions need to be taken based on evidence and fact, rather than stereotypes and hunches. […] implicit bias is likely to be relevant to many areas of an institution's work, for example appraisals and grievances, Research Excellence Framework submis-sions, student admissions and course evaluations [… and] recruitment and selection (http://www.ecu.ac.uk/publications/unconscious-bias-in-higher-education/ accessed 15 September 2017).

Read from an institutional racism perspective this statement is what Ahmed (2004) would call a 'declaration of whiteness' in which 'admissions' of 'bad practice' become signs of 'good practice'. This declaration of whiteness could be called an 'unhappy performative' because by its own admission 'the conditions are not in place that would allow such declarations to do what they say' (Ahmed 2004). The conditions are not in place because (un)conscious bias as an alibi for anti-Black and people of colour racism textures the (im)possibility of their emergence.

(Un)conscious bias (also called implicit bias in the ECU report) impacts all aspects of academic life and remains impervious to remedy because of the affects (called emotions by the ECU above) attached to anti-Black and people of colour 'stereotypes and hunches' which pervade the very walls of the institution as well as dynamise its culture, processes, ideologies and actions. For our purposes here we can say that there is a 'libidinal economy' (Wilderson 2010) of racism attached to unconscious bias in place in UK HEIs.

Wilderson (2010, 7) sets out the operation of libidinal economy as related to both affiliation and phobia which he claims is as objective as political economy. As we have seen above in the ECU quote, affiliation and phobia impact political economy as well. Libidinal economy structures psychic and emotional life and as such is resistant to change as, indeed, would be (un)conscious bias because:

> libidinal economy functions variously across scales and is as 'objective' as political economy. It is linked not only to forms of attraction, affection, and alliance, but also to aggression, destruction and the violence of lethal consumption … it is the whole structure of psychic and emotional life … something more than but inclusive of or traversed by … a 'structure of feeling'; it is a dispensation of energies, concerns, points of attention, anxieties, pleasures, appetites, revulsions, phobias capable of great mobility and tenacious fixation.

This 'dispensation of energies, concerns, points of attention, anxieties, pleasures, appetites, revulsions, phobias', underlies the construction of (un)conscious bias as a tool for the erasure of anti-Black and people of colour racism. We can see this tenacious but mobile fixation of anti-Black and people of colour racism if we look at how it impacts employment and promotion within UK HEIs.

The political economy of anti-Black and people of colour racism and 'misogynoir' in these contexts is reproduced in UK academic institutions as illustrated by employment statistics. The term 'misogynoir' was coined by Moya Bailey in 2010 to describe Black African descent women's specific experiences of sexism and racism and is reflected in the following employment statistics (https://mic.com/articles/152965/meet-moya-bailey-the-black-woman-who-created-the-term-misogynoir#.BylkkdjQ2 accessed 21 December 2016). According to the Higher Education Statistics Agency database for 2013/2014 the total number of UK academics in 2013/2014 was 194,240. Of these, 153,675 academics are white, that is, 79.1% of all academics with only 1.48% of Black academics. At professor level 83.5% are white and 0.50% are Black. Gender negatively impacts Black women's promotion prospects once in academia as there were 60 male Black African professors and 5 female Black African professors, 15 male Black Caribbean professors and 10 female Black Caribbean professors and 5 male Black Other professors and 5 female Black Other professors. This is how 'stereotypes and hunches' act to hinder progress on racial equality through their tenacious attachment to what the Black (wo)man is and can become.

These 'stereotypes and hunches' that are the manifestations of (un)conscious bias come out of 'racialising assemblages' (Weheliye 2014) in which the Black (wo)man's and (wo)man of colour's bodies emerge out of the 'complex social and historical interstices of whites' efforts at self-construction through complex acts of erasure vis-à-vis Black people [people of colour]. These acts of self-construction, however, are myths/ideological constructions predicated upon maintaining white power' (Yancy 2005, 216). The Black and (wo)man of colour's material, epistemological, social and political body is erased so that white power and privilege can be maintained. Erasure occurs through a peculiar kind of social recognition that distorts reality such that white people mis-see themselves as 'civilized superiors' and non-whites as 'inferior savages' whilst producing a 'collective amnesia' about the past of Empire, colonialism and enslavement (Mills 2007).

Such mis-seeing and peculiar social recognition implicates (un)conscious bias as a part of the maintenance of such power, especially if we think through the lens afforded us by the Racial Contract and its epistemologies of ignorance (Mills 1997). Mills' (1997) Racial Contract inserts an analysis of the operation of white supremacy within the Social Contract invented by Western political philosophers. The Contract and its epistemologies enable white supremacy and its racial entitlements to remain unseen by those racialised as white (Mills 1997, 2007) through incantations of unconscious bias. (Un)conscious bias enables a continuation of white privilege and power as those racialised as white and non-whites who have been co-opted continue to benefit from the world which they have created and maintained where:

> Both globally and within particular nations, then, white people, Europeans and their descendants, continue to benefit from the Racial Contract, which creates a world in their cultural image, political states differentially favouring their interests, an economy structured around the racial exploitation of others, and a moral psychology (not just in whites, sometimes in nonwhites also) skewed consciously and unconsciously toward privileging them, taking the status quo of differential racial entitlement as normatively legitimate, and not to be investigated further. (Mills 1997, 40)

Mills' (1997) Racial Contract extends from culture, to politics, to economy, to moral psychology which is 'skewed consciously and unconsciously' towards white supremacy, and 'a differential racial entitlement' – white privilege – which is simply taken as a given. If we say that a world is made in which both those racialised as Black/people of colour and white see white privilege as 'normatively legitimate' then this means that (un)conscious bias relates to norms. Norms are not racism neutral but drag the coloniality of white power (Quijano 2000; Gutiérrez Rodríguez 2016) into universities, impacting epistemology, institutional hierarchies and ideas about who counts as human which begin from whiteliness as the norm (Wynter 2003). Norms as expressed through institutional culture, practices like recruitment and selection and processes like curriculum construction are not unconscious but maintain the privilege of those racialised as white and non-whites who support whiteliness (Mills 1997, 2017; Yancy 2008, 2012). Black and people of colour phobia lives on within the libidinal economies of white institutions organised 'by trajectories of repulsion rather than attraction, by phobic strivings "away from" rather than philic strivings "toward"' (Ngai 2005, 11). This is the normative anti-Black and people of colour life of universities which is relevant for assertions of (un)conscious bias in equality, diversity and inclusion environments. As phobic opinions and attitudes which it is said that 'we are not aware' that we hold but which influence our actions, (un)conscious bias seems to be one aspect of the epistemologies of ignorance which are part of the Racial Contract instantiated by whiteliness (Mills 1997). To put it otherwise, (un)conscious bias is part of the apparatus of maintaining white racialised power by calling on the idea of ignorance, of not knowing that what is being done or said is racist because it was not wilfully said or done to hurt, to discriminate, to be racist. It came from somewhere over which we have no control – i.e. the unconscious.

Equality, diversity and inclusion policies are a normative expectation of twenty-first century UK higher education institutions. However, this normative expectation erases anti-Black and people of colour racism and silences their daily experiences of racist, sexist, ablest, classist, ageist, transphobic and homophobic exclusion, harassment, bullying and discrimination. This erasure is enabled by the increasingly prevalent institutional norm of relating discriminatory institutional culture and individual acts to unconscious bias which we can be trained to 'unlearn'. This 'unlearning' has itself become a normative expectation in which 'confession' is necessary for anti-racist progress to be made institutionally. However, as Dovidio, Kawakami, and Gaertner (2002) argue, overcoming the impacts of unconscious bias depends on two elements. First, there must be opportunity, the time to reflect rationally on our implicit attitudes, the space to interrogate our automated responses. The second element – and the one that is most crucial – is motivation: implicit attitudes are more prevalent and more powerful when the motivation to address them is absent. Yet the challenging of (un)conscious bias by white institutions and white individuals would require challenging the Racial Contract itself, it would require an acknowledgement of participation within systems of racism that privilege whiteliness. Actually overcoming (un)conscious bias, then, requires a motivation to challenge the very system which has provided white privilege, a motivation that, intrinsically, puts the continuing benefits of white privilege at risk. Here is where the project of overcoming (un)conscious bias threatens to move beyond palatability and challenge the Racial Contract. Consequently, here is where the potential of unconscious bias training within universities breaks down, risking as it does the benefits to whiteliness that continuation of the Racial Contract offers. Here it is then where 'white fragility' and self-forgiveness emerge as key discourses focused on minimising risk to these benefits while keeping institutional racism in place.

Decolonising 'white fragility': self-forgiveness as an approach to institutional racism

Let us change tack a little and look to another meaning of bias. That is, 'a direction diagonal to the weave of the fabric'. It is taking this diagonal approach to thinking which we will try to establish as we look at the 'white fragility' which is linked to unconscious bias and its attached self-forgiveness as an antidote to institutional racism. In equality, diversity and inclusion understandings, we have to confess to unconscious bias to move towards diminishing institutional racism. This confession instantiates 'a fantasy of transcendence in which "what" is transcended is the very "thing" admitted to in the declaration' (Ahmed 2004).

What Ahmed speaks about here are very unreflective confessions of doing wrong which will not have the effect of diminishing institutional racism. As Saul (2013, 55) avers, 'a person should not be blamed for an implicit bias of which they are completely unaware that results solely from the fact that they live in a sexist [racist] culture. Even once they become aware that they have implicit biases, they do not instantly become able to control their biases and so they should not be blamed for them'. Confessions of (un)conscious bias within the context of training in equality, diversity and inclusion can (re)centre white supremacy by removing blame and its accompanying shame and guilt which is part of the process of unlearning white supremacy. White fragility emerges as vulnerability, anger, fear, for which the only balm is self-forgiveness because you simply did not actively know; your racism was unconscious – after all, unconscious bias begins from the premise of inevitability and normalisation. However, self-forgiveness is inactive as an approach to institutional racism because it relies on introspection on the part of the white self and institution which is what Yancy (2015) calls a 'distancing strategy'. (Un)conscious bias is a strategy to distance the white self from the charge of racism and, indeed, that one can be implicated in its perpetuation. (Un)conscious bias does this by occluding the extent of white supremacy and its impact on Black people and people of colour and on white people themselves by focusing on the white suffering that results from 'irrational claims' of anti-Black and people of colour racism. (Un)conscious bias maintains white supremacy and, indeed, its very definition insists that racist culture and environment are crucial to its existence. The need to focus on white suffering, white fragility, to say it is not your fault, produces a paradox at its centre where those racialised as white are victims of the racism from which they benefit.

Let us use an example from the ECU report (2013, 6) cited earlier to look further at why confessions of unconscious bias do not lead to diminishing institutional racism. In this report, higher education institutions are asked to consider whether:

> shortlisting can be done anonymously. Particularly for professional and support positions, human resources (HR) processes could be adapted to remove information such as name, school, university, all monitoring data, and anything else that is irrelevant to the application.

Leaving to one side the difficulty of doing this for academic positions because of the publications aspect, what this approach denies is the impact of organisational culture on who is hired once they are in the interview.

The culture of the organisation is a zone of 'suturing' (Yancy 2015) of whiteliness to white power and privilege which is not undone through confessions of unconscious bias. This is so because white supremacy remains stubbornly in place as it is not challenged by the beneficiaries of the Racial Contract who, as we recall from Mills (1997) above, can also include non-whites. Through an engagement with literature and training in unconscious bias, white people and white institutions simply feel that they need do nothing at all apart from to confess to having unconscious bias. Here we have the Racial Contract in action, where white power and white supremacy as the norm do not need to be investigated any further because 'whiteliness is not the problem, racism is, everybody can be racist including Black people and we are not white supremacists or have right wing politics so we can't be racists'. Does this distancing strategy meant to avert the gaze from whiteliness sound familiar? The charge of Black racism does not take into account the systemic nature of racism, empire, colonialism nor the white constructed 'racializing assemblages' (Weheliye 2014) that ensure white supremacy, for example. To assert that only self-proclaimed white supremacists are racist is to continue to not see one's part in maintaining whiteliness which remains a 'non-knowing [which includes] both straightforward racist motivation and more impersonal social-structural causation … also moral non-knowings, incorrect judgements about the rights and wrongs of moral situations themselves' within which Black people and people of colour can be implicated (Mills 2017, 57). Confessions of unconscious bias seek temporary solace from the charge of anti-Black and people of colour racism and its lived experiences. (Un)conscious bias cannot fix institutional racism because racist white relationalities extend from and to the white self through the process of white subject formation that restrict access to understanding the extent of white racism through epistemologies of ignorance. (Un)conscious bias is about protecting whiteliness from its noxious self through ensuring the non-occurrence of normative white disruption. However, it is this normative white disruption that is necessary if we are to get beyond unconscious bias to thinking about how we can dismantle the toxic culture of institutional racism.

To bring about such normative white disruption, what we have to engage in is the other meaning of bias, a thinking diagonally, against the grain in other words, which ruptures white fragility and the culture of thinking 'it's unconscious bias what done it'. This bias, this diagonal thinking is about opening the white self and the non-white co-opted self to the alterity that it has itself created, to that epistemology which is not seen as knowledge, that morality which is seen as immoral, those affects which are seen as irrelevant for institutional life. Thinking diagonally means, to paraphrase Yancy (2015), that we choose to lose our way, we practice becoming unsutured to whiteliness and we seek to not see it as the normative expectation.

From this space of criticality, this bias, we can come to terms with the fact of whiteliness and our complicity with and involvement in maintaining a white 'racist second skin' (Tate 2018) which extends from the individual to the social and back again in a feedback loop. It is this white racist second skin which remains intact and that needs to be dismantled as it underlies the white epistemologies of ignorance of/ about anti-Black and people of colour racism which are so entrenched. Thinking diagonally instantiates a decentring of whiteliness which does not return it as centre or return to it as fragile or vulnerable but acknowledges it as supremacist, a site of the coloniality of power and a location which is inimical to everyone's psychic health, both Black and people of colour and white. It is only through a refusal of this return that such bias can enable a form of thinking which dwells on the question of the uneasy feelings, practices and processes caused by white racism's impacts institutionally and personally rather than eliding them through a focus on unconscious bias. Dwelling on uneasy feelings, practices and processes means that the relationality between the white self and anti-Black and people of colour racism cannot be seen from a distance. Dwelling with unease rather than its elision could enable us to challenge and address racism within 'post-race' contexts where racism is seen as only being committed by white supremacists and members of the far right or alt-right and Black people can be racist too. Equality, diversity and inclusion's unconscious bias denies the need for institutional action because it focuses on the individual, volunteerism and minimising white fragility. Senior leaders must go beyond unconscious bias, foreground the Racial Contract underlying institutional life and prescribe the necessity for anti-racist change which can only emerge when we see racism and white supremacy as problems.

Conclusion

In *Look A White!* George Yancy (2012) reminds us that the white self is a location of opacity in terms of its own racism. (Un)conscious bias keeps people racialised as white and the non-white co-opted spoken about by Mills (1997) entombed within white racism. This white racism sets the boundaries of who they are and what they can become as it makes them complicit in its operation because they benefit (Mills 1997; Yancy 2012). The ECU (2013) definition with which we started pointed us to the fact that to understand unconscious bias we cannot merely look to the individual psyche but also to our institutions' cultures and practices. We have to continuously look diagonally, from the bias, at that culture for the signs of anti-Black and people of colour racism and think about what this has done to our understandings of ourselves in the world that we inhabit. It is from this bias that anti-racism can begin to reconstruct subjectivities, institutions, epistemologies, discourses on the human and regimes of recognition.

Disclosure statement

No potential conflict of interest was reported by the authors.

ORCID

Shirley Anne Tate 🆔 http://orcid.org/0000-0003-3060-9880

References

Ahmed, S. 2004. "Declarations of Whiteness: The Non-performativity of Anti-racism." *Borderlands E-Journal* 3 (2). https://www.borderlands.net.au/vol3no2_2004/ahmed_declarations.htm
DiAngelo, R. 2011. "White Fragility." *International Journal of Critical Pedagogy* 3 (3): 54–70.
Dovidio, J. F., and S. L. Gaertner. 1991. "Changes in the Nature and Expression of Racial Prejudice." In *Opening Doors: An Appraisal of Race Relations in Contemporary America*, edited by H. Knopke, J. Norrell, and R. Rogers, 201–241. Tuscaloosa: University of Alabama Press.
Dovidio, J. F., K. Kawakami, and S. L. Gaertner. 2002. "Implicit and Explicit Prejudice and Interracial Interaction." *Journal of Personality and Social Psychology* 82 (1): 62–68.
Dovidio, J. F., K. Kawakami, C. Johnson, B. Johnson, and A. Howard. 1997. "On the Nature of Prejudice: Automatic and Controlled Processes." *Journal of Experimental Social Psychology* 33 (5): 510–540.
Duguid, M. M., and M. C. Thomas-Hunt. 2015. "Condoning Stereotyping? How Awareness of Stereotyping Prevalence Impacts Expression of Stereotypes." *Journal of Applied Psychology* 100 (2): 343–359.
Easterly, D. M., and C. S. Ricard. 2011. "Conscious Efforts to End Unconscious Bias: Why Women Leave Academic Research." *Journal of Research Administration* 42 (1): 61–73.
Equality Challenge Unit. 2013. "Unconscious Bias and Higher Education." Accessed September 15, 2017. http://www.ecu.ac.uk/publications/unconscious-bias-in-higher-education/
Equality Challenge Unit: Advancing Equality and Diversity in Universities and Colleges. 2017. "Unconscious Bias." Accessed December 1, 2017. https://www.ecu.ac.uk/guidance-resources/employment-and-careers/staff-recruitment/unconscious-bias/
Goldberg, D. T. 2015. *Are We All Postracial Yet?* Cambridge: Polity Press.
Green, A. R., D. R. Carney, D. J. Pallin, L. H. Ngo, K. L. Raymond, L. I. Iezzoni, and M. R. Banaji. 2007. "The Presence of Implicit Bias in Physicians and Its Prediction of Thrombolysis Decisions for Black and White Patients." *Journal of General Internal Medicine* 22: 1231–1238.
Gutiérrez Rodríguez, E. 2016. "Sensing Dispossession: Women and Gender Studies between Institutional Racism and Migration Control Policies in Neo-liberal Universities." *Women's Studies International Forum* 54: 167–177.
McConnell, A. R., and J. M. Leibold. 2001. "Relations among the Implicit Association Test, Discriminatory Behavior, and Explicit Measures of Racial Attitudes." *Journal of Experimental Social Psychology* 37: 435–442.
Mills, C. 1997. *The Racial Contract.* Ithaca, NY: Cornell University Press.
Mills, C. 2007. "White Ignorance." In *Race and Epistemologies of Ignorance*, edited by Shannon Sullivan and Nancy Tuana, 11–38. Albany: State University of New York Press.
Mills, C. 2017. *Black Rights/White Wrongs: The Critique of Racial Liberalism.* New York: Oxford University Press.
Moule, J. 2009. "Understanding Unconscious Bias and Unintentional Racism." *Phi Delta Kappan* 90 (5): 320–326.
Ngai, S. 2005. *Ugly Feelings.* Cambridge, MA: Harvard University Press.

Quijano, A. 2000. "Coloniality of Power, Eurocentrism and Latin America." *Nepantla: Views from South* 103: 533–580.

Saul, J. 2013. "Implicit Bias, Stereotype Threat and Women in Philosophy." In *Women in Philosophy*, edited by Katrina Hutchison and Fiona Jenkins, 39–60. Oxford: Oxford University Press.

Steinpreis, R. E., K. Anders, and D. Ritzke. 1999. "The Impact of Gender on the Review of the Curricula Vitae of Job Applicants and Tenure Candidates: A National Empirical Study." *Sex Roles* 41 (7/8): 509–528.

Sullivan, S., and N. Tuana. 2007. "Introduction." In *Race and Epistemologies of Ignorance*, edited by Shannon Sullivan and Nancy Tuana, 1–10. Albany: State University of New York Press.

Tate, S. A. 2018. *The Governmentality of Black Beauty Shame: Discourse, Iconicity and Resistance.* London: Palgrave.

Tate, S. A., and P. Bagguley. 2017. "Building the Anti-racist University: Next Steps." *Race, Ethnicity and Education* 20 (3): 289–299.

Weheliye, A. G. 2014. *Habeas Viscus: Racializing Assemblages, Biopolitics and Black Feminist Theories of the Human.* Durham, NC: Duke University Press.

Wilderson, F. 2010. *Red, White and Black: Cinema and the Structure of US Antagonisms.* Durham, NC: Duke University Press.

Wilson, T. D., S. Lindsey, and T. Y. Schooler. 2000. "A Model of Dual Attitudes." *Psychological Review* 107 (1): 101–126.

Wood, M., J. Hales, S. Purdon, T. Sejersen, and O. Hayllar. 2009. *A Test for Racial Discrimination in Recruitment Practice in British Cities: Research Report No 607.* London: Department for Work and Pensions.

Wynter, Sylvia. 2003. "Unsettling the Coloniality of Being/Power/Truth/Freedom: Towards the Human, after Man, Its Overrepresentation – An Argument." *CR: The New Centennial Review* 3 (3): 257–337.

Yancy, George. 2005. "Whiteness and the Return of the Black Body." *The Journal of Speculative Philosophy* 19 (4): 215–241.

Yancy, G. 2008. *Black Bodies White Gazes: The Continuing Significance of Race.* Lanham, MD: Rowman and Littlefield.

Yancy, G. 2012. *Look a White! Philosophical Essays on Whiteness.* Philadelphia, PA: Temple University Press.

Yancy, G. 2015. " Introduction." In *White Self-criticality beyond Anti-racism: How Does It Feel to Be a White Problem*, edited by George Yancy, xi–xxvii. Lanham, MD: Lexington Books.

Index

.

Printed in Great Britain
by Amazon

68871031R10099